DIRECTORS OF EDUCATION

Directors of Education

TONY BUSH
Lecturer in Educational Administration, The Open University
and
MAURICE KOGAN
Professor of Government and Social Administration,
Brunel University

London
GEORGE ALLEN & UNWIN
Boston   Sydney

**George Allen & Unwin (Publishers) Ltd,
40 Museum Street, London WC1A 1LU, UK**

George Allen & Unwin (Publishers) Ltd,
Park Lane, Hemel Hempstead, Herts HP2 4TE, UK

Allen & Unwin, Inc.,
9 Winchester Terrace, Winchester, Mass. 01890, USA

George Allen & Unwin Australia Pty Ltd,
8 Napier Street, North Sydney, NSW 2060, Australia

First published in 1982

British Library Cataloguing in Publication Data

Bush, Tony
    Directors of education.
1. Education—England   2. Local officials and
employees—England
I. Title   II. Kogan, Maurice
379.1'53'0942   LB2831.826E/

ISBN 0-04-379001-1
ISBN 0-04-379002-X Pbk

Library of Congress Cataloging in Publication Data

Bush, Tony.
    Directors of education.
Includes bibliographical references and index.
1. School superintendents and principals—England.
2. School superintendents and principals—Wales.
3. Educational surveys—England.   4. Educational surveys
—Wales.   I. Kogan, Maurice.   II. Title.
LB2831.626.G7B87   371.2'01'0942   82-4038
ISBN 0-04-379001-1   AACR2
ISBN 0-04-379002-X (pbk.)

Set in 10 on 11 point Times by Inforum Ltd, Portsmouth
and printed in Great Britain
by Mackays of Chatham

Contents

Contents

Preface

This book is a sequel to *County Hall* (Harmondsworth: Penguin, 1973), in which one of us (Maurice Kogan, together with Willem van der Eyken) discussed the role of the Chief Education Officer with three recently retired CEOs, Dan Cook, Claire Pratt and George Taylor. That work was carried out before local government had been reorganised, except in the London area, and before the corporate management revolution had reached its peak. Many other changes have occurred in the educational world in the past decade, and in this study we seek to assess how they have affected the role of the CEO, or Director of Education as he is often now styled.

Edited versions of the interviews conducted in 1972 with Cook, Pratt and Taylor have been included in this volume for readers who want to make their own detailed comparisons with statements about the role of the CEOs in the 1980s. Their thinking remains relevant to the issues being tackled now. The main sources of comparison are the 1980 interviews (by Tony Bush) with four present and former CEOs. The interviews were recorded on tape and subsequently transcribed; they have been amended, where necessary, and edited. The result is a discussion of the major issues affecting local education in the 1970s and 1980s by men who are, or were recently, immersed in these issues on a day-to-day basis. We are grateful to these busy people as well as to their predecessors for their important contributions to this book and for the co-operation given in the collection and processing of the material.

Our interviews inevitably produced statements about how events appeared to individuals in the particular settings of the authorities they served. We have put their impressions into a broader setting by carrying out a postal survey of the other directors in England and Wales; this covered the same issues as were discussed in the interviews. We are grateful for the support of the Society of Education Officers in encouraging its CEO members to respond to our questionnaire. In the event sixty-one of the 101 CEOs approached found time to reply. All respondents were guaranteed anonymity, so their names and LEA's cannot be identified. Table 1 shows a breakdown by type of authority. Although the bulk of responses showed little variation according to type of authority or region, such differences as emerged are noted in Part One of the book. What we cannot say is whether or not our non-respondents have different perceptions from those who replied.

The material derived from the interviews and survey has been drawn on extensively in Part One, where we deploy our data against some of the other studies in the field. Among these is an unpublished study carried out in 1974 by Myron Atkin, at present Dean of the School of Education, Stanford University, USA, and Helen Simons, now of the London University Institute of Education. We are grateful for access to their material. A general list of references is given at the end of Part One. We are indebted to Professor Ron Glatter, Daphne Johnson and Tim Whitaker for their constructive criticisms. We also wish to express our thanks to Tricia Glover, who carried out a thorough analysis of the survey material. Sally Harris coped admirably with the large amount of correspondence, transcription and typing produced by the study.

Table 1   *Responses to Survey of CEOs (England and Wales)*

Type of authority	No. of LEAs approached	No. of responses	%age of responses
English counties	39	25	64·1
Welsh counties	7*	5	71·4
Metropolitan districts	35*	19	54·3
London authorities	20*	12	60·0
TOTAL	101	61	60·4

*South Glamorgan and Coventry were not included in the survey. Hillingdon was omitted also, because the CEO's post was vacant.

Part One

THE DIRECTOR OF EDUCATION
IN 1972 AND IN 1980

Chapter 1

The Purpose of This Book

The first and most important purpose of this book is to allow seven Chief Education Officers (CEOs) to speak to the reader over the period of eight years between the publication of this book and its predecessor. Our interviewees speak in their own words, if not directly, because the questioner has acted as intermediary, yet with as much directness as is possible through the medium of lightly structured interviews recorded verbatim.

The three CEOs who joined our study in 1972 discussed issues that still remain critically important. Their perceptions are the starting point for the achievement of the further objective, namely, to illustrate the major changes that have, sometimes dramatically and sometimes barely perceptibly, taken place in the role and working context of the Chief Education Officer.

In particular, we elucidate some of the main themes that affect the working lives of Directors of Education, such as the effects of local government reorganisation, the increasing importance of corporate management, of politicisation of local government and of changing central-local relationships. These issues are illuminated with evidence from both our interviews, and the sixty-one questionnaires.

Chapter 2

The Context: Changes in the 1970s

The Directors of Education who are the subject of this book worked in a period – the 1970s – which was a decade of turbulence for education. It is doubtful if any previous time was so packed with incident or produced so much change. The precise point in time when expansion gave way to a steady state or reduction is open to debate (Fowler, 1980), but in 1970 the numbers of pupils and teachers in the system were still growing and administrators still sought to provide enough accommodation for increasing demand. By the end of the decade, contraction dominated educational planning. The schools expected to have 13 per cent fewer pupils by 1985 than at their peak, and 750,000 pupil places were to be taken out of the school system if local authorities followed the guidance stated by central government. Teacher training had undergone painful reduction and reorganisation after virtually tripling its numbers, at government's behest, in the 1960s. The impact of contraction was aggravated by economic problems and financial limitations, especially following the election of the Conservative government in 1979.

Not only a contracting service, but reduced certainty about the place of education as a force for good, is the context in which contemporary educational administrators work. For example, in 1972 Dan Cook could speak of the growing support and involvement of middle-class parents in the publicly maintained system. That support has given way to anxious concern, particularly as comprehensive schools find it difficult to meet their terms of reference to provide a better education for the whole of the population. Higher education, too, expanded on generous lines to meet the demands for it predicted in the 1960s, has suffered first a drop in recruitment rates and now, as we write, absolute reductions in capacity induced by government policy. Yet all Chief Education Officers will have come from a generation that regards securing a higher education as a worthy achievement. The assumption that education would make the mass of the people wiser, happier and more productive must have strongly substantiated the power of the first postwar generation of CEOs. That buoyancy of public support lasted for at most twenty-five years before the pessimistic and restrictive mood set in.

The 1970s was also an era of structural change. Following the Local Government Act 1972, local government in England and Wales (outside London) was reorganised and the number of local education authorities (LEAs) reduced from 162 to 104. (141 to 83, excluding London). After the Maud Committee's Report on Local Government Organisation (1967), then the Bains Report (1972), many of the new LEAs sought to adopt more integrated decision-making structures which produced 'corporate management', a notion borrowed, as were many managerial concepts of the time, from American business management theories. The effects of the corporate approach on the local education service have been far-reaching, although few developments had the dramatic consequences experienced in the new county of Avon, as described in Part Two by Derrick Williams.

The political system seemed almost casual in producing changes which effectively countermanded the changes just carried through. For example, a partial reversion to the former county borough system was envisaged by the proposals for 'organic change' put forward by the Labour government in 1978, four years after massive reorganisation.

The Department of Education and Science (DES) itself did not escape scrutiny, although with few obvious consequences. Following a review by the Organisation for Economic Co-operation and Development (OECD, 1975), the role of the DES was examined by the House of Commons Expenditure Committee (Fookes Committee, 1976). The role of Her Majesty's Inspectorate (HMI) has also been studied by select committees. Following the 'Great Debate' on the curriculum and educational standards initiated by James Callaghan in 1976, the HMI appeared to be creating a stronger leadership role in these areas.

As our respondents testify, the relationship between central and local government changed in this period. The 1976 Education Act, requiring LEAs to submit schemes for comprehensive reorganisation, followed the Tameside case, where the LEA challenged the secretary of state's right to impose comprehensive schools on an unwilling LEA. The 1980 Local Government Planning and Land Act will reduce local freedom by penalising local authorities who go beyond centrally determined spending limits.

The relationship between LEAs and their institutions came under the spotlight with the William Tyndale affair, culminating in the dismissal of the head and six of his staff following a public inquiry (Auld, 1976). The role of school governing bodies has also been reviewed by the Taylor Committee (Taylor, 1977).

Pressure groups have been more active in many areas on such issues as school closures and comprehensive reorganisation. Union activity has increased also, with the teachers' unions fighting cuts in educational expenditure, especially in those areas where they go beyond those required by falling pupil numbers. Here, as elsewhere, the unions have sought to link the issue of educational standards to a natural concern with the welfare of their members.

The Director of Education has been at the centre of many of these developments. He is expected to interpret the trends and respond to them, to advise the LEA and the schools and colleges, to contribute to national policy-making and local decision-making. In the past it could be assumed that CEOs were among the main agents of change. In the period that we describe he emerges at least as much as the recipient as the promoter of the main changes.

Chapter 3

The Background of the Director

The 1944 Education Act required each LEA to appoint a CEO. This requirement remained in force following the 1972 Local Government Act, despite opposition from some who felt it infringed local authorities' discretion to determine their own arrangements for managing the education service.

Education is like other local government services, where the chief officer and, indeed, most senior officers have a professional qualification or background. The general administrator usually has a supporting role and cannot aspire to the top posts unless the appropriate professional qualification is acquired; it is only chief executives among the most senior local government officers whose qualifications are not specialist. Three former CEOs have become chief executives. Most chief executives are either lawyers, or finance officers, by training. This model contrasts with the civil service, where the professional has an advisory role and the permanent secretary posts and other administrative jobs are reserved for the generalists.

The respondents to our survey all conform to the established pattern (Rendel, 1968) that CEOs start their careers as graduate teachers. All sixty-one are graduates and all have teaching experience. Most (forty-seven) have a teaching qualification and a number (thirteen) have a higher degree. The average teaching experience is six years, although one CEO taught for only one year, while another had twenty-five years' experience. Fifty-five respondents have experience of secondary schools, while only nine have taught in primary schools and nine in further or public-sector higher education. Twelve have experience of adult education. Four have taught in universities. On leaving teaching, they served an apprenticeship in subordinate posts, usually entering administration as Assistant Education Officers (AEOs), administrative assistants or professional assistants. The great majority (fifty) were Deputy CEOs before becoming CEOs. On average our respondents held administrative posts for ten years before securing the top job.

In this respect, at least, little appears to have changed since 1972, when three CEOs were interviewed. Dan Cook entered educational administration in 1939, after taking his degree at Liverpool University, research at London and Cambridge and five years' secondary teaching experience. He was an AEO and then a deputy for twenty years before becoming Devon's CEO. Claire Pratt, a graduate of London University, entered administration in 1944, after teaching for five years in a public school and nine years in a teacher training college. She had twenty years' administrative experience before becoming Hillingdon's CEO. George Taylor entered administration in 1945, after taking degrees at the universities of Manchester and London. He taught in secondary schools for twenty-two years, for the last eight of which he was a headmaster. He had five years as a Chief Inspector and Deputy CEO before becoming CEO for Leeds in 1950.

Our four 1980 interviewees have similar backgrounds. Fred Adams, a Cambridge graduate, taught in a Quaker boarding school and in adult education. He first became a CEO in Bradford in 1967, after twelve years' administrative experience. Eric Briault, also a Cambridge graduate, taught in secondary schools for fourteen years. He became an inspector in the former London County Council, then was a deputy education officer for fifteen years before becoming (Chief) Education Officer in 1971. Derrick Williams is the third Cambridge graduate among our interviewees. He taught for a year in a grammar school, and in adult education here and overseas. He became CEO for the new Avon authority in 1974, after experience in Oxfordshire, West Suffolk and, as an AEO and deputy, in Bristol. Robert Aitken is rather unusual in that he acquired a taste for administration as a young school-leaver. He subsequently took a degree at Nottingham University and gained teaching experience in primary and secondary education specifically to prepare for a career as an educational administrator.

There is little doubt that CEOs themselves regard teaching experience as essential to the satisfactory fulfilment of their role. Robert Aitken expresses it in colourful terms: 'I have found usually in the end it takes a monkey to deal with a monkey. My staff and I have been teachers and we know the tricks.' Fred Adams puts a similar point: 'There is a recognition that if you are dealing with schools and teachers, you want to know the language of teachers and the realities of the classroom.' Derrick Williams also emphasises the importance of teaching experience: 'It's essential for the future welfare of the service that he (the CEO) has the confidence of his teaching force, and that almost certainly means he must have taught and know the workings of a school.'

Chapter 4

From Teacher to Director: Do Values Change?

CEOs serve a long apprenticeship as teachers and administrators before reaching the top post. What is it that leads teachers to take on a role that has become increasingly difficult and demanding? Aitken was early committed to administration and 'would not have been happy painting on the canvas at school level; I need a bigger brush and a broader canvas'. Adams admits that 'there is a strong element of ambition . . . it is a sense of feeling that you are making some impact on an important area of public life . . . I think inevitably a desire to be near to the centre of power was part of the motive'. Briault originally wanted to become a headmaster but instead became an LCC inspector to maintain his interest in geography, and because as a former conscientious objector, he considered he had little chance of securing a headship, a disability unlikely to operate now.

Directors consider that they have a significant influence on the development of the education service in their areas. The term 'dynamic', used by several CEOs, suggests that they assume far more than a regulative or controlling role. Taylor in 1972 believed that there were two kinds of management: 'One is the control or regulating . . . and the other is dynamic. And I would prefer to regard my job as being not a controller but infusing or directing the machine to new enterprises.' Briault agrees but recognises that 'in seeking to shift education in the direction that one believes is right one can only do it by convincing the people who in the end make the decisions'. For Aitken, the CEO 'needs to have a catalyst role to stimulate and to break out of moulds if that is necessary'. His distinct contribution is that he is the forward-thinker, the appraiser of where the vehicle is going.

Our interviewees and respondents, in regretting the increased managerial emphasis of their role (see pages 10–12), suggest a commitment to the values of the teaching profession. But are different values held by a class teacher, a head, or a Chief Education Officer working with his service, within the corporate team and within the national system of education?

For the most part, teachers' values are primarily 'educational' and concerned with the development of the cognitive and affective skills and the well-being of the pupil. The same teacher may, in his pastoral role (Johnson *et al.*, 1980), take up a wider range of tasks which draw upon values associated not only with individual development, but also with social control or the development of a sense of community or the school acting as a surrogate parent. As the educator moves from the classroom and becomes a head, he does not lose the values held by the classroom teacher; but the emphasis changes as the functions become wider. The managerial tasks involve values connected with maintaining coherent and reliable institutions, working confidently and maintaining the boundaries with the outside environment. Some of these issues have been explored in the distinction made between the executive and the professional leader functions of the head (Hughes, 1973). Yet outsiders may perceive the changes of perception more clearly than heads themselves. Heads see themselves primarily as 'master-teachers', emphasise the charismatic and pastoral aspects of headship (Bernbaum, 1979) and regard managerial ability as much less significant. Fiske commented in 1969 that 'many only tolerate the managerial and administrative part of their duties' (Glatter, 1972). Heads must perform management tasks and cannot ignore the fact that they are at the centre of a political system in which different groups' views have to be reconciled within the curriculum and activities of the school (Kogan, 1980). They might even in times of crisis and contraction find themselves leading a pressure group (Wood, 1980). If, then, the transition from teacher to head broadens functions and reorders values, we can assume that when the educator enters the even wider system, as a CEO, an even sharper change in the hierarchy of values occurs.

The Director of Education, in all of our material, claims a devotion to the values of the classroom teacher and regrets the increasing diversion of time and energy towards coping with an ever-complex managerial and political system. The CEO is concerned to ensure that schools play their full part in, and get their full share of, the activities and resources of the total local authority system. At the same time, however, the CEO has also to reduce demands into the proportions supportable by the resources likely to be secured. The CEO, as the head on a smaller scale, must then become concerned with such notions as equity – ensuring that resources are allocated fairly between competing educational interests – with the promotion of due process, so that complainants and clients get a fair hearing; and that they do not get their way simply by the exercise of pressure, but by systematic consideration of the arguments that they put up as against other arguments. Some might call these bureaucratic or machine-minding values. In fact, they also rest upon more fundamental issues of the balance of rights of individuals as against the whole community that the education system must equally serve. This is not to say that this balance is always fairly struck, or that any group of administrators does not include those that mistake the process for the issues that the process is supposed to serve.

The CEO, then, shares the values of teachers from whom he is recruited. But he also participates in the management of a system which might develop its own ethic. And he feels his role to be less obviously professional and more managerial. A decade ago Claire Pratt could say: 'I think I went round the schools a great deal more than some CEOs because I have felt this to be so important. It is part of my way of personal contact.' This personal and outward-looking approach was a feature of the CEO's role in the 1960s. It was personified perhaps by Hertfordshire's former CEO, John Newsom, who was said to go about the county with a trumpet in one hand and a trowel in the other. Now, a majority may well agree with the director of a London borough who asserts:

> Far too much time is spent on managing resources and adminis-
> tering parts of the system which could be left to others at the
> expense of the very responsibility which only the education officer
> by qualification and profession can discharge, namely, ensuring that
> children are well taught.

This emphasis on the managerial components of the CEO's role at the expense of the professional aspects is related to the development of corporate management to which we refer later in this part of the book. The trend away from concern with content is compounded by the apparently endless financial crises. As the CEO of a Welsh county puts it, 'cutbacks inevitably generate complaints, deputations, demands to address meetings, lengthy correspondence, petitions, etc.'

The reluctance many directors feel towards being 'managers', rather than 'professionals', is suggested by the comment of the CEO of an eastern county: '[The CEO] is less obviously a front-line leader but rather one who by sacrificing himself to the role of handling the machine, corporate and political, allows others to get on with the "real" work.'

As the work of the director becomes more managerial in nature, it is much more difficult to identify the distinct contribution of the professional CEO to the development of the local education service. What is it that the CEO can do as well, or better than, others concerned with schools and colleges in an LEA? Our interviewees seem to suggest that a wide-ranging and positive leadership of the service is now the essence of the role.

Briault's emphasis on the CEO as 'leading professional' may be difficult to sustain, in view of the evidence of our survey respondents that the managerial component of their role is now the dominant feature. Williams feels that the balance is moving away from the educational aspects of the position:

> No longer then is his distinctive contribution, as I see it, primarily as an educationalist, though he must be that. He must also have the skills of modern leadership, of representation and negotiation as well as administration.

As the managerial element of the role increases, at the expense of the professional component, the justification for a professional head of the local education service is more difficult to make. The thought of a non-professional CEO is anathema to Adams:

> If the idea of some of the practitioners of corporate management ever got a hold, that you don't need to be an educationalist, that you only need to be a manager, I think that would be a disaster . . . [But] I think it is further away now than it was ten years ago.

CEOs AND A POWER ELITE?

If there are functional and value differences associated with different roles in education, are there also social and power networks that hold them together? Certainly, the representatives of the local authority and teacher associations are always at negotiation meetings with their DES counterparts, and there are also informal occasions when some at least meet at each other's conferences and seminars.

These informal links do not, however, add up to a single system working towards shared aims. The connections are discontinuous and not systematic. The three principal levels of authority among full-time and permanent leaders of the education service are the heads of schools and colleges, the directors of education (and their most senior staff) and the administrators in the DES.

Relationships between individual directors and individual officers of the DES may be cordial but they possess none of the collective attributes of a 'ruling class' or 'power elite'; 'consciousness, conspiracy or coherence' (Crewe, 1974). Some CEOs become prominent within national policy-making, because they represent their peers either through the Society of Education Officers, or through the officer committees of the national associations concerned with education. Others are selected for nationally important tasks by DES ministers and officials. But there is virtually no career interchange between them. No DES administrator has become a CEO. Two distinguished deputy secretaries, Sir Toby Weaver and Jack Embling, spent some of their early years in local authority administration but both entered the civil service during the war when recruitment was open more widely.

One of the present DES under-secretaries, most unusually, is a former head teacher. Two HMIs, J. Stewart Mason and Sir Graham Savage, became Director of Education and Education Officer for Leicestershire and London, respectively. But HMIs are, of course, former teachers. Interchange between CEOs and DES administrators is, therefore, occasional rather than expected. It must be hypothesised that civil servants within the DES look at least as much towards the Treasury for the shaping of *their* values, and the priorities which they advance, as towards the needs of education as represented by CEOs.

Chapter 5

Local Government Reorganisation

The reorganisation of local government, which took effect in 1974, was the first major structural change outside London since 1888. Before 1974, the education service was provided by fifty-eight county councils and eighty-three county boroughs. The latter were all-purpose authorities and generally, but not always, comprised the larger towns and cities. The 1972 Act abolished county boroughs and established a two-tier system throughout England and Wales, comprising county and district councils. In six English conurbations metropolitan county councils were established but most major services, including education, are provided by the second-tier metropolitan district authorities. Elsewhere in England and Wales education is the responsibility of the first-tier non-metropolitan county councils. Since 1974, therefore, there have been 104 LEAs. There are thirty-nine English and eight Welsh counties, thirty-six metropolitan districts, twenty outer London boroughs and the unique Inner London Education Authority, which has the education function in the former LCC area.

Many CEOs faced personal change as the local education service had its first major shake-up of the century. The number of LEAs, and hence CEOs, was cut by about one-third and local government officers outside London experienced the trauma of applying for their former (or other) jobs. Four of our survey respondents lost rank as a result of reorganisation. As former CEOs, they became deputies in the new (larger) LEAs in 1974, but subsequently, of course, they again became CEOs.

Fifteen respondents moved from one LEA to another at the time of reorganisation: four had to move to retain their rank, three moved because posts looked more secure in the new LEA, while three took the opportunity for an external promotion. The other five did not give a reason for the move. Thirteen CEOs gained promotion within their existing or analogous authority. Four of these were in the new metropolitan districts and nine in the counties.

Two of our 1980 interviewees were personally unaffected by reorganisation: Briault remained in the ILEA, which was not subject to the 1974 reorganisation; Aitken remained as director in Coventry, whose boundaries were unaffected, although it became a most-purpose metropolitan district rather than an all-purpose county borough. Williams was Deputy CEO in the former Bristol county borough before reorganisation and became CEO of the new Avon county council in 1974. He was understandably pleased to have gained promotion to the top post in a larger authority: 'It was an exciting opportunity, of being in on the beginning of a new authority, based on Bristol which had been a progressive authority with a total commitment to education.' Adams had been CEO in Bradford since 1967 but the new metropolitan district expanded to take in part of the former West Riding. He was forced to reapply for the CEO's job and was shattered to find that the post went to former West Riding AEO, Richard Knight: 'I can only say that it was as near to breaking my heart as anything that has happened to me short of bereavement.' Within three weeks, he was appointed as CEO for South Glamorgan which 'softened the blow'.

WORKING WITHIN THE REORGANISED AUTHORITIES

With these personal uncertainties only a few months behind them, many CEOs were faced with administering the education service in authorities different from those they served before. A major consequence for many was the amalgamation of all or part of former authorities into larger LEAs. Thirty-six of our forty-nine respondents outside London refer to this. Twenty-four CEOs mention the problems that amalgamation had created. Nine were especially concerned about the need to establish equal levels of provision for staffing, capitation, and so on, throughout the new LEA. Many CEOs hoped to establish the best current practice of the former LEAs within the new authority but some were frustrated by the economic difficulties which have prevailed ever since reorganisation. Williams, for example, had hoped 'that we could apply to all schools the most generous standards of staffing and capitation we had inherited, but Avon was born at a time when public expenditure was being reduced and we had to compromise'.

Nevertheless, Avon did reach a position of equality 'on a reasonable basis within the first two years', but one CEO of a north-western district replies that his LEA had still not achieved equal levels of provision by 1980, while a northern county CEO refers to a levelling down of standards of provision as a result of financial stringency. The director of a northern district reports that rationalisation 'has, in practice, tended to accept the lowest level rather than the highest level of service'. A minority (seven) of CEOs mention such benefits of reorganisation as a 'levelling up of educational provision', more resources being made available; or the new LEA being stronger, more cohesive and better balanced than its predecessors.

Twenty-six CEOs said that the new LEAs were more political than their predecessors. This was especially true of formerly 'non-political' county authorities. Nineteen CEOs of English counties mention increased political activity. 'Greater political awareness', 'increasing political influence on all key decisions' and 'emergence of a party machine' are typical of the comments made. A CEO of a western county replies that 'a non-political county became intensely political – the county borough politicians overwhelmed the more gentlemanly county members'. By contrast, only seven directors of metropolitan districts report increased political activity and none of the Welsh CEOs do so.

The two interviewees most affected by reorganisation were conscious of a lingering parochialism among members of the new counties. Avon included the former Bristol and Bath county boroughs and parts of the counties of Somerset and Gloucestershire. Williams feels that 'in the early years many, if not most, members remained loyal first to their local areas, particularly since the great majority of them had been senior councillors in their previous authorities. The Somerset faction particularly remained strong'.

South Glamorgan comprises the former county borough of Cardiff and part of the former county of Glamorgan. Adams, too,

> can identify those members who are Cardiff-oriented, those members who are county-oriented. Attitudes die very slowly and it is not at all unusual to hear people in the education committee talk about education in this city. They haven't adjusted.

Nine of the survey respondents mention a residual parochialism. This was more evident in the metropolitan districts (five CEOs) and in Wales (two) than in the English counties (two).

It is a nice question whether these differences are a hangover from earlier artificial political alliances, or whether they derive from geographical and historical loyalties which statutory change cannot break down. Reorganisation has been alleged to be affected by political bias, by 'a very longstanding Conservative desire to neutralise the radical propensities of the cities by placing them under the umbrella of the Conservative voting Shires' (Sharpe, 1978). Not surprisingly, the inheritors of this kind of formula did not always settle down together. Nor do new arrangements, it has been argued by Sharpe, meet their principal objectives, that local government should follow population settlement patterns and that their larger size should improve standards of service, and that they should be more democratic than their predecessors.

It is not, therefore, surprising that there were many more references to the problems arising from reorganisation than to the benefits of the new structure. Reorganisation was not seen to be to the advantage of the education service, although there had been powerful arguments for the change, many of them of particular relevance to education. A major argument concerned the differential sizes of the 141 pre-reorganisation LEAs (outside London), a point particularly backed up by the evidence of HMIs to the Redcliffe-Maud Royal Commission which suggested a minimum size for LEAs of 250,000. Before reorganisation, seventy-four provincial authorities had populations below this figure, while thirty-two had less than 100,000 people. Following reorganisation, only seventeen of the new LEAs have a population below 250,000, although fourteen outer London boroughs are also below that level. It was thought that larger LEAs are able to provide larger and more specialist advisory and careers services. It is now argued that the specialisation of the largest has disadvantages of separating different strands of policy and of making 'central' politicians remote from the schools, teachers and parents.

CONTINUING UNCERTAINTIES IN THE REORGANISED LOCAL
AUTHORITIES

Under reorganisation, many towns and cities lost their county borough status and their education powers, and resented their reduced role. Peter Shore, then Labour Secretary of State for the Environment, proposed that nine[1] of the larger cities regain certain powers, including education, in a process of 'organic change'. There were strong political overtones in this proposal, because the cities concerned often had a Labour majority but now formed part of counties which tended to be Conservative-dominated. The proposal died with the advent of the Conservative government in May 1979. While, as Adams points out, not all former boroughs wanted further change, CEOs must have been acutely aware that their very employment base could be changed at political will.

Another case of the same uncertainty, upon which Eric Briault comments fully, is the initiative by the Conservative group in London, led by an MP, Kenneth Baker, which argued that the Inner London Education Authority should be abolished and its power allocated to the twelve inner London boroughs and the City of London. Baker's arguments for change rest primarily on the issues of financial control and democratic accountability and, thus, speak very much in the language of the early 1980s. As the reader will see, Briault refutes Baker's claims that ILEA members are not directly accountable, that ILEA's educational achievements are low and that a unified service should give way to one broken up among the boroughs. The defence of ILEA became somewhat more difficult, when in 1980, HMIs published criticisms of secondary schools in London which were eagerly picked up by ILEA's opponents (HMI Report, 1980).

EDUCATION AND LOCAL GOVERNMENT

The example of ILEA as a free-standing education authority pre-cepting on its constituent boroughs leads Briault to argue that the concept should be generalised: 'Given a free choice, I think I would go for independent education authorities.' Other directors, however, went even further and in the mid-1970s in the aftermath of reorganis-ation there was some disenchantment with any form of local govern-ment among educationists, including CEOs. In 1975 Manchester's CEO, Dudley Fiske, argued that education is essentially a national service and wondered if education should remain under local authority control at all. He concluded, too, that if the price for education staying within local government was too high, new *ad hoc* education author-ities should be created.[2] The merits of local government as providers of personal social services such as education is, of course, an issue that has occupied the minds of politicians and political scientists over a long period of time (Regan, 1979).

In 1980 the Society of Education Officers (SEO) established a working party on the 'Future organisation and financing of the education service', which will consider its relationship with local government. Fiske also returned to this theme in 1980.[3] The major issue was and is the corporate management structure adopted by many of the new local authorities. For many CEOs, corporate management and the education service are uneasy partners.

Chapter 6

Corporate Management

During the period before reorganisation, there was considerable thought about the internal management of local authorities. The subject was first scrutinised by the Committee on the Management of Local Government under the chairmanship of Sir John Maud, whose report *Management of Local Government* (1967) set out most of the arguments that were then taken up in detail by a second study group appointed by the Secretary of State for the Environment, Peter Walker, and the local authority associations, chaired by Kent's chief executive, M. A. Bains.

Both reports confirmed tendencies already emerging in local government. The Maud Report referred to a 'long tradition of associating a particular committee with a specific service' and of delegation of functions to specialist committees, which was convenient to local authorities but 'disperses direction and control'. While many local authority services have little in common, 'the separateness and individuality of the various services can be over-emphasised': 'Planning for the development of the community, the allocation of priorities for finance and for space on the drawing board, the timing of the various schemes all demand a co-ordinated approach.' Maud, therefore, promoted the notion of a managing board to provide the necessary co-ordination and focal point. The report also endorsed far more clear delegation to officers, who should be allowed to get on with their work without too much interference by politicians. The clerk was to be the undisputed principal officer of the authority and his co-ordinative powers would, it was implied, discourage the proliferation of departments and the 'other disadvantages of pseudo-professionalism'. These principles were elaborated further, and also modified, in the Bains Report five years later.

In his Preface to the Bains Report, Peter Walker, in applauding its main recommendations, thought that reorganisation would provide 'a unique opportunity to study carefully the best management practices within local government' and to see that they were carried out. John Stewart of the Institute of Local Government Studies, who was influential in helping local authorities to clarify their new arrangements, also thought that 'the moment of changing local authority structure has been the moment to begin to implement these new ideas and new concepts' (Atkin and Simons, 1974).

Twenty-seven of our respondents believe that reorganisation was the impetus towards corporate management in their LEAs, although in some cases it was built on the existing system rather than something completely new. The CEO of a northern county replies that 'much of the corporate planning represented a refining of, and improvement upon, what was already in progress prior to 1974'.

Whatever the stimuli, CEOs now operate in a sharply different management environment from that preceding the Maud and Bains Reports. Oxfordshire's CEO, John Garne (Atkin and Simons, 1974), said that 'the most significant change for me as a Chief Education Officer within the English education system, between the pre-April 1974 period and now, is corporate management in local government'. In 1972 Claire Pratt, whose outer London borough had been created in the earlier London reorganisation, recognised that change was on the way: 'I do accept the fact that we were simply a part of the rate-borne services and that we must not live in splendid isolation.'

Chief Education Officers were not hostile to the concept. Williams, who had more reason than most to doubt its value, appreciated 'the need for corporate planning and for a corporate outlook towards the generality of public services a local authority provides'. But Cook who advocated working closely with other departments did not favour an extension of the role of central departments: 'Why, for example, should a clerks' department clerk an education committee, prepare the agendas and write the minutes?' To him, this could obviously be done by someone engaged in the day-to-day work of education. In our 1980 survey, the director of a Welsh county refers to 'a constant battle to maintain control of certain aspects of the service and to ward off the efforts of certain members and officers who wish to see a greater corporate control over its activities'.

Altogether, forty-three of the survey respondents give examples of decisions formerly taken within the education committee but now taken in other departments or committees. These include the acquisition, disposal and maintenance of sites and buildings, the preparation of minutes and agendas as well as major decision areas to which we will refer in detail later.

These changes add up to a major shift of discretion from the education service towards authority-wide decision-making. Whether this is simply a corrective to what Bains described as the traditional independence of the education service from the central organisation, or whether it constitutes an infringement of the legitimate rights of the education service, depends on where one is standing and obviously varies from one LEA to another. Birmingham district council, for example, in 1976 passed a resolution damning corporate management and declaring it a complete failure productive of excessive centralisation, duplication of work, laborious documentation and serious administrative inefficiency (Haynes, 1978).

The examples derived from our interviews and questionnaires demonstrate the diversity of views about the ways in which major decisions should be made. Resource allocations, and the way in which they are made, demonstrate underlying philosophies about the distribution of power and participation in decision-making. What should be the power of those who represent workers within the institutions, such as teachers within schools and colleges, as compared with those who have to take a more holistic view of the development and running of a large and complicated civic system? Who is accountable for what? And should the collective plan begin with a total view of how much money should be spent and then broken down by those whose main expertise is in determining the total spending framework; or should budgets be a composite of those who know the needs of particular services without, perhaps, being able to place them in priority order with the needs of other services?

The issues seemed to have emerged, however, less as theoretical concerns than as feelings about the style and personal relationships resulting from changes in management structures. Many non-educationists might have shared discomfort at what one leading chief executive once called 'kidology'. If so, it is possible that they asserted themselves strongly when corporate management gave them a chance:

> There is a distinct feeling in local government that the 'across the board' officers believe themselves to be somehow superior to their colleagues. There are too many people whose main function now appears to be to co-ordinate, monitor and, at times, interfere. (Fiske, 1975)

Aitken well contrasts the calculative style of corporate management with the political sense required to run a service:

> Politics is about pleasing a whole host of individuals ... It's not logical and it doesn't fit tidy, refined, measured processes ... scientific management could not quite come to grips with the political situation.

It is obvious from our interviews and questionnaire material that corporate management appeared in many different forms in the 1970s in England and Wales. These variations had become evident even before the Bains Report appeared and had begun to take effect (Greenwood and Stewart, 1972).

STRUCTURE AT MEMBER LEVEL

Bains (1972) maintained that there should be a policy and resources committee to 'be responsible for allocating and controlling the financial, manpower and land resources of the Council'. The central committee should have a supporting structure of subcommittees. 'The more routine matters requiring member participation should be dealt with by three resource subcommittees each dealing respectively with one of the three main resources.' A performance review subcommittee was also advocated. Bains was fuzzy on the role of service committees such as education, but it was clear that they were to be subordinate to the policy and resources committee. There is now considerable variation in the practice of LEAs.

Fifty of our respondents make reference to a major central committee. Twenty-five of these are called policy and resources committees, fourteen are called policy committees, while eleven have other similar titles. Apart from Briault, in the unique setting of ILEA, all our interviewees work in authorities with central policy committees. Coventry's policy advisory committee is composed of members of the majority party only and evolved from a similar structure which pre-dated Bains. Aitken does not consider that this set up has adversely affected the role of the education committee: 'Before I had experience of the system in Coventry, I might well have said that it was leaving the education committee weaker, but in practice the position of individual committees is respected.'

South Glamorgan's policy committee includes the chairman and some of the deputy chairmen of the main committees and representatives of the opposition party. Adams says that 'few education issues ever go to the policy committee', so there appears to be a continuing and important role for the education committee. In Avon a resources co-ordination committee was established along with resources committees for finance, personnel and land and buildings. Education is one of several programme area committees. Williams was concerned at 'a trend towards decisions being taken within the resource committees at the expense of the programme area committees'.

STRUCTURE AT OFFICER LEVEL

Bains (1972) advocated the appointment of a chief executive in the new local authorities, who shall be 'the head of the Council's paid service and shall have authority over all other officers so far as this is necessary for the efficient management and execution of the Council's functions'. There should be also a principal chief officers' management team, which 'should be responsible, under the Chief Executive's leadership, for the preparation of plans and programmes in connection with the long-term objectives of the Council and for the general co-ordination of the implementation of those plans'. For education authorities, that is, metropolitan districts and non-metropolitan counties, Bains suggested the inclusion of the CEO, or director of educational services, as a member of the management team.

Fifty-one of our respondents refer to a chief officers' management team, while six others mention looser groupings of chief officers. Forty-seven of those CEOs are full members of the management team and three claim a specially influential position, two as deputy chief executives and one by virtue of being head of the largest department in the authority. There are few comments on the role of management teams, but the CEO of a Midlands county claims that his membership 'impinges little on my departmental role', while the attitude of a north-western CEO is unlikely to lead to a meaningful corporate approach: 'My role is to remind other chief officers that their departments and problems equate more with the school meals service than the whole service in relation to size, budget and manpower.'

South Glamorgan has a chief officers' management team of which Adams is a member. He feels it has worked well with a time limit on meetings, so that 'we wouldn't waste time and energy on some sort of ideological conformity to corporate management'. Avon has a chief officers' team also but Williams was concerned that, instead of undertaking corporate planning, 'resources officers particularly were tempted into claiming day-to-day management responsibilities in the programme areas', thus dispersing rather than unifying management control. Coventry had a chief officers' team as early as 1969 and Aitken has been a member of the team from the beginning. He found the approach to be satisfactory and stimulating, except that there was an overemphasis on rational management which 'could not quite come to grips' with the political realities of determining priorities.

All our interviewees have worked with chief executives except for Briault, who, as education officer, was effectively ILEA's chief executive. It is clear that the chief executive is significantly different from the pre-Bains town clerk, whose power to co-ordinate the main services of an authority was uncertain. In South Glamorgan the chief executive is 'the chief officer with the ultimate control and the ultimate responsibility for advising the county council', although the specialist chief officers are left to run their own services. Adams accepts, though, that the corporate approach leads to the possibility of interference in professional matters by other officers:

> You can waste an endless amount of time imagining that you are facilitating corporate development, when I really couldn't comment seriously on whether there should be a link road with the M4 and I wouldn't expect the Director of Environment and Planning to

be able to determine whether French should be part of the core curriculum.

Aitken accepts that Coventry's chief executive has a managerial, rather than simply a co-ordinating role: 'The exception was, and had to be, in the professional disciplines of an individual chief officer . . . advice on education was my responsibility.'

The CEO's membership of the chief officers' management team and the need to develop good relationships with the chief executive have influenced the nature of his role. In 1974 Atkin and Simons remarked on the change:

> The new management role the CEO had to assume under reorganis- ation clearly challenged the way many CEOs had worked in the past, particularly their taking pride in the degree of personal contact with local schools, teachers and parents. Sheer pressure of workload at the corporate level in the new structure now prevented them from spending much time at the grassroots.

The switch in emphasis from the professional educator role to the corporate management role is symbolised by the change of title given by many LEAs to their chief officer. Before the Bains Report, most authorities used the style 'Chief Education Officer' or occasionally 'County Education Officer', suggesting a professional emphasis. In 1980 a majority use the term 'Director', which tends to have managerial connotations. The shift is especially marked in urban authorities. This could be explained by the fact that it was the urban authorities that were more affected by the 1974 reorganisation, but the change is also significant in London, reorganised in 1965. See Table 2.

Table 2 *Changes in Titles of Chief Officers (1971–80)*

	1971		1980	
	Director	Education Officer	Director	Education Officer
English counties*	14	30	11	27
Welsh authorities	12	5	7	1
County boroughs	41	38	—	—
Metropolitan districts	—	—	25	11
London authorities†	4	17	13	7
TOTAL	71	90	56	46

*Cornwall has a Secretary for Education.

†In 1980 Barnet has a Director of Educational Services and Chief Education Officer.

Sources: Education Committees Year Book, 1971–72 and *Education Authorities Directory, 1980.*

MANAGEMENT PROCESS IN LEAS

It can be seen that three of our interviewees and the great majority of our survey respondents work within a structure of corporate management very similar to that postulated in the Bains Report. This may mean that Bains correctly judged the movements already in train, or simply that the new authorities had to establish a management structure in a hurry and found in Bains an officially blessed blueprint which they took on board without a detailed consideration of their own authority's needs. The apparent uniformity of structure may conceal a diversity of practice, however. A study of *process*, rather than *structure* alone, reveals this diversity and offers insights into the benefits and demerits of different approaches.

REVENUE SPENDING

Traditionally the revenue budgets of local authorities were built up service by service, approved by the relevant spending committee and then put to the council, which would either accept or cut them, often across the board rather than discriminating among its services. In this process the CEO and the education committee had a major impact on priorities and often on the total level of educational spending, too. Cook in 1972 was asked whether the allocation of resources rested with him: 'It lies with me in the sense that I advise the committee on how much money we need and they help me to get as much as we possibly can from the authority.'

The 1980 interviewees worked in a context very different from that outlined by Cook but their LEAs also differ considerably among themselves. The position in Avon contrasts sharply with that in pre-reorganisation Devon:

Budgets for all the services were prepared in the Treasurer's Department and submitted to the Finance Committee, finally approved by the Resources Co-ordination Committee and in effect passed to the Education Committee as its budget for the year.

Once approved, much of the budget was controlled by committees other than the education committee, which therefore had little scope for changing its priorities through exercising virement. South Glamorgan operates a system which is a source of concern to Adams: 'If you are looking at resources only then the risk is that you are not going to pay any regard to the level or the needs of the service.' The South Glamorgan approach is dominated by the supply side, the amount of money to be made available, in contrast to the demand-led process of pre-reorganisation Devon. The education committee does have virement within its budget, but subject to the approval of the finance committee.

Coventry has a process of almost continuous budgeting with the policy advisory committee seeking from spending committees a series of programme levels at figures plus or minus the current level. Once the level of spending is fixed, priorities within the education budget are determined by the education committee except that the policy advisory committee may stipulate that a particular area, perhaps the pupil–teacher ratio, may not be cut.

Thirteen of our respondents report that some aspects of revenue budgeting, formerly determined within the education service, are now settled by policy or finance committees. One director of a north-western district comments that his LEA's finance committee 'refers back or overrules some decisions on spending even within the approved budget'. The CEO of a Midlands county refers to the 'extension of financial control by policy and resources committee to an extent where various budget panels suffocate the service committees'.

CAPITAL SPENDING

Control of capital spending has been complicated by the fact that much of education's building programme is 'key sector'. This means that the loan approval is specific to a particular project or a particular area of spending, for example, secondary school building. Moreover, the level of 'key sector' spending is fixed by the DES, although the LEA could decide to spend less than the full sum allocated.

Both Adams and Aitken note the potential for conflict between the priorities of the education service and the overall priorities of the authority:

> The policy advisory committee controls and allocates the whole capital programme for the whole council and for all committees . . . [but] the DES capital building programme is an important determinant of the education capital programme. (Aitken)

If Adams and Aitken feel that they have been able to carry out their capital programmes without any real problems, Williams found that Avon's version of corporate management created difficulties in the implementation of the agreed programme:

> It was the Land and Buildings Committee which accepted tenders for building projects, and decided the cash limits to be applied to each, without reference to the Education Committee. The total programme of building projects could be frustrated by a decision made by the Land and Buildings Committee to accept a tender significantly above the estimated costs for one project.

The project to be dropped would be determined by the accident of which first received the approval of the committee, rather than reflecting the priorities of the education service.

Six of the survey respondents refer to decisions on capital spending, formerly determined within the education service, which are now settled by the policy committee or one of its subcommittees. The director of a West Midlands district replies that 'the policy committee has on occasion frozen all capital projects other than those already committed'.

But it is not only the relationship with the central committees that raises issues. There is also potential tension between the local authority's wish to determine priorities for capital spending across the whole range of its services and the ability of central government departments to prescribe levels of capital spending through the 'key sector' mechanism. The local authority associations believe that all capital spending should be 'locally determined'. The 1980 Local Government Planning and Land (No. 2) Act appears to go some way towards meeting that objective. The Act empowers the minister to specify an amount of prescribed expenditure for each year 'for such purposes as the authority thinks fit'. While he retains the right to direct that a specified part of the sum may be spent only on a specified project, he can do so only if that project is of national or regional importance. We cannot be certain, but the DES may seek to retain 'key sector' status for some or all of education spending. On the face of it, though, this appears to herald a major change and one unlikely to be welcome to CEOs, because it may well increase the power of central departments and reduce the ability of the education service to determine its own capital programme. Aitken describes the proposal as 'a cloud on the horizon', partly because he anticipates that it will be accompanied by tight limitations on the level of capital spending: 'You have freedom to scrap among yourselves about a much more limited amount of resource.'

PERSONNEL POLICY AND CONTROL

The Bains Report 1972 gave a high priority to the development of personnel management in the new local authorities. The head of the personnel department should have a major role with improved status and direct access to the chief executive, although Bains was vague about the relationship between the personnel officer and the departmental chief officers. Bains also advocated the establishment of a personnel subcommittee of the policy and resources committee.

The development of a centralised personnel service has been one of the major consequences of reorganisation, certainly from the standpoint of the CEO. Half of the survey respondents (thirty) make reference to personnel issues as examples of decisions now taken outside the education service. Most of these decisions have been 'lost' to the personnel subcommittee or its equivalent. A particular bugbear concerns the irksome procedures often required before vacant posts can be filled. The director of a West Midlands district describes what happens in his authority:

> All the chief officers have to go to the chief officers' management team to seek approval for the filling of any post, even though the post is established and provision is made for it in the estimates . . . Having obtained their approval, the chief officer then has to obtain the approval of his own service chairman, and then to attend a special meeting once a fortnight with the chairman of the policy committee and chairman of personnel.

Twenty-five respondents report that decisions concerning non-teaching staff matters, formerly under the control of the education service, are now taken elsewhere, usually by the personnel committee. This happens in South Glamorgan but Adams is not unduly concerned about it: 'I would accept entirely that when you are talking about clerical and secretarial and administrative duties, there should be one common yardstick for all the county council's employees.' Aitken, too, accepts the logic of common policy but feels that there ought to be more delegation to departments within a policy framework. Williams, by contrast, felt that in Avon the personnel committee and department were so strong, with power to approve the establishment of a non-teaching post or to fill a vacancy, that the unified management of the education service was threatened. They also became responsible for the supervision of the non-teaching staff in schools.

For the sake of consistency, one might have imagined that teaching staff matters would also be the responsibility of the personnel committee. In practice these issues have been left with the education committee and the CEO almost everywhere. The impression from the interviews and the survey responses is that this would be a major sticking point for all professionals in the service, including the CEO, and as a result local authorities have not sought to transfer power away from the education service. One West Midlands director describes how 'I have always struggled to keep teaching posts out of the clutch of personnel'. Aitken also feels strongly about this: 'Just occasionally questions are raised as to why are teachers different . . . I do not believe that I could really help in the management of the service and of schools . . . if the professional side of it was not within the compass of the education service.' Adams, too, asserts that 'teachers are a different breed'. One LEA which did initiate action on this issue is Rotherham, which in 1977 sought to have teacher appointments confirmed by the director of personnel and resources and not by the education department. The proposal was opposed by the director, the chairman of the education committee, local teachers associations and the SEO, who sent a deputation to meet a special subcommittee of the policy committee in April 1978. Marginal changes followed during 1978, and the role of the education department was strengthened following a restructuring of some departments in 1980. The position now is that advertisements are placed by the personnel department but applications are then made to the director of education and, subsequently, processed within the education service.

Chapter 7

The Avon Education Service and Corporate Management

An aspect of corporate management which emerges clearly from the survey evidence and our interviews is that the generic term conceals great diversity. Even where management structures appear similar, the management process and the location of influence and power vary significantly. Adams and Aitken are broadly satisfied that corporate management, as it operates in South Glamorgan and Coventry, is not to the detriment of the education service. They can live with it, even thrive on it, but it appears in different guises, and Williams found that he could not accept Avon's version of corporate management and resigned to take a senior post in higher education. Since his resignation, Avon has become synonymous with the less satisfactory aspects of corporate management. Because it appears to represent one extreme in the continuum of corporate management, the Avon affair is instructive and merits separate attention.

Following reorganisation in April 1974, the new county of Avon was born. It encompassed Bristol, Bath and parts of Somerset and Gloucestershire but as a new authority had an excellent opportunity to carve out a completely new management structure. Relying on management consultants, Avon produced a structure similar to that advocated by Bains but with different terminology. The policy and resources committee became a 'resource co-ordination committee'. Instead of subcommittees, committees for 'finance and general purposes', 'land and buildings' and 'personnel' were established with the authority to control those key resources. As perceived by Derrick Williams, these changes were not beneficial. There was uncertainty and confusion as to the responsibilities of committees, and resource committees took decisions at the expense of the programme area committees. There was confusion of responsibility between the programme area officer, who was supposed to manage his service, and the resource chief officers, who were also responsible for the use of resources. This had a direct impact on the schools and colleges:

> From the point of view of heads of schools, there were too many unco-ordinated managers. Heads of schools found themselves responsible to four or five chief officers and my own officers in the Education Department were left uncertain about their roles.

If the structure appeared unsatisfactory to him, the decision-making process confirmed the dominant role of resource committees and resources officers by comparison with the education committee and the CEO. The land and buildings committee accepted tenders for building projects without reference to education committee priorities. The education budget was determined by the treasurer's department and the finance committee. Approval to establish new non-teaching posts in schools, or to fill existing vacancies, was at the discretion of the personnel committee. The only major responsibility left with the education committee was the management of teaching staff, and even here Williams was not confident of the position:

> I always feared that the time would come in Avon when the Personnel Department would be responsible for the County's establishment and the number of teachers in each school.

Eventually Williams felt that neither he, nor the education committee, 'could effectively manage the education service even though we had the nominal, indeed the statutory, responsibility. Too many cooks were stirring the broth'. In October 1976 Williams tendered his resignation, significantly, to the education committee:

> The management of the education service is fragmented between so many committees and administrative departments of the Council that there is no united or effective direction of it. The Education Committee cannot exercise that direction, nor can I.[4]

Williams's resignation provoked a stormy reaction from educationists both within Avon, and outside it. The Avon Teachers' Consultative Committee made the following statement:

> We applaud his [Derrick Williams's] courage in exposing the true facts of the situation. This concern has been felt by teachers since the formation of Avon in 1974. No notice has been taken of our repeated representations to the Education Department, the Education Committee, and the Chairman of the County Council to express our deep disquiet over the permanent damage being done to the education service by the Avon County Council's interpretation of Corporate Management.[5]

The Society of Education Officers (SEO) was 'gravely anxious' about the state of affairs in Avon:

> The Society finds it impossible to reconcile the idea of an effective education service within local government with an education committee shorn of the support of a coherent management and

advisory service provided by an education department led by a professional CEO.[6]

The SEO advised any of its members contemplating service with Avon first to make contact with the Society at its London office. Lord Alexander[7] referred to:

> a worrying tendency in local authorities not to recognise the intention of the Education Act on the position of the Education Committee, which is intended as a statutory committee of the authority to be given responsibility for administration of the service, subject always, of course, to financial and major policy decisions of the authority.[8]

The Avon case is significant not just because it provoked the resignation of the CEO, serious though that was, nor even because Williams received full support from teachers within Avon and others outside it. It throws into sharp relief many of the issues surrounding corporate management. Corporate management is, in fact, an ambiguous concept. One version – that which prevailed in Avon – assumes that the corporate whole has a life of its own and that unitary objectives can or should override the values of the contributory elements. An alternative version would respect the integrity of the individuals, of the prime institutions, working within such services as education, social work and housing and would not seek to compress diverse values into a single set of norms. In this view the local authority would seek to enhance pluralism in public activity. It would recognise that client needs may be mediated through demands for different services and in different ways through contacts with different kinds of professions, and it would do its best to enable all groups to get a measure of what they want and need. At times, of course, priorities have to be asserted so that there will be winners and losers. But the presumption in the weaker version is that of collegial interaction between diverse groups, rather than the imposition of a single, and technocratic, system of control.

Michael Harrison, then President of the SEO, expressed the hostility of many to Avon's version of corporate management, and in so doing, shifted the ground of objection to that of concern for the 'seamless garment' of education:

> Events in Avon . . . seem to say that local government . . . is putting a higher value in some places . . . on its functional management than on the quality of its education service. This is a condition in which integrated administration of an education system can be destroyed, and with it the key role of the chief education officer working with his education committee.[9]

Chapter 8

The Political Framework

The relationship between administrators and politicians is a recurrent issue and all commentators on it (as summarised by James, 1980) emphasise the difficulty of finding and generalising data about the relationship. Prescriptive statements, as in the Maud (1967) and Bains (1972) committee reports recognise that, while policy finally rests with the members and administration with the officers, policy development is strongly conditioned by the expertise, information and full-time resources of the officers, while members have a legitimate interest in detailed issues involving their constituents. In any event, the pre-1970 literature tilts towards displaying how officers strongly affect the determination of policy. Our 1972 interviews showed how CEOs certainly saw themselves responsible for instigating changes within the system. Studies written in the 1970s (White, 1974; Donnison *et al.*, 1975) showed how the CEO acted as an information gate-keeper and as an initiator of change. Saran (1973) concluded that officers initiate changes not seen to be politically sensitive.

By the time we approach the end of the 1970s, however, major changes have occurred. Local government is more politicised, and this affects not only the substantive issues, but also the degree to which different voices will have a say in decision-making. What might have been considered a technical matter in the past, such as the closure of a village school, or a change in the balance of provision within a local area, is now highly political.

During our period, control of the local authority has been regarded increasingly as a worthwhile prize. 'Without a doubt, the shadow elections of 1973 in England and Wales were a dramatic leap in party political control at the local level' (Jennings, 1977). Whereas in many local authorities councillors have always met in party groups to determine their approach to policy issues, such meetings have acquired a new importance. Where one party has a clear majority, the party group meeting is often the effective decision-making forum and the formal committee system may simply ratify decisions already made. The CEO of a southern county emphasises the role of the party group in policy-making:

All major educational decisions are taken by the controlling group in caucus and then ratified by the education committee and the council ... it is now necessary for a chief officer to persuade the controlling group, meeting privately, before he can obtain a decision from the education committee, meeting publicly.

Although they were not asked directly about it, twenty of the directors in our survey refer to the significance of the party group. Fourteen of the thirty-one respondents in urban LEAs mention the group, while only six of the thirty county directors do so. However, Adams, a county director, acknowledges the importance of party groups: 'On any major step they will reach a decision in the group and then you will know in advance what at the end of the day will come out of it.' Aitken feels that in Coventry the one party 'Cabinet-style' policy advisory committee may reduce the significance of the caucus, though it remains important:

I believe it does bring out the caucus or the otherwise secret considerations more into the open to share with the council's officers. That is not to say that on occasions a debate is not stopped with typically the words, 'well, I think we shall have to take this to another place'.

Jennings, in his study of six LEAs, also emphasised the importance of the group:

Political action centres on the party groups, especially the majority party group. It is a focal point for power and decisions about policies and the policy making process. (Jennings, 1977)

Twenty-eight respondents report on increasing politicisation of decision-making over a wide range of issues. Seven CEOs refer to financial matters and eight to staff appointments, but the issues mentioned cover virtually the whole range of educational decision-making. Although only three of the twelve London respondents refer to increasing politicisation, these LEAs have mostly had strong political control since their inception in 1965.

Briault found there was a developing tendency for members to become involved in executive action. He complains that 'a particular subcommittee chairman demanded to be told of every suspension of every child that took place. Now I thought that was ridiculous'. Aitken detects little change except for the establishment of performance review committees to investigate particular issues. Williams felt that there had been little change: 'The councillors are far too busy to concern themselves with the details of administration, unless it is going wrong somewhere.'

THE DIRECTOR AND THE CHAIRMAN

The increased power of party caucuses and the tendency in many areas for an increasing number of decisions to be taken at the political level sharpens the importance of the CEO's relationship with members. Traditionally, the key relationship is with the education committee chairman. Pratt, for example, hinted at the desirability of a CEO–chairman alliance: 'They should have sufficient respect for each other's point of view to be able to come to a reasonable agreement before the thing comes before the committee.' Another and perhaps unusual example of relationships in an earlier period is that of George Taylor's quarrel with the chairman of the service of youth subcommittee. This invoked not only a demarcation of responsibility between a chief officer and a committee chairman, but also a style of relationship that is certainly not likely to exist now. 'I then sent for the chairman. I invited him to come and see me. I didn't tell him why.' The chairman explained that he told his chief officer what replies to make to correspondence, but Taylor replied 'Well, you wouldn't if you were chairman of the education committee, because I wouldn't tolerate it'.

The great majority (fifty-six) of our survey respondents believe the relationship with the education chairman remains central. Thirty-nine of them qualify that statement in one way or another, referring in particular to the power of the party group and its leadership, and the role of the leader of the council. Much depends on the personal qualities of the chairman and his standing within the majority party. This is emphasised by the CEO of a northern county: 'the strength of the CEO–chairman axis clearly depends much on the strength of character of the chairman of the education committee and the influence which he wields in the majority group.'

Our interviews and questionnaires give some evidence that, in the context of corporate management, the education chairman may not always have the personal qualities or the standing within his party which he had before reorganisation. This possibility is acknowledged by Aitken:

It can happen that you have a chairman who does not pack a clout inside the party. I had one who was a dear man, very committed to education but wasn't very articulate . . . Inside the party he often couldn't manage it. So you work with other members of his party to see that they supplement the chairman.

Adams accepts that the position of education chairman 'marginally . . . has been downgraded. The mere fact that there is a committee which can override the education committee is indicative of that'.

There is considerable variation among LEAs on this issue. The director of a north-western borough, for example, replies that: 'from the early days of local government reorganisation the most able councillors ended up on the education committee and this has in many ways coloured (to the obvious advantage of the education service) the views of the council.'

Where the growth of corporate management has reduced the power of the committee chairman, the CEO must cultivate additional relationships at the political level. In Avon 'the power caucus within the council is likely to be the chairman of the county council and the chairman of the resource committees rather than the chairmen of the programme area committees'.

The CEO of a north-western county reports that the CEO and the education committee:

> have to carry with them the majority party [and] the chairmen of the council, policy and resources, finance and personnel committees [and] the chief executive, treasurer and city secretary . . . the leadership of the authority, at the strategic level, has been put into a commission of senior chairmen and chief officers.

The need to maintain good relationships with so many individuals and groups is demanding but many directors feel it is essential if their position is not to be eroded. One CEO of an eastern county argues that the 'tendency for power to drift elsewhere can only be countered by eternal vigilance so that regular attendance at more meetings is vital'. The director of a northern district refers to 'a greater sophistication and intensity of political life', and adds:

> we may measure our skill these days by the sensitivity and rationality we can bring to bear on the officer–member relationship. It is all virtuous, no principles are compromised. We walk with care always. It is a time-consuming and exhausting way of life!

It is difficult to draw firm conclusions about the centrality or otherwise of the CEO–education chairman relationship, because it appears to vary so much from one LEA to another and is subject to change within LEAs with changes of party control and personnel. Clearly, it remains an important relationship. 'Each chief education officer relies on the chairman of the education committee as a conduit into the controlling party and the committee system' (Jennings, 1977). Equally, the director must foster links with other political leaders. The more that key decisions are taken outside the education committee, the greater is the importance of these other relationships. The CEO of another eastern county replies that 'it has become just as important to brief and persuade the chairmen of policy and resources, finance and even personnel, too'. Where the education chairman is not politically influential, the CEO's contacts with other political leaders may be vital, if the education voice is to be heard where the key decisions are made.

Chapter 9

Relations with Central Government

Relationships between local and central government have been, and remain, an area of uncertainty and constant change. The underlying relationship is that of two bodies each relying upon legal powers, but central government clearly has the upper hand. For one thing, it is able to reconstruct, through legislation, the areas, powers and duties of local government. And whatever its declared intentions, it retains key controls over the activities of local authorities.

The relationships between the centre and local authorities have given rise to a considerable normative literature, that is to say, discussion on what the relationship ought to be. Most commentators recognise that there are differences in the perspective of those responsible for national and those responsible for local policies. While they need not be in conflict with each other, there are national considerations such as the maintenance and development of the economy and the maintenance of law and order. And a national sense, whether acted on in any substance, that services should be reasonably equal irrespective of the place of residence of the recipients, which determine the framework policies made by the DES. The somewhat vaguely stated precept of section 1 of the Education Act 1944 did, indeed, call upon the secretary of state to

> promote the education of the people of England and Wales and the progressive development of institutions devoted to that purpose, and to secure the effective execution by local authorities, under his control and direction, and the national policy for providing a varied and comprehensive education service in every area.

But, as J. A. G. Griffith remarked (1966), that section means less than it says. For one thing, local authorities are not the same as health or water authorities, but are elected. This gives them a direct political legitimacy of their own and also assumes that there are local values to be articulated and to put into operation through local policies. The fact that it might be difficult to identify what is specifically local about a particular policy does not mean that there might not be differences of style and purpose which the local political system derives from its sense of what its own constituents want. But if that is so, there is plainly room for continuing tension and conflict between the centre and the local authorities. In the working life of the Chief Education Officer, in any event, the tensions are present and are yet another set of conflicting forces to be reconciled.

Local authorities have an independent source of finance in local rates. These legal, democratic and financial considerations combine to ensure a significant measure of discretion for local authorities. Their financial autonomy is limited to the extent of local authorities' dependence on the rate support grant (RSG) provided by central government. The extent of dependence on RSG varies according to the wealth of individual authorities and from year to year; in 1980–81 RSG provided some 61 per cent of local revenue, but this is to fall to 60 per cent in 1981–2. Once the grant is received by an authority, it is free to decide its own level and pattern of spending, subject to statutory requirements. As we shall see later, these arrangements are about to be changed.

LEAs have a number of statutory requirements to fulfil. They must, for example, provide education for all children aged 5–16 and must provide grants to all students taking degree courses at UK universities, polytechnics and colleges. The nature and level of provision in most parts of the education service are determined locally, however, and the wide variation among LEAs in key policy areas like the pupil–teacher ratio and capitation levels is testimony to the readiness of many authorities to set their own standards (CIPFA, 1980). As Dearlove (1973) suggests, 'there are firm grounds for claiming that local authorities are by no means the passive agents of the central government but have scope to develop their own policies'. In 1972 our three CEOs saw themselves 'within a national system of gently suggested guidelines rather than strong national prescriptions'.

The central-local relationship is not static. Some authors (Burgess and Travers, 1980) maintain that local authority freedom is all but extinguished. Most of the survey respondents take a less extreme view but detect some change in the nature of the relationship. Thirty-five CEOs believe that the centre is more powerful in relation to the local education service than it was a decade ago. Twenty-four of them refer to increased financial control and in particular the imposition of cash limits which has replaced the former policy of giving LEAs a supplementary grant to cover inflation. Many CEOs are concerned at the probable impact of the 1980 Local Government Planning and Land Act on local government freedom. The new proposals are too complex to discuss in any detail here but the Act gives the government power to strongly influence the level of rates in individual local authorities. 'The Secretary of State [for Environment] may reduce the amount of rate support grant payable to a local authority for any year if the uniform rate for that authority's area in that year exceeds the notional uniform rate.' The notional uniform rate would be determined by the secretary of state and appears to give new powers to the government to limit local government spending. Burgess and Travers (1980) claim that the effect of the Act 'will be within a very short time to replace genuine local government by the dependent outposts of a large central bureaucracy'. The director of a London borough describes the Act as 'changing the ground rules of the central-local relationship'. Aitken, Adams and Williams all feel that the Act is part of a trend to greater centralisation in financial matters. Adams refers to 'the way that the Department of the Environment can and does attempt to control local authority expenditure in a way that never happened up to about three years ago'.

Thirteen of the survey respondents refer to increased central influence over the curriculum. The recent spate of material, from the DES and HM Inspectorate in particular, is thought by the director of a London borough to 'constitute a plethora of official documents and reports which have to be considered by the LEA'. The CEO of an eastern county detects 'a firm move towards influencing curriculum which is new compared with ten years ago'. Adams sees 'no diminution of what I suppose Jim Callaghan in his Ruskin speech triggered off, namely, that the secretary of state has some responsibility for the level and quality of education which is being provided'. But Briault thought that, though the DES had shown more interest in the curriculum in the last year, that did not amount to increased control over authorities.

The growth of interest by the DES in the curriculum is not, of course, new. In the early 1960s it became evident that those powers which ministers had exercised over many decades meant that they could not evade some of the major issues of curriculum and educational organisation. For example, ministers used their powers to determine the structure of secondary school examinations and it was they, and not local authorities, who decided that there should be General Certificate of Education examinations and, later, the Certificate of Secondary Education. In these cases they solicited and considered the advice of the Secondary School Examinations Council as they now seek the advice of the Schools Council on the Curriculum and Examinations. But the decision was theirs, and it is simply not possible for a minister to decide, let us say, whether English language shall be a compulsory subject for pupils taking any GCE examination, or whether subjects must be taken as a group of four or five, or can be taken singly, without taking a view of the nature of secondary school education as they want it to be.

At the same time, ministers said, and seemed to mean it, that it would be for the schools and the local authorities to determine the content of education. The initiative taken by James Callaghan in his

Ruskin College Speech in 1976; the creation of the Assessment of Performance Unit in the DES a year or so before; Shirley Williams's 'Great Debate'; the succession of DES and HMI papers (1977, 1980a, 1980b) on a core curriculum and encouraging local authority initiative in monitoring the curricula of their schools in a somewhat more structured way than hitherto, all add up to a significant trend. But in the view of the authors, Briault is right in maintaining that this does not involve increased control. There is a difference between acting as a promoter in stating a view of the curriculum as both the DES and HMIs have done separately (1980a, 1980b), and in causing local authorities and schools to follow set curricula laid down by the centre. The DES may well cause more pressure to be placed on local authorities by stating its view of what might be provided, so that local electors, governors, parents and pupils will have sharper expectations of what is provided. Also the requirement in the 1980 Education Act that schools must state their educational objectives and publish some of their examination results will certainly affect the performance of the schools. These changes are, however, more by way of tightening up the general procedures for public accountability on the curriculum than for establishing a more prescriptive role of the DES in that environment of stronger accountability. Nevertheless, the increased interest of the DES and HMIs reflects a changing climate and leads many CEOs to feel that the traditional freedom of schools in these matters is being eroded.

Although finance and curriculum are the areas most frequently cited by CEOs, many other examples are offered to support the majority view of a trend to greater central influence and control. Five CEOs mention the 1976 Education Act, which required LEAs to introduce comprehensive education (although that has now been repealed). Other factors mentioned include the 1980 Education Act, with its imposition of appeals procedures concerning pupil admissions to schools, and increased control of further and higher education.

Much of this perceived centralisation is occurring in a framework overtly intended to reduce central control of local government. Although the 1980 Local Government Planning and Land Act removes some minor, and little used, controls it has done little to change the prevailing view among CEOs that local democracy is under threat. The director of a London borough says that 'the centre . . . will always talk of local democracy, appear to be patient with it, and in fact regard it as a clog'. The CEO of a northern county suggests that 'the greater freedom perhaps consists in greater freedom to do less and less'.

Although the majority of our respondents consider that central control has increased, four CEOs argue that the centre is less powerful, while seventeen perceive no significant change. Examples of reduced central control include the ending of the requirement to provide school milk and the abolition of the DES-determined fixed prices for school meals. Some CEOs refer also to the failure of Shirley Williams to earmark in-service training provision within the rate support grant. Derrick Williams attributes this to declining DES influence within central government. Arguably, though, that is compatible with a general grant which has been the basis of central support for education since 1958, and there is no significant recent change here in principle.

Education experienced central government intervention from sources other than the DES in the form of the increasing role of the Manpower Services Commission (MSC) in educational and quasi-educational activities. Aitken expresses his concern about its developing role in education:

> The budget of the Manpower Services Commission is now about equivalent to the total budget for further education. And really much of that work is being done on an agency basis within the education service. It would be better done and more accountably done by the education service direct. We've been squeezed out in a major way. The DES has been too mild and lacking in impetus, dynamism and leadership on this issue. I think it shows in other ways too.

If relations between central and local government are again in a state of flux, the main changes, except in the uncertain case of the curriculum, are being expressed through departments other than the DES. It is the Department of the Environment which is changing the rules of local government expenditure. It is the Department of Employment which in the view not only of our CEOs, but also in evidence given to the Select Committee (Fookes, 1976), is taking over parts of the post-school educational domain through the work of the Manpower Services Commission at the very time when local education authorities' scope for development is restricted. The director of a northern district comments on the changing significance of these three central departments:

> The DES is less powerful. The Department of the Environment is obviously more so because of the ever-increasing constraints on public expenditure and its power over the Rate Support Grant, and the Department of Employment via the MSC is more so because of the riches it brings!

HER MAJESTY'S INSPECTORATE

The DES is similar to other government departments in its hierarchy of career civil servants, led by a permanent secretary. It is unusual, however, in having a particularly influential group of professional staff. They are HM Inspectors (HMI), who are almost all former teachers. There are (in 1980) 478 HMIs in England and Wales, headed by the Senior Chief Inspector (SCI), who has deputy secretary rank, and by a Chief Inspector for Wales.

The HM Inspectorate has traditionally been referred to as 'the eyes and ears' of the DES. 'It shall be the duty of the Minister to cause inspections to be made of every educational establishment at such intervals as appear to him to be appropriate.'[10] This duty is exercised by HMI but appears to have been a declining aspect of their role for some time. As long ago as 1968 a Select Committee noted the change. 'HM Inspectors regard themselves in the main as advisers and consider such inspections as they hold incidental to their advisory work.'[11] The shift from inspection to an advisory role is noted by thirty-six of our survey respondents. This is attributed to deliberate policy, under-manning or the increasing activity of local advisers. A few respondents note a parallel reduction in emphasis on the local aspects of the HMI role and enhancement of their national role. The CEO of a southern county replies that there are now 'few if any inspectors with detailed and prolonged knowledge of local schools', while another southern county CEO asserts that 'they are now virtually invisible'.

Six CEOs specifically mention a recent re-emphasis on inspection and other aspects of the local role of the HMIs following a period of retrenchment. The CEO of an eastern county comments on an 'increased emphasis on the inspectorial role including the revival of the formal inspections'. A stronger role is noted also by Aitken:

> There is no doubt that HM Inspectorate waned in influence sub-stantially in the 1960s and . . . they withdrew from inspection, on a regular basis, of schools . . . Latterly, since the time of the 'Great Debate', and under the present Senior Chief Inspector, they have been trying to get back on track.

One chief inspector quoted by Atkin and Simons in 1974 claims that there was no real change in role, only of style:

> The only difference is the inspectorial practice – that we no longer have routine inspections. But basically our role is assessment; it's not advice. I can't see any point in an Inspectorate which doesn't assess.

Many directors welcome HMI involvement at local level and do not appear concerned about a possible duplication with LEA advisory services. Briault made this distinction between the two roles:

the London inspectorate is very directly involved . . . in the detailed
working of the service, whereas HMI is more removed from those
direct relationships and able therefore to advise against the national
background and to complement the perhaps more localised point of
view of the inner London inspectorate. I think that the one helps the
other.

Some CEOs endorse Briault's view, which is similar to that expressed
by the present Senior Chief Inspector, Sheila Browne,[12] but the CEO
of a western county adds a caution: 'If central government is to
influence the curriculum, clearly HMI is one of the tools to hand.'

There is a problem here for CEOs and the LEAs they serve. They
generally welcome the advice of the HMI. As the CEO of a northern
county puts it, 'they make a first-rate contribution as a national
monitoring force'. But many do not want the centre to increase its
involvement with the curriculum. The CEO of a London borough
refers to a 'gradual incursion into curriculum matters which I regret
will inevitably grow over the years'. So long as the HMI are perceived
as independent of the DES, the issue is largely avoided. Certainly,
Aitken perceives and welcomes a stronger central role for HMI:

> they are also fighting their corner more in the DES, and power to
> their elbow! So, in a way, we are witnessing something of a power
> struggle going on. I would welcome, certainly in the DES, a greater
> influence from the Inspectorate.

The CEO of a northern district also mentions a DES power struggle
and illustrates his argument with a reference to 'the nonsense over the
present documents on the curriculum, some of which come from
the inspectors and separate ones which come from politicians and
administrators'.

Most directors distinguish between the HMI and DES roles on
curriculum, welcoming the one and being at best suspicious about the
other. One CEO of a Welsh county, however, regards the more active
role of HMI on curriculum issues as a 'symptom of HMI's closer
alignment with the DES than in the past'. If this view becomes widespread, then the attitude of CEOs towards the national role of HMI is
likely to become markedly more cautious than at present.

Chapter 10

Governing Bodies

The 1944 Education Act provided for all secondary schools to have governing bodies and for all primary schools to have managing bodies. LEAs chose to interpret this requirement in a variety of ways. Some set up individual governing bodies for each school, some established governing bodies for groups of schools, while a few established a subcommittee of the education committee to carry out this responsibility for all schools (Baron and Howell, 1974).

The Taylor Report (1977) recommended individual governing bodies for all schools. Twenty-nine of our survey respondents indicate that their LEAs have individual governing bodies for all their schools, while twenty-five have a mixture of individual and group governing bodies and six have group governing bodies for all their schools. Forty-nine of our respondents say that the nature and role of governing bodies has not changed significantly since 1977. Six LEAs have expressly made changes in line with the major Taylor recommendations.

Few of the respondents comment on the role of governors, but those who do indicate a slight increase in activity. The director of a north-western district replies that 'bodies seem more active, pass more resolutions to have improvements made, some very slight indication of more interest in curriculum matters'. Of course, it is difficult for CEOs to be confident on this issue, because they have to aggregate their impressions from many different governing bodies which may have differing levels of involvement.

CEOs tend to be ambivalent about governing bodies. They accept that they are part of the system with a (largely undefined) role to play. Yet they are reluctant to cede power to them. In South Glamorgan there are individual governing bodies with teacher and parent representation, but Adams admits to being a 'reactionary' in relation to their functions:

> I would strongly resist a governing body which saw itself as really determining the daily operations of the school. And I wouldn't wish them to have freedom to pursue policies which might be in conflict with the wider requirements and priorities of the county council.

In many ILEA schools 'the managers and governors were pretty heavily involved with the way in which the school was being run'. By contrast, in Avon, Williams felt that their role was nominal: 'They often found it difficult to relate their own interest in the school to the interests of the authority. They are a somewhat uncomfortable part of the system because so few functions are delegated to them.' Few functions are delegated to governing bodies because further power could be at the expense of the LEA itself. Where LEAs contemplate expanding the role of governors, it is rarely at the expense of their own authority. Aitken explains how Coventry members want to strengthen the role of governors:

> I think they would want to see more involvement of parents, more accountability of the head and the teaching profession for what is actually going on. I don't think they really are that committed to handing over control over resources and maybe they are realistic about this.

The few respondents who refer to the functions of governing bodies mostly take a similar view. The director of a northern district says that 'governors are encouraged to become involved at a more detailed level in the affairs of the school'. The CEO of another northern district emphasises the role of the authority in the development of competent governing bodies: 'We continue to help them to mature, for example, by having the education committee send papers to them for discussion and reaction – on issues of curriculum, school management, structure of the education service and so on.'

The teacher unions are concerned that governing bodies will increase their authority at the expense of the head and his staff and have resisted many of Taylor's recommendations. NUT General Secretary Fred Jarvis, for example, described Taylor's proposals on new powers for governing bodies as 'unworkable, impracticable and undesirable on educational grounds'.[13] A meaningful role for governors may infringe what are perceived as the rights of either the elected members, or the teachers. 'It is difficult to avoid the conclusion that governing bodies fall largely under the dual control of heads and local authorities and play a mainly marginal and symbolic role' (James, 1980). The conclusion reached by George Taylor in 1972 still rings true for some CEOs:

> I find it difficult to see what is the future role of governors. In as much as they are democratic institutions I am sympathetic with them, but in practice I find it very difficult to see what their role is.

Our survey data cannot show the enormous variations in quality of governors, the extent to which they are helped and encouraged by heads to fully realise their functions and the quadrilateral relationship that emerges between the governors and those whom they are supposed to represent; the head and teaching staff; the Chief Education Officer and other officials; and the local authority. For example, some governing bodies welcome visitors to their meetings and regard it as a matter of principle that, save for confidential matters, they should be open to the public. Others are shocked at the very thought that 'strangers' should be present. Some take seriously the doctrine implicit in the Taylor Report that the curriculum is derived not only from the expert knowledge of teachers, but also from the needs and expectations of pupils and other client groups. On this view, the teaching staff would take account of the views of parents and pupils and others about what the curriculum might become and how it should be administered. The final decision and power might rest with them, but they would be reflexive to the needs of their clients. In this construct the governing body would be one of the more important testing grounds for the interaction between the professionals within the school and the clients who use the school. This type of assumption appears in virtually none of our witness evidence in 1972 or now. And the testimony of CEOs must be contrasted with an evaluation made in 1980 in *The Times Educational Supplement*: '10 years of campaigning have brought success to the National Association of Governors and Managers.' Nor do they echo Tyrrell Burgess's claim that NAGM's

real success has been to rewrite the educational case for the governing body. We have rewritten the philosophy of the school, and given a practical example of how it could be done without legislation, through parents, teachers, the local community and the LEA.[14]

Chapter 11

Interest Groups

As the pace of change in education accelerated in the 1970s, there was a parallel increase in pressure group activity at national and local levels. The comprehensive issue, in particular, led to a proliferation of interest groups both for and against individual and LEA-wide comprehensive proposals (James, 1980). In the late 1970s pressure groups fighting school closures became active.

Yet the literature on interest groups, in education as elsewhere, is, on the whole, in the direction of that summarised by James (1980): there is certainly evidence that some politicians and officials oppose increased participation as unnecessary, expensive, time-consuming and frustrating. Their reaction is often to restrict access to information and ignore reactions to information. 'What participation there is becomes a manipulative exercise in "educating" for participation. "Token" participation is no more than a means of legitimising proposals already decided upon.' But if officials find interest group activity, and the growing demand for participation, difficult or undesirable to handle, that does not dispose of the question of whether they take any notice of it.

The CEOs in the survey largely confirm the impression of an increase in interest group activity. The overwhelming majority (fifty-three) of our sample refer to increased activity in their areas. One CEO of a northern county notes decreased activity following the resolution of the secondary reorganisation issue in his area, but even he expects 'a renewed surge of pressure group activity arising out of the consequences of falling rolls and the implications of the Education Act 1980 on admission policies and appeals'.

More than twenty different types of group are named by our respondents, ranging from legitimised[15] groups like teachers' unions to the definitely non-legitimised and often *ad hoc* bodies such as 'humanitarians' or inner-city groups representing one-parent families or the unemployed. The CEO of a western county says 'they range from the worthwhile to the peripheral and misguided', without saying which groups are in each category. Briault was cautious about pressure emanating from 'unrepresentative and extremist' teachers' groups: 'I followed the policy of giving them a hearing but one didn't take their view quite so seriously, except to the extent that one had to make sure that they were not unduly influential when it came to the formal consultation or local decisions.'

The largest number of directors (twenty) refer to parent–teacher associations and other parent groups as being of greatest significance, while twelve consider teachers' unions* to be most important. Ten directors, including seven from London authorities, refer to the role of local branches of CASE and other national client groups as being of particular importance.

The survey respondents also identify a wide range of issues as being of greatest significance in terms of pressure group activity in their areas. Twenty-eight CEOs name issues related to falling rolls as of particular importance. These include school closures, amalgamations and the viability of small schools. Fifteen CEOs refer to reaction to financial retrenchment, while ten, all in London or the counties, mention secondary reorganisation. Five county CEOs refer to resistance to transport charges, a proposal eventually defeated in the House of Lords. Some fifteen separate issues are singled out in the responses.

It is evident from the responses that CEOs perceive an increase in pressure group activity from a range of different groups and over a wide range of different issues. It is perhaps rather surprising, however, that the great majority of them (thirty-eight) also claim that pressure groups can directly influence policy-making. Adams argues that consultation is not perfunctory in South Glamorgan but equally does not guarantee that the group consulted is going to get its own way:

> I am not very keen on the thought that policy is made as a result of who cries the loudest and we have tried very hard to project the idea that policy, the distribution of resources, goes according to the merits of the case rather than who makes the loudest noise.

However, Adams acknowledges that there is also 'some regard paid to the relative strength of pressure groups' by decision-makers. It is at the political level rather than the officer level that 'pressure' is likely to be effective. Most CEOs, like Williams, 'recognise the sectional character of a pressure group and equally . . . give weight to interests . . . not vigorously pressed'. Politicians, with an eye on the next election, cannot afford to be quite so rational in their approach to policy-making.

The survey respondents name nine different policy areas where pressure groups have directly influenced decision-making. Fifteen directors refer to groups which prevented the closure or amalgamation of schools. Nine of these were in the counties, where parents have sought to preserve small rural schools, but groups are active in urban areas also. In some cases pressure or anticipated pressure results in

---

* This result as stated is surprising but might derive from the form of our question, which asked directors to give examples of 'pressure groups' that influence policy. They may not have regarded teachers' unions as 'pressure groups'.

decisions considered unwise by the CEO. Briault found that ILEA's plan to close Bow School in East London was thwarted by local reaction. The director of a London borough replies that pressure on members in his area led to 'reluctance to plan for the whole LEA for falling rolls ... because it would mean declaring some schools as possible closures'.

Four CEOs mention secondary reorganisation as an area of policy influenced by groups, while seven refer to opposition to cuts in staffing or capitation and four discuss school transport charges. Other issues include school meals and corporal punishment, while the director of a West Midlands district replies that 'the lobby for the retention of nursery and under-5s education resulted in non-statutory parts of the service being saved at the expense of the statutory service'. The CEOs of five English and Welsh counties also testify to the strength of the nursery lobby in their areas.

The testimony of our survey respondents that lay pressure groups are not only more competent and active, but have successfully influenced decision-making across a wide range of issues, contradicts conclusions reached by other writers. Dearlove (1973) shows that councils can be autonomous 'against a backdrop of apathy, ignorance and powerlessness'. James (1980) suggests that parents have limited influence:

> There was little evidence of members or officers attaching much importance to the need to take account of parental opinions ... Decision-making has become increasingly closed and centralised and parental opinion is not generally seen as a potent electoral influence.

A possible explanation for this contradiction lies in the nature of the major issue identified by our respondents, that of school closures or amalgamations. Here is a specific issue which parents can comprehend and which is often perceived as threatening the social fabric of an area, especially in the villages. James argues that parents 'are unlikely to mobilise their group power by voting as a bloc to bring pressure on their local authority', but the issue of school closures, and the related issue of school transport charges, have produced just such a mobilisation and our respondent CEOs acknowledge its impact on decision-making. Whether parents are able to have similar impact on more general and longer-term issues is doubtful, because 'they are less able to press their case continuously as are the teacher groups' (James, 1980).

The relationship between the CEO and legitimised groups has changed. The traditional relationship is perhaps as described by Briault:

What Bill Houghton* understood extremely well ... was the importance of the right relationship between administrators and the teachers' professional associations . . . [Their] public utterances are really a kind of façade as often as not and . . . the real agreement is reached across the table between people like Vic Shaw [then London NUT Secretary] and Bill Houghton.

These informal contacts remain strong and influential only if the participants can make any agreements stick at other decision-making levels. There is evidence, within and outside education, that union leaders cannot now commit their members with as much confidence as in the past. The development of corporate management within local government means that the CEO also speaks with less certainty at such informal meetings. He has to convince a wider range of groups and individuals of the value of a particular policy line. Where agreements reached between the Chief Education Officer and union leaders cannot be honoured, it is inevitable that these groups will seek to direct their pressure to those who are perceived to have decision-making authority. Adams finds that people in higher education in particular 'want to address themselves to the leader of the council or the chief executive rather than to the education committee'. Williams believes that corporate management makes it more difficult for groups to identify decision-makers and 'the further away a group is from the real decision-makers, the more loudly it feels it must make its case – the more too it will go public with its concern'.

The tendency for teachers' unions to seek political rather than professional links is noted also by Jennings (1977) in his study of six LEAs:

officers report that the distance between teachers and administrators as fellow professionals is growing, because teachers are courted by politicians. Informal contacts between officers and teachers seem fewer and less important. Union and association leaders sometimes prefer and promote their objectives directly with party leaders, by-passing officers and even education committee chairmen.

The increasing activity of pressure groups over a wide range of issues and with perhaps increasing influence poses considerable problems for the CEO. This is especially true if some pressure group activity passes him by, because power is perceived to lie elsewhere. It is difficult to keep up with the new noises in a wider and more insistent political system.

* Sir William Houghton, Eric Briault's predecessor as ILEA's Education Officer.

Chapter 12

The Director and Schools' Contraction

CEOs almost everywhere are now managing a contracting service. Only two of our respondents anticipate an increase in school populations in the next decade. The total number of births in England and Wales fell by 35 per cent during 1964–77. A majority (thirty-five) of the survey respondents express concern about the maintenance of morale among groups concerned with the education service: CEOs refer to reduced opportunities for teacher employment, lack of promotion opportunities and the effects on educational provision and standards. Eighteen respondents make particular reference to the problem of morale among teachers. A London borough director says that 'staff faced with reduced career opportunities can become disheartened', while the CEO of a West Midlands district 'wonders just how far goodwill can be stretched before it snaps'.

Fifteen CEOs mention the need to convince politicians that expenditure cannot be reduced in direct proportion to falling pupil numbers, if standards are to be maintained. The director of a Welsh county refers to 'difficulties of redistributing resources . . . in a contracting situation, while at the same time demonstrating that economies of scale are not always financially proportionate, nor educationally practicable'. An eastern county CEO writes of 'educating members against the idea that you can cut expenditure pro rata to the decline in pupil numbers'. Aitken tries to overcome this by relating his arguments to individual schools:

> Although that school has lost twenty-five children that only may mean three pupils per class and you still need the school, and the caretakers and the cleaners; it begins to be seen that you can't always relate every cost to the number of children. There are premises-related costs: there are child-related costs.

Twenty-three CEOs refer to problems concerning school closures and fourteen to issues of redeployment as significant aspects of falling rolls. Ten other CEOs refer to difficulties in maintaining curriculum coverage in the schools. Another difficulty mentioned by nine CEOs is the reluctance of members to tackle the problems of contraction. One southern county CEO refers to 'summoning up and retaining the political will to act resolutely' on falling rolls. Briault, who carried out a major piece of research on falling rolls during 1978–80,[16] feels, however, that 'many authorities now are beginning to consider the implications and to make plans to meet it, including closures of schools in some cases'.

Often it is the CEO who has to take the initiative in persuading politicians to face up to the problems of contraction. The director of a London borough feels that he must 'bear the responsibility for pointing out to members the effects of population decline and financial restriction'.

The CEO and his colleagues are perhaps just as vulnerable to problems of morale as the teachers. The director of a northern district argues that the management of contraction 'is unremittingly harder than the management of expansion . . . and generally management manpower is thinly stretched, the pay relativities (education officers– teachers) are ludicrous, and morale has to be nursed'.

Aitken is rather more sanguine about the difficulties of contraction:

> Every age has problems. It is challenging to meet the needs of the job and if that means changing your style, developing new skills, then that's all part of the excitement, the stimulation of the challenge.

It will be difficult for Aitken and his CEO colleagues to maintain such a positive approach as the twin problems of falling rolls and economic constraints continue to mount. Yet in previous periods of restriction a few CEOs, such as Henry Morris, who introduced village colleges to Cambridgeshire (Reé, 1973), concerned themselves with improving the content and institutional forms of education at the individual school level. As the CEO of a southern county suggests, directors must become 'more inventive to keep the service moving forward despite the difficulties'.

CONTRACTION AND SCHOOLS' DISCRETION

Falling pupil numbers are seen to combine with financial constraints in reducing the discretion of schools and their ability to operate as independent units. These are clearly considerations that never had to be taken on board in the early 1970s. Thirty-nine of our survey respondents either believe that schools' freedom has already been curtailed as a result of these twin difficulties, or anticipate that discretion will be limited in the near future. Williams, too, argues that 'contraction encourages very much greater control and the assumption by the centre of responsibilities which in more ordinary circumstances you would expect to be exercised by heads'.

The CEOs identify a wide variety of different constraints on schools but two problems are given particular prominence by them. Twenty-one of the survey respondents describe how, as numbers fall, staff might face redeployment and schools either cannot replace departing staff, or must accept teachers redeployed from other schools in the authority. Twelve of the thirteen LEAs examined by Briault and Smith (1980) operate a scheme of compulsory redeployment. This must mean the director and his colleagues become far more directive than before. The shift in the locus of decision-making is emphasised by the CEO of a southern county:

> The exporting school in the last analysis has to accept the CEO's judgement about who should be redeployed, and the receiving school has to accept that they cannot choose anyone but a redeployed teacher to fill a vacancy.

This view contrasts sharply with Pratt's assessment of appointing procedure in a period of expansion:

> The heads don't 'appoint' their staff, but any CEO with sense allows the head to pick his staff and the CEO advises him if he thinks this necessary but allows him his say because he has got to work with them.

The other major issue arising from contraction and economic difficulty concerns the curriculum. Eighteen CEOs refer to the impact on curriculum resulting from falling staff levels. Other issues mentioned include greater control by CEOs over admission arrangements to schools, reduced in-service training and the threat to sixth forms in schools. Coventry recently tackled this last problem of small sixth-form teaching groups in a co-operative manner, as Aitken describes:

> We shared this problem with the heads. They themselves have come up with consortia groupings. They themselves have said there are certain subjects which don't fit, and they are leaving me to decide about those . . . Now, surely it is much better to have got to that position through open discussion and recognition than to be forcing the issue, and I think we are the stronger for it, all of us.

The effects on teacher attitudes are not yet clear. Heads working in consortium no longer have so strong a managerial authority over their staff, whose feeling of belonging to the school as their own institution may weaken. Being 'in the employment of the authority' may take on a stronger and less satisfying reality.

Chapter 13

Accountability and the Director

Accountability has become an increasingly prominent issue in education. This reflects a growing concern that the freedom traditionally assumed by British educational institutions should be conditioned by a view of what are the best interests of the community and clients they are there to serve. The director is not immune from these demands for increased accountability. Members and the electorate expect the CEO to take responsibility for the education service in his area and to answer for any perceived weaknesses or limitations, wherever they may be found.

Constitutionally the CEO must be regarded as accountable to his employer, which is the council as a corporate body. Thirty-one CEOs in our survey expressly state that they are accountable to the council, although three imply that this is only the theoretical position. Eleven of the thirty-one claim that their accountability to the council is exercised through the education committee, one through the policy committee and two through the chief executive. Seven refer only to their accountability to the council, without any mention of the way in which the accountability is mediated.

Traditionally, the CEO's accountability to the council has been mediated through the education committee. Forty-three of our respondents refer to their accountability to the education committee, twelve more than mention the council. If this appears surprising, even that degree of acknowledgement of the role of the council is a significant change since we discussed the matter in 1972 with our three CEOs:

> The council is the supreme governing body to whom CEOs must defer. Yet it quickly becomes apparent that the whole council as a formal entity has little place in educational decision-making. Note how none of the chief officers refers to it.

Twenty-four CEOs refer to accountability to both the education committee and the council. Adams also notes this joint responsibility: 'If I say the county council I am stating a legal position. Of course the county council as such won't know very much about what is going on here. I am accountable to the education committee.' Ten CEOs

mention only the education committee and do not explicitly acknowledge the position of the council itself.

The emergence of corporate management systems in most LEAs has
led to some diffusion of accountability. Only two CEOs mention
responsibility to the policy committee, but as many as twenty-eight
acknowledge the position of the chief executive and three CEOs refer
only to their accountability to him. Thirteen of the twenty-eight CEOs
mention both the council and the chief executive, effectively mediating
their accountability through the latter. This would have seemed
astonishing to the CEO of the early 1970s. The 1972 interviewees
scarcely mentioned the clerk, the chief executive's predecessor, but
where they did, it certainly was not to acknowledge any responsibility
to him. Cook rather took an opposing view: 'There are quite a number
of authorities where the clerk of the county council takes too close an
interest . . . I personally just can't understand why this should be so.'

The 1980 interviewees recognise the position of the chief executive,
although not all acknowledge accountability to him. Williams was
'clear that the chief executive was my senior officer', while Adams
'acknowledges a certain amount of accountability to the chief executive'. Briault, however, referring to the general position rather than the
special case of Inner London, 'does not take the view that he [the
CEO] is directly answerable to the chief executive', while Aitken does
not mention the chief executive in his response.

Twenty-two of the survey respondents mention accountability to
both the education committee and the chief executive. Such a position
of dual accountability cannot be comfortable for the CEO. The CEO
of a southern county mentions accountability to the education committee, and adds: 'I should expect the chief executive to be on my tail, if
my performance were below par.' The director of a northern district
emphasises the limitations of accountability to the chief executive:
'This is largely a fiction, since accountability requires the ability to ask
the question as well as the capability to answer it, and my friend the
chief executive wouldn't pretend to have adequate depth of knowledge
about education to ask many real questions.'

The accountability of the CEO to the council appears to be mediated
through either the education committee, or the chief executive, or in
some LEAs, both. The differing emphasis on corporate management
in LEAs may explain the different perceptions of CEOs on this issue.
The director of a northern district feels unable to respond on the
nature of his accountability: 'the LEA has refused to promulgate the
functions of the Chief Education Officer.' Few CEOs are that uncertain about their position, but in most LEAs the corporate approach
ensures that accountability is less direct and clearcut than it was before
the Bains revolution. The significant point is, however, that the issue
would hardly have mattered fifteen years ago.

Some directors feel that, in addition to their managerial account-ability, they have a professional responsibility to the teachers and pupils in their educational institutions, although the two terms are used as if interchangeable. Williams explains it in these terms:

> I always held strongly that I had another accountability, 'profes-sional' accountability, which I owed to the local community for the efficiency of the education service, and indeed to the county's force of teachers, for whom the CEO is leader.

Aitken also refers to professional accountability as do fifteen of the survey respondents. The CEO of an eastern county thinks that 'accountability is a two-way process, not simply vertically hierarchical. Therefore, I feel accountable to heads of schools/colleges, to the teaching profession as a whole, to my own staff and to the public'. Although CEOs acknowledge responsibility to pupils and teachers in their schools, they are not really accountable to them. Accountability means answerability to a body or individual with the power to impose sanctions for non-compliance. Teachers and pupils have no direct sanctions comparable with those available to the council. What some CEOs acknowledge as accountability is perhaps more accurately described, in the words of a northern county CEO, as 'a moral res-ponsibility'. Moral responsibility may be felt towards almost everyone concerned with the education service but formal accountability is owed to the LEA, which has the legal right and duty to provide that service.

ARE THE SCHOOLS ACCOUNTABLE TO THE DIRECTOR?

The education service differs from other local government services in that the great majority of employees work within institutions separate from the town or county offices. Schools and colleges are separate entities, staffed largely by professionals who expect and enjoy dis-cretion in carrying out their teaching role. The relationship between the CEO and head or principal is not, therefore, that of a manager–subordinate, as is found in the social services, or housing or other local authority departments. Both are senior professionals, yet both work within a setting of public accountability.

Our 1980 interviewees all refer to the importance of their links with heads of institutions. Aitken regards it as 'the key relationship. One at which I have had to work and learn'. Briault, in the largest authority, emphasised the need for an active relationship between his profes-sional staff and the schools:

> I would see my responsibility to be in direct contact with as many of them as possible, and if I couldn't do that myself, to make sure that

my administrative and advisory arrangements made sure that there was somebody directly relating to them and advising and helping them and in a position to draw me in if necessary.

Twenty-six of the survey respondents make particular reference to the value of good, friendly relationships with their heads. One CEO of a southern county says that this 'has helped to carry us over some sticky patches without confrontation', but directors, perhaps inevitably, became vague when asked about the nature of the relationship. Taylor denied that his relationship with heads was a managerial one: 'All I would do was to set out the case, try to persuade them, and if they didn't accept my advice, to accept the decision.' Eight years on, Adams takes a similar view: 'I can't very well wish to direct them. It would be impertinent for someone who left the classroom thirty years ago to think that he could tell a school how it should do its job.' Aitken talks of 'a shared common professional purpose among respected

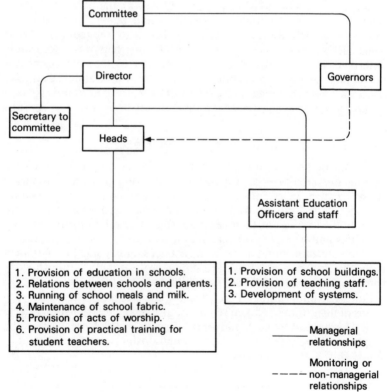

Figure 1 *Head accountable to Director of Education.*

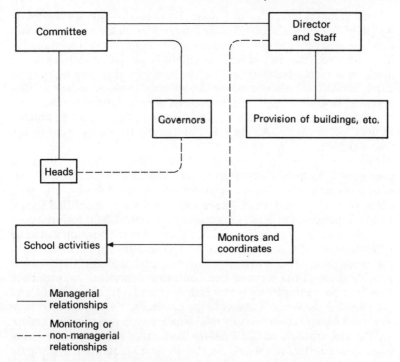

Figure 2   *Head accountable to education committee.*

colleagues', but 'at rock bottom, you are the head of the service and you expect to be able to give directions'.

The survey evidence throws up conflicting perceptions about the relationship with little agreement emerging. One CEO of a West Midlands district points to the ambiguity of his links with heads. Schools 'fluctuate from dreams of unrealisable and unrealistic autonomy, for example, sixteen- to nineteen-year problems not faced easily, to calling for help when things get rough, for example, mid-day break'. A CEO of a Welsh county suggests that corporate management within local government 'has tended to forge a stronger link between officers and leaders of institutions in defence of the education service'. Few are as deterministic as the CEO of a western county, who feels that the CEO should be 'a near benevolent despot, though I would qualify despot . . . to imply a person willing to listen to the institutions, striving to get an agreement but in the end having to make the decision.'

Some of the unresolved issues raised in *County Hall* are still un-solved by our data. The CEO's authority over heads and over the schools remains largely non-specific. Particular powers can certainly be found in local authorities' disciplinary codes, in the procedures laid down formally for distribution of resources, but the actual relationship becomes specified only when extremely large decisions have to be made: when schools are to be closed or to change their nature, or to be amalgamated, or when a major disciplinary problem arises so that action at levels beyond the school must be contemplated. The main area of doubt concerns whether schools and colleges are accountable to the CEO or the LEA. The CEO of a northern county says this is a 'moot point'.

The issue as put in *County Hall* is as follows: the committee is accountable to the council for the operational activities of the local education authority. But it has to delegate most of the work to paid employees. Is the pattern of delegation as in the very simplified Figure 1? In this pattern, the heads are accountable to the CEOs for what goes on in the schools. But, in Figure 2, we show what the position would be if heads were not accountable to the CEO, but directly accountable to the committee. This structure would assume that the CEOs must provide some of the services that constitute education – appropriate buildings, for example, without which no school is legally a school, and they provide these as *collaterals* to the heads. But they would also have a monitoring and co-ordinating role, which means that they can ensure on the committee's behalf that the committee's policies are being implemented. But they would be able to do no more than investigate and report to the committee. They would not have managerial authority over the school.

It should be emphasised that there is a difference between possessing managerial *authority*, which a CEO would need if he is to be accountable for the work of the schools, and an *authoritarian* style of the kind eschewed by many of our respondents. 'Hire and fire' is not essential to managerial authority, in all or any of the public-sector organisations.

Forty-one of the survey respondents feel that there is some accountability from institutions to the CEO, though few are as certain as one CEO, who replies that it is 'line management'. The majority are probably closer to the position set out by the CEO of a southern county: 'In practice, the committee, the teaching profession, governors and parents expect the CEO to promote effective education in good schools and to intervene to get things right when they are going wrong.'

Thirteen CEOs write that institutions are accountable to their governing bodies, but ten of these feel that there is responsibility to the CEO as well. The director of a northern district distinguishes between the accountability of the head to the CEO and institutional accountability, which is mediated through governing bodies to the education committee. However, this clear distinction between professional and political systems is rather more blurred in practice. The CEO's staff normally clerk the governing bodies, for example, and it is the LEA's professional advisers who judge the quality of education in the schools. Consequently, institutional accountability is at minimum mediated through the CEO. Briault suggests that heads 'have an accountability . . . for the health of the institution to the employing authority, and the manifestation of that employing authority I would think is the CEO . . . As a chance phrase a number of heads would speak of me as "the boss" '. The director of a London borough argues that 'increasingly teachers are seeing themselves professionally responsible to the statutory officer (as the LEA's professional representative), fearing direct professional accountability to laymen'.

It seems certain that CEOs do not engage in a managerial relationship with the schools, if that means that they undertake detailed monitoring or 'fine tuning' of the heads' decisions on the core activities of teaching, encouragement of learning, curriculum development, relationships with the community, and so on. Instead, they either on their own authority, or as proxies for the education committee, lay down the general boundaries within which discretion over these key activities is exercised by the head and the staff.

In the particular circumstances of Avon heads were unable to maintain a direct line of accountability to CEO Williams. This was

> regretted both by me and I know by heads and principals. Clearly, their accountability to an individual in an authority would be simpler, more direct and more professional. Their situation and mine in Avon was made difficult because other departmental officers claimed the responsibility of heads to themselves for the management of resources.

The increasing emphasis on accountability may bring in its train a reduction in institutional discretion. In 1972 Cook was able to say that 'within reasonable limits the headmaster and his staff are free to run the school as they think best and to have the sort of curriculum they think best'. If schools are required to explain their actions, the subsequent interaction may lead to a modification of behaviour and, hence, a limitation of their discretion. This possibility is suggested by the CEO of a large metropolitan authority:

> CEOs in order to be efficiently accountable to committees, MPs and the public, need accurate information. Schools and colleges are therefore increasingly required to provide this. A recent example is a curriculum analysis of each secondary school. The curriculum is the school's concern but the CEO needs to know in how many schools, for example, French is taught in mixed-ability classes until

the fourth year. This knowledge carries the threat of a directive that this practice be stopped.

Five other CEOs in the survey mention the curriculum implications of tightening lines of accountability. The majority of respondents (forty), though, feel that there has been no discernible impact on institutional discretion. Where reduced freedom is noted, it is more often attributed to financial constraints than increased accountability. The main example here concerns limitations on replacement of staff. One CEO of a southern county says, 'in a few instances there is conflict because of wishes of governors to be seen to govern'. Most LEAs, however, still appear to value institutional discretion. The director of a north-western district describes the attitude of his LEA in this way: 'The authority continues to prefer professionals who make decisions and act as they judge best to those who dither and constantly seek to have their hands held.' Aitken believes that 'accountability is a form of questioning; it is the arrogant professional who thinks he should never be questioned . . . any profession ought to be big enough to be held accountable'.

Chapter 14

William Tyndale Junior School

Directors proclaim their relationships with school heads to be those of friendly colleagues. But what happens when CEOs feel that a school is going wrong? Our interviewees acknowledge their responsibilities. Aitken says that

> if an institution is really failing, and if it is basically the fault of the head or he or she is the cause of it, then you do something about it. You seek the removal of the head in the final analysis.

Before that arises, the director would expect the appropriate adviser to have counselled the head and, only then if necessary, to inform the director of the problems. However, as Cook pointed out: 'the difficulty here is to decide when a school is going downhill, if it is, and at what speed it is going downhill.'

Manchester's CEO Dudley Fiske (1979) has written of 'the almost total lack of agreed grounds on which to assess the health of a college or school'. This difficulty was evident at the William Tyndale Junior School in Islington, within the ILEA area, during 1974–5. Briault, then ILEA's education officer, approached problems in schools in a similar manner to other CEOs:

> I did leave it to the [ILEA] Inspectorate. I didn't think my role in these relationships was to get personally and actually involved in the difficulties or problems. If I became aware of them, it was my job to put in train the necessary support or help or advice or surveillance, but not to get involved in it.

From March 1974, the principal agent of 'support' at Tyndale was the new district inspector, Don Rice. He attended a crucial meeting between teachers and managers in July 1974 and presented a report to the chief inspector and ILEA officials. A further, and more critical, report was made in March 1975 and received by Harvey Hinds, chairman of the ILEA schools subcommittee. At a subsequent meeting, Hinds told three of the school's managers that 'the reports were not so critical as to justify instituting a full inspection' (Auld, 1976). This view was expressed in the knowledge of an anticipated fall of eighty in the school population in June 1974– September 1975.[17]

Briault acknowledges that the supportive approach was maintained too long:

> The kernel of the Tyndale problem would always I think be the kernel of such a situation, and it is really, at what time do you move from support and help to disciplinary action and who decides to make the move. Don Rice of the District Inspectorate sought to adopt an advisory and supportive and helpful position in the hope of so moving the situation as to avoid a final showdown. And looking back, I think probably he and we went along that line just too long.

It was just over a year between Rice's first report on Tyndale (9 July 1974) and the decision of ILEA's schools subcommittee to institute a public inquiry preceded by a full inspection of the schools (24 July 1975). In view of the dramatic nature of events during that year, we can only agree with Briault that a formal investigation of Tyndale was required earlier, and preferably much earlier, than July 1975. The inspection began on 22 September in the absence of the head, Terry Ellis, and seven of his staff, who withdrew their labour and closed the school. Ellis went ahead with the school closure, despite a direct appeal from Briault: 'I did my best, personally on the phone to him . . . to make it clear to him that he had no right to close the school. It wasn't his school to close.'

Briault regards the refusal of Ellis to heed this appeal as 'a major defiance of the proper responsibility to his employing authority':

> He didn't regard me as his boss. Ellis had to be dismissed because he was shown in a disciplinary hearing to have failed to carry out his duty, so badly failed as for it to be irresponsible for the authority to leave him with that responsibility.

The informal approach of the district inspector, Don Rice, was maintained too long and was unsuccessful. By the time a formal approach was taken by ILEA, confidence in the school by parents had gone beyond the point of redemption, as had confidence in ILEA by the Tyndale staff. The ultimate decision to close the junior school (and to amalgamate it with the infants school) was predictable long before it happened. Tyndale was a failure for almost everybody involved, including the education officer. It is, however, a story full of lessons for those who think that schools can be managed on a simple accountability model, even if stronger application of local authority power would have been appropriate in this case.

Chapter 15

Conclusion: A Changing Distribution of Power and Authority

In this introductory part of the book we have collated from our interviews and questionnaires the views of directors on the several conflicting movements that have affected them over the last decade. While the background and values of directors have hardly changed, their working context has been subject to the push and pull of increased politicisation; the movement to make them responsible to a corporately managed local authority, rather than to their own education committee; the demands for more direct responsiveness to 'external' groups working through governing bodies and pressure groups and the changing relationships with central government.

In taking note of these often conflicting changes and pressures we can identify two issues that can be taken further before we invite the reader to consider the text of our interviews with the seven CEOs. First, what can be said about the new distribution of power and authority as far as the director is concerned and, secondly, what model of decision-making is implied in the changed structures? The number of groups with a direct interest in the administration of education has increased. If the number of players increases, some of these must have lesser roles. But there are also the effects of changing the actual power held by any individual player. What does our evidence show? Figures 3 and 4 show how the main linkages which the CEO must make, have been greatly elaborated in recent years.

The education subgovernment (Manzer, 1970) used to be quite self-contained. We have displayed evidence, showing how corporate pressures have reduced departmental power and reinforced the roles of the chief executive and the chief officer management team. In many of the larger authorities the CEO cannot maintain a personal relationship with heads of schools and colleges. Sometimes, as in Avon, other chief officers control resources deployed in schools and, hence, splinter the accountability of the heads. If governing bodies gain in authority, it may be at the expense of the CEO. Teachers' unions may sense that decision-making power lies outside the education office and seek to influence the chief executive and political leaders, as well as the CEO.

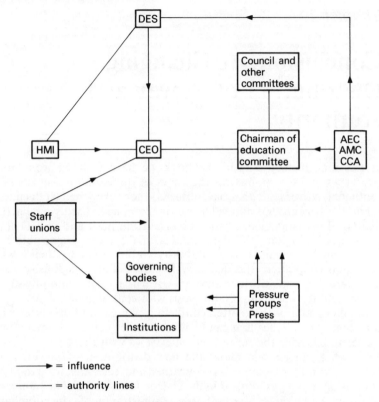

Figure 3   *The CEO's relationships before the Bains Report.*

Where does all this leave the director? The web of relationships is much more complex than it was a decade ago and, arguably, the CEO is no longer at the centre of the web. The authority once accorded and assumed as of right has been replaced by a position more uncertain, more managerial and more political. Often there is no overt reduction in authority, let alone of accountability, but changes are made barely consciously and accountability and responsibility are not clarified. This hurts. A former deputy education officer, John Mann, commented (1978) 'by blurring the process of making decisions, and failing to make accountability explicit, the system has become what NEDO called "a minimising environment with few rewards for real success and negligible sanctions for failure" '. The Director of Education has had to become used to living in a political world and has seen his educational influence decline. As one respondent put it: 'There is now no place for those unwilling to consult or unable to act with sensitivity.'

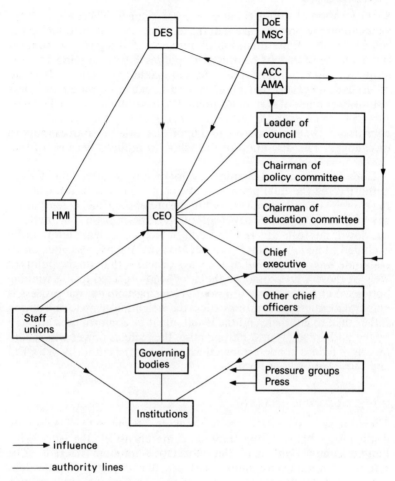

Figure 4 *The CEO's relationships' increase in complexity (1980)*

In spite of all the difficulties, the CEO still has a powerful position within the local authority, widespread opportunities to influence objectives and relationships, and often considerable satisfaction from his work. One director on the point of retirement, responds:

and yet it is a fine job . . . One deals with committed and honourable people in the service, sees results over the years, is stirred up by the controversy and research and feels, quite often, exhausted in a good cause.

So the location of authority and power has changed. There are, indeed, views about the precise nature of the displacement. In introducing the concept of the 'finite quantum of authority' Fowler (1979) concentrates on the effects of contraction upon authority, arguing that the scope for discretion and real decision-making is reduced. It could be argued, however, that officials tend to get more rather than less authority in times of scarce resources. We have already remarked how the CEO must exercise authority when schools must be closed, or consortia between schools insisted upon, and other resources reduced or changed. The discretion of the school is reduced because of that factor.

Does increased participation by more groups affect the CEO's authority? At the final point of implementation, a decision, which is the exercise of authority, represents closure of the issue, at least as far as a local authority is free to act without DES permission. The matter is cut down, interests are reduced and objections at least temporarily excluded as action begins. As a decision-making process goes on its elaborate way, options fall by the wayside and with them the points of view of those who promoted them, or who objected to the winning options. Yet, when many different groups participate, the process is elaborated, many more groups affect the weighting given to one option rather than to another, and the result might be compromises affected by the additional groups. Participation thus affects power which conditions, if it does not determine, the exercise of the authority of a CEO and those with whom he works.

MODELS OF POLICY-MAKING

There are several models of policy-making. Dennison (1975) usefully distinguishes between the 'rational-comprehensive', the 'successive limited comparisons' and the 'normative-optimum' models. The rational-comprehensive model assumes that objectives and values associated with them are clarified before an analysis of alternative policies is attempted. Ends are isolated before the means for their achievement are considered. The resulting analysis is as comprehensive as possible. The successive limited comparisons approach accepts the difficulties presented by the values of different groups and individuals and assumes there is no general acceptance of objectives, or that ends and means cannot be separated. This approach accepts the limitations of intellectual capacity, time and information to complete it, and this leads, in Lindblom's terms, to the strategy of 'disjointed incrementalism'. Dennison creates a compromise between the two approaches in a 'normative-optimum' model, where objectives are clarified, alternatives are identified and there is negotiation between desirability and feasibility.

Much of our new material in 1980 centres on the growth of corporate management which, for the most part, tends to reinforce the first of these styles. For example, when there is a total budgetary and investment plan which then cascades down into predetermined budgets for the service areas, officials in the corporate management role may become dominant if only because of the technocratic nature of the calculations to be made. It is not officials representing services who become dominant, but those who are concerned with maintaining the total system. Although our evidence is not conclusive, many of our respondents suggest that politicians who become dominant are also those concerned with large-scale and comprehensive development, rather than with the promotion of the needs of particular services. The system managers, rather than the service providers, win in this model.

Corporate management makes for convergence of plans and policies that were previously negotiated unsystematically. As we have already seen, however, there is simultaneous diffusion and uncertainty in the political system which leads to incrementalism rather than rationality. Thus, the CEO faces potentially incompatible notions of how education within local government should be controlled and administered.

The mood of our 1980 respondents inevitably reflects the general pessimism surrounding British political life and the economy. They also make their views heard at a time when Britain is entering a particular cycle of belief and ideology about the role of public institutions and the extent to which the community will be prepared to support them. It is for this reason that we think it important to remind readers of the views being advanced only eight years ago. The dominance of public good as against private values and effort no doubt goes through cycles, and we write as a period of twenty-five years of advance and hopefulness is, if not coming to an end, then at least severely affected by general economic and social changes. In the transcripts of dialogues that follow – the 1972 and 1980 interviews – the reader can see what remains unchanged and what is affected by the baffling and difficult changes in the environment which these public servants have to face.

Appendix: Tabulated Results of Survey of CEOs, England and Wales, 1980

The results presented in this appendix are based on a postal survey of directors of education carried out in 1980. One hundred and one CEOs in England and Wales were approached and sixty-one of these replied to the questionnaire. The survey has been referred to as appropriate throughout Part One but the major findings are tabulated here so that they can be considered together.

Table 3 *Consequences of Reorganisation Specified by Respondents*

Type of LEA	'Amalgamation caused problems'	'Amalgamation caused benefits'	'Increased political activity associated with reorganisation'	'Impetus towards corporate management associated with reorganisation'
English counties	12	2	19	16
Welsh counties	4	1	0	3
Metropolitan districts	8	4	7	8
TOTAL	24	7	26	27

Table 4 *Decision Areas Formerly Determined within the Education Service Now Settled by 'Central' Committees or Departments*

Type of LEA	Revenue budget	Capital budget	Personnel matters	Clerking, education committees	Sites and buildings	Other	No change
English counties	4	2	13	1	7	2	8
Welsh counties	0	0	3	1	0	1	2
Metropolitan districts	6	3	10	4	1	1	4
London authorities	3	1	4	2	0	1	4
TOTAL	13	6	30	8	8	5	18

Table 5 *The Relationship between Director and Education Chairman*

Type of LEA	Relationship remains central	'Centrality'* Qualified	No longer central
English counties	22	15	3
Welsh counties	5	3	0
Metropolitan districts	17	13	2
London authorities	12	8	0
TOTAL	56	39	5

*The 'centrality' of the relationship between the director and the education chairman was qualified by rival relationships with the council leader, majority group leader, policy committee chairman; with alternative power centres such as the majority group, policy committee and other power distributions; and by the chairman's authority within the group.

Table 6 *Interest Groups of Particular Significance*

Type of LEA	Parents/ PTA	Teachers' unions	Non-teachers' unions	Branches of national groups	Ethnic groups	Rate-payers	Others
English counties	6	3	1	0	0	1	4
Welsh counties	2	2	0	1	0	0	1
Metropolitan districts	8	5	1	2	5	1	1
London authorities	4	2	1	7	1	2	0
TOTAL	20	12	3	10	6	4	6

Table 7 *Main Issues Subject to Interest Group Activity*

Type of LEA	School closures	Secondary reorganisation	Nursery education	School transport	Adult education	Cuts (general)	Others
English counties	12	5	4	3	2	7	3
Welsh counties	3	1	1	2	0	3	1
Metropolitan districts	7	0	3	0	2	4	6
London authorities	6	4	1	0	0	1	2
TOTAL	28	10	9	5	4	15	12

Table 8 *Issues Where Interest Groups Are Said to Have Directly Influenced Decision-Making*

Type of LEA	School closures	Secondary reorganisation	Nursery education	School transport	Cuts (general)	Other
English counties	6	2	3	2	3	2
Welsh counties	3	1	2	2	2	0
Metropolitan districts	2	0	1	0	2	1
London authorities	4	0	0	0	0	1
TOTAL	15	4	6	4	7	4

Table 9   *The Director's Accountability to Different Bodies*

Type of LEA	Council	Education committee	Chief executive	'Professional'	Other
English counties	13	17	12	7	3
Welsh counties	3	4	2	1	0
Metropolitan districts	8	14	11	4	2
London authorities	7	8	3	3	0
TOTAL	31	43	28	15	5

Notes

1   Bristol, Derby, Hull, Leicester, Nottingham, Plymouth, Portsmouth, Southampton and Stoke.
2   Reported in *Education*, 21 November 1975.
3   Fiske, D., 'Education – going national', William Walker Lecture, November 1980.
4   *The Times Educational Supplement*, 8 October 1976.
5   *Education*, 15 October 1976.
6   ibid.
7   Former Secretary of the Association of Education Committees.
8   *Education*, 15 October 1976.
9   Letter to the *Guardian*, 19 October 1976.
10 Education Act 1944, section 77(2)(London: HMSO, 1944).
11 *House of Commons Select Committee on Education and Science, Part 1 Her Majesty's Inspectorate (England and Wales)* (London: HMSO, 1968). (HC 400–1).
12 See, for example, *DES Evidence to the Expenditure Sub-Committee*, 1976.
13 Quoted in *The Times*, 24 May 1978.
14 'Governors are a good idea', *The Times Educational Supplement*, 6 June 1980, p. 21.
15 For a discussion of these terms, see Kogan, M., *Educational Policy Making* (London: Allen & Unwin, 1975).
16 Briault, E. and Smith, F., *Falling Rolls in Secondary Schools* (London: NFER, 1981).
17 In May 1974 there were 213 pupils on roll. By May 1975 numbers had fallen to 144. Rice expected the roll to be 125 in September 1975 but the actual figure was 114.

References

Atkin, M. and Simons, H., 'Education policy-makers in Britain in the seventies' (unpublished, 1974).

Auld, R., *William Tyndale Junior and Infants Schools Public Inquiry* (London: ILEA, 1976).

Bains, M.A., *The New Local Authorities – Management and Structure* (London: HMSO, 1972).

Baker Report, *Education in Inner London*, report of a committee of London Conservatives, chaired by Kenneth Baker, MP, 1980.

Baron, G. and Howell, D.A., *The Government and Management of Schools* (London: Athlone Press, 1974).

Bernbaum, G., *Schooling in Decline* (London: Macmillan, 1979).

Briault, E. and Smith, F., *Falling Rolls in Secondary Schools* (London: NFER, 1980).

Burgess, T. and Travers, T., *Ten Billion Pounds* (London: Grant McIntyre, 1980).

Chartered Institute of Public Finance and Accountancy, (CIPFA), *Education Statistics: 1980–81 Estimates* (London: CIPFA, 1980).

Coates, R.D., *Teachers' Unions and Interest Group Politics* (Cambridge: Cambridge University Press, 1972).

Crewe, I., *British Political Sociology Yearbook, Vol. 1, Elites in Western Democracy* (London: Croom Helm, 1974), Introduction.

Dearlove, J., *The Politics of Policy in Local Government* (Cambridge, Cambridge University Press, 1973).

Dennison, W.F., 'The application of planning, programming, budgeting techniques to the expenditure of English local education authorities', doctoral thesis, University of Newcastle upon Tyne, 1975.

DES, *Local Authority Arrangements for the School Curriculum*, report on the Circular 14/77 recommendations (London: HMSO, 1979a).

DES, *Aspects of Secondary Education in England. A Survey by HM Inspectors of Schools* (London: HMSO, 1979b).

DES, *A View of the Curriculum*, HMI Series, Matters for Discussion, No. 11 (London: HMSO, 1980a).

DES, *A Framework for the School Curriculum. Proposals for Consultation by the Secretary of State for Education and Science, and for Wales* (London: HMSO, 1980b).

Donnison, D.V., Chapman, V., Meacher, M., Sears, A. and Urwin, K., *Social Administration Revisited* (London: Allen & Unwin, 1975).

Fiske, D., 'LEAs: can they afford to stay local?', *Education*, 21 November 1975.

Fiske, D., 'Accountability: a chief education officer's perspective', *Educational Analysis*, vol. 1, no. 1, Summer 1979.

Fowler, G. (Unit 16, E222), 'Influence or control?' Open University, Reading 3, *The Effects of Contraction*, 1979.

Fowler, G., 'The changing nature of education politics in the 1980s, Annual Conference of the British Society for Comparative Education, Cambridge, 1980.

Glatter, R., *Management Development for the Education Profession* (London: Harrap, 1972) (now distributed through NFER).

Greenwood, R. and Stewart, J.D., 'Corporate planning and management organisation', *Local Government Studies*, vol. 1, no. 3, October 1972.

Griffith, J.A.G., *Central Departments and Local Authorities* (London: Allen & Unwin, 1966).

Haynes, R.J., 'The rejection of corporate management in Birmingham in theoretical perspectives', *Local Government Studies*, vol. 4, no. 2, April 1978.

HMI Report, *Educational Provision by the Inner London Education Authority* (London: DES, 1980), DS/380.

House of Commons Select Committee on Education and Science, *Her Majesty's Inspectorate (England and Wales)*, Pt I (London: HMSO, 1968), HC 400–1.

House of Commons Expenditure Committee, *Decision Making in the DES*, 10th Report (London: HMSO, 1976), HC Paper 621.

Hughes, M.G., 'The professional as administrator', *Educational Administration Bulletin*, vol. 2, no. 1, 1973.

James, P., *The Reorganisation of Secondary Education* (London: NFER, 1980).

Jennings, R.E., *Education and Politics* (London: Batsford, 1977).

Johnson, D., Ransom, E., Packwood, T., Bowden, K. and Kogan, M., *Secondary Schools and the Welfare Network* (London: Allen & Unwin, 1980).

Kogan, M., 'Policies for the school curriculum in their political context'. *Cambridge Journal of Education*, vol. 10, no. 2, 1980.

Lee, J.M., *Social Leaders and Public Persons* (London: Oxford University Press, 1963).

Mann, J., 'A critical look at decision making and accountability at management level', *Education*, 15 September 1978.

Manzer, R.A., *Teachers and Politics* (Manchester: Manchester University Press, 1970).

Maud Committee Report, *Management of Local Government*, Vol. 1 (London: HMSO, 1967).

OECD, *Educational Development Strategy in England and Wales* (London: HMSO, 1975).

Redcliffe-Maud Report, *Report of Royal Commission on Local Government in England 1966–1969*, Vol. I (London: HMSO, 1969), Cmnd 4040.

Ree, H., *Educator Extraordinary. The Life and Achievement of Henry Morris* (London: Longman, 1973).

Regan, D.E., *Local Government and Education*, 2nd edn (London: Allen & Unwin, 1979).

Rendel, M., *Graduate Administrators in LEAs*, University of London Institute of Education, Appointments Board, 1968.

Saran, R., *Policy Making in Secondary Education* (Oxford: Clarendon Press, 1973).

Sharpe, L.J., 'Reforming the grass roots, an alternative analysis', in D. Butler and A.H. Halsey (eds), *Policy and Politics, Essays in Honour of Norman Chester* (London: Macmillan, 1978).

Taylor Report (DES and Welsh Office), *A New Partnership for our Schools* (London: HMSO, 1977).

White, P.T., 'The reorganisation of secondary education in Bath and Southampton' (unpublished M.Phil dissertation, Southampton University, 1974).

Wood, T.H., 'Falling rolls and the pathology of closure' (unpublished dissertation, Brunel University, Department of Government, 1980).

Part Two

INTERVIEWS WITH DIRECTORS OF EDUCATION

INTERVIEWS HELD IN 1972

Dan Cook

Devon

Dan Cook was educated at elementary and secondary schools in Cumberland and at Liverpool and London universities. He was a research fellow in modern history at Liverpool University, where he worked on parliamentary history. After six years' teaching in university, schools and adult education, he became an assistant education officer in West Sussex. He then joined the Devon Education Authority, where he was Deputy Chief Education Officer for twenty years and Chief Education Officer for five years. Dan Cook has been a member of the University Grants Committee and of the Committee on the Education of the Visually Handicapped.

BACKGROUND

I was brought up in a Cumberland village which was an industrial village, but within sight of Pillar Rock in Ennerdale, and I'm certain that both have always influenced me. I come from a mining family living in an area where there was great poverty and unemployment in the 1920s and 1930s, with just in the background some of the most wonderful scenery in England. They influenced me, by making me decide to work in education or in politics. I'm always being told that educational change merely reflects change in society. I was – without realising it for a long time – brought up to think differently, and I still work on the principle that education can, and does in fact, improve society.

BECOMING AN ADMINISTRATOR

What, then, was the appeal of administration rather than teaching, or, for that matter, research?
Remember that at that time many young people just had to go into teaching because it was all they could get a grant for. If I had not promised to take up teaching, I could not have gone to the university. It became clear that, if I wanted to go into educational administration, I should go into teaching first, and I still think it essential for CEOs to have had teaching experience.

THE ELEMENTS OF THE JOB

Now that you have been a CEO, what are the main elements of the job?
I've heard it said – more than once – that the CEO is in charge of the
secondary activity in education. That is, he is not a front-line man,
but enables other people to do the front-line job. I don't think this is
entirely true, especially nowadays. I think that CEOs have to do a
great deal of initiating work in the front line. As to the main
elements, he has, first of all, to let the authority and the community
know and advise them on the objectives of an education authority.
He's got to tell them the sort of resources he needs and expect their
backing for getting most of those resources. He's got to be a good
organisation man; he's got to keep a vast machine running. After all,
education is the most highly personalised of all local government
services. In my own authority there are 7,000–8,000 people –
teaching and non-teaching staff – to consider, apart from 70,000
children. This is a big organisation, and most of the time of a CEO
must be spent in the day-to-day work of just running the machine
and making it possible for those within his own office, but particularly for those within their schools, to do their job better. One other
job that a CEO should do and very few of us find time to do, and
often haven't the resources to do, is to assess from time to time what
we have done and what the value of it is. I am thinking now, say, of
one comparatively small part of the area in which I work, which has
had about £1·5 million injected into it in new buildings and more
teachers and which has had some carefully planned reorganisation. I
would like to know, in a few years time, to what extent this injection
of money and resources has improved the life of that community,
improved the quality of life. So assessment is part of a CEO's job,
which for one reason or another he does not do particularly well. But
then evaluation within the education service generally, even if
attempted, is inadequate.

*You have mentioned four or five main elements or tasks within the
CEO's role. But the way, the style, with which they are done affects the
quality of the whole school system, doesn't it? Can you identify points
of style that you have employed in performing those tasks?*
Basic to the work of a CEO must be concern for children and
increasingly for the whole community. He is influenced in the way he
goes about his job by the sort of area in which he works, by the
people – lay and professional – he has to work with. He cannot in any
way influence the choice of elected representatives, but if he is there
long enough, he can build up a staff of varied skills and interests and
talents through whose work as well as his own he can imprint style on
his authority – yes, if there is a perceptible style it is probably, and

should be, the authority which is seen to have it. A CEO will help to develop this style by his own way of operating, by his enthusiams and persistence, by his choice of staff and by his credibility with councillors and teachers. Probably, the most important responsibility is in the appointment of staff both in the office, and in the schools. To me, it is much more important to spend my time in getting to know all I can, directly or indirectly, about the health of each individual school and college in the area than in so many of the other things in which a CEO can get involved.

CHANGES IN THE JOB

You've been in educational administration in West Sussex and Devon for thirty years. Could you say something about the general changes in the objectives and assumptions about education that you have witnessed during your time and how your role as an administrator has changed as a result?

There have been some most remarkable changes. Some of them we've brought about ourselves. One of these is the public interest in education. We've made life much more difficult for ourselves just by telling people more about education, letting them know what we are about, what we are trying to do; as a result, we are getting pressures of all kinds which twenty-five years ago we didn't have. Then there is the difference in the attitude in the DES. The former Board of Education often seemed to be almost supine in its approach to problems, but now the department is taking a much more positive part and I, for one, welcome it. Another thing that is so much more obvious is the greater activity of teachers. The pressure from the teachers has changed from simply being for an improvement of their lot, to demanding improvement in the conditions in the schools and a greater involvement in planning. Again, this is something I welcome. One thing that I am aware of is the developing interest of the middle classes in the maintained education system. There is, of course, something very middle class still about the whole of our educational system, but many middle-class parents are now helping by drawing public attention to what is needed – not all of them who are doing this are sending their children to these maintained schools – but there is this activity going on which, to my mind, is of very great value. On the political side, there is a change which seems to me to be significant. Over and over again now, we are getting a national government of one party with local government controlled by the opposition party. This has particularly affected the argument about 'going comprehensive'. There is, too, a developing interest in the role of the educational administrator. It is being accepted more that an expensive public service needs good management. Ideas and assumptions are changing about what kind of service schools should be providing for children. The administrator must take account of this and of such developments as the need to link education more closely with the welfare services or the move away from purely intellectual and cognitive concerns to the social development of the child as a whole.

THE ROLE OF LOCAL GOVERNMENT

You've been describing a change of public opinion towards a far more expansionist attitude to education, which has produced both stronger public support, and stronger public pressure on the educational administrator. Could we move on now to the LEA itself? What are the main purposes or objectives of a local authority's work?

Let me start by saying that I am a believer in both strong national government, and in strong local government. I believe that the job of the local authority is, on the whole, to implement national decisions – in doing this they interpret those decisions to suit their own particular area or parts of their area. I say this about strong national government, because it seems to me quite wrong that educational provision should vary so much from area to area as it still does.

I believe that one of the purposes of central government is to create more equality in that way. One of the main purposes of an LEA is to see that the resources needed for a strong and lively education system are made available, and it is one of the jobs of an education officer, through his education committee, to get the LEA, the town or county council to acknowledge the size and importance of the education service in the community and to give it sufficient to make it, and keep it, healthy.

The main activities of an LEA are fairly obviously to provide teaching and learning processes for people in this area. There are a few other things, like providing school meals, which take a great deal of resources and effort as well. But what about the broader aspects of an education authority's work?

The education system as we know it now has developed over sixty years or so. We are in education departments doing many things, mainly because originally there was no other agent to do them, and so an education officer finds himself not only looking after the education of children and the welfare of the community, but to some extent he's also a transport manager and a catering manager, and he has all manner of other such sidelines that he must attend to. I believe that with the growth of local government, we ought in education to shed some of these activities, so we can concentrate more on the essential work of an education department, which is the encouragement of teaching and learning. I don't see, for example, why an education authority should run a school meals service if there is a catering service in the community which can do it with greater expertise. Nor do I see why we should have in the education department a so-called welfare service when, in the same authority, there is a social services department which should be able to do the work with greater resources and sensitivity. And so I believe that one of the great responsibilities of education committees and education departments in the future is to try to cease to be largely self-sufficient, self-contained empires. They must go out to work closely with all the other departments of their councils.

OTHER OFFICERS

Could you also say something about the way in which an education department is controlled and restricted by some of the control parts of the whole council, like, say, the clerk's department or the treasurer's department?
There are quite a number of authorities where the Clerk to the Council takes too close an interest, apart from the legal and general interest which he must take anyway in the administrative work of the education department. Personally, I just can't understand why this should be so. Why, for example, should a clerk's department clerk an education committee, prepare the agendas and write the minutes? That seems to me to be a time-wasting exercise, and one which can be done very much better by the people who are engaged in the day-to-day administration of the education system. But, on the whole, it seems that with the development of small groups of principal chief officers who interest themselves in the whole activities of the council, the sort of interference which one could fear is diminishing.

EDUCATIONAL EXPENDITURE

Your county disposes of £20 million a year on education. The allocation of these resources presumably lies with you. Is that correct?
No, it wouldn't be correct to say that. It lies with me in the sense that I advise the committee on how much money we need and they help me to get as much as we possibly can from the authority. It isn't correct in the sense that the committee and its officers can spend the money more or less just as they wish. It's well known that over 90 per cent of the expenditure of an LEA is not really under their control, in the sense that they can alter it significantly. They have freedom really to spend about 7 or 8 per cent of their annual expenditure.
One of our troubles in the education service, in the offices and the

schools, is that we are doing so much that has been done for so many years that we just don't seem in any authority to be able to sit back for long enough to question the basis on which some of our expenditure is built up. We still hesitate about cutting off or allowing to wither away something which has been acceptable for years without question, in order to spend the money on something else.

Did you feel yourself constrained by the law of education, by statutory constraints, did you feel that the flow of circulars, administrative memoranda and other advice, guidance, or instruction from the DES got in the way of exercising the right level of freedom in the local authority?
I would say that the main Education Act and the subsequent education acts are so wide-reaching in scope that they cover most of what a local education authority would wish within its resources to do. There are things which should be altered, and there is something to be said for a new Education Act about once every quarter of a century. But, on the whole, I have not found that CEOs are seriously inhibited in their work. Indeed, they are helped by the operation of the Act or the information which comes from the department.

THE DEPARTMENT OF EDUCATION AND SCIENCE

What about the DES's control over building programmes, or the operation of 'stop–go' as it affects the work of a local authority?
If we are to accept that there has to be national control of financial resources, then I can understand and accept the needs for major building programmes, and personally, I have found that officers of the department are most helpful in detailed examination of claims. I'm impressed by the knowledge they acquire of the needs of areas and of places within those areas.

The picture you're giving of the DES runs contrary to that which has appeared in quite a bit of recent literature. The assumption has been that civil servants are amateurs and aren't really concerned with the area they administer.
I think that is plain nonsense. Over the years, I've found that most of the people I've dealt with in government departments have been thoughtful and compassionate people and some highly gifted. I have been deeply impressed by the amount of work they can get through and, on the whole, their general helpfulness. I'm also sensitive to the way in which they can change with changing governments.

HER MAJESTY'S INSPECTORS

The role of the HMI is changing. This is, we're told, a hand-picked body of men and women, and for many years many of them were, to my mind, engaged on rather trivial work, chasing round an area or indeed all round the country. Now, it does seem to me, when they are specialising more on themes or on projects and becoming more deeply involved in in-service training, that they are doing much more valuable work. I'm quite sure that most heads and teachers in schools still welcome a visit from an HMI. Sometimes I find myself wishing, however, that HMIs would be prepared to act in the tougher, old-fashioned way with a school that has gone soft. As a CEO, I like to feel that I can see the district HMI once or twice a month and discuss with him, quite informally, what is going on within the authority.

DEVELOPMENT

You said before that there is a need for both strong local and national government in education. Where does the impetus for development come from?

It surely comes from a number of sources. The universities are very active. There is a certain amount of cynicism about their activities and understandably so, but there is some extremely good work coming out of universities which is of direct help to the work of education authorities. The teachers themselves should be giving, all the time, an impetus to development and should be innovating. They are getting great encouragement and help now from the Schools Council, though here again there is cynicism and sniping.

And it is here I believe that the administrators – the CEO and his staff – can do much in their front-line work. They collect, analyse and sieve ideas. They should be doing this, passing them out to the schools, to individual teachers, to groups of teachers at teachers' centres, and throughout the in-service system generally. The good school, too, is an incentive to further improvement both within itself, and beyond.

For major structural changes the department must act, but the government does not always initiate change in the sense that it originates the idea and then implements it. In fact, it could be argued that however powerful, compassionate and imaginative ministers and senior civil servants might be, it is difficult for them in education to take the initiative in the sense of getting things done or seeing that they are done. So much of what has been done in education began in localities, was developed there and then picked up in one way or another by HMIs or by the department and gradually began to influence policy thinking.

COUNCILLORS

Could you talk about the role of the councillor in policy-making and in the administration of education locally?
We must bear in mind that I happen to work in an authority which operates on non-party lines. There are no political divisions in my particular authority. Now, I personally welcome this. I believe that political decisions should be made nationally. I don't see why they should have to be made again locally and sometimes at several levels locally. I wonder whether the service does not have too many laymen poking about in it. I'm not saying this, I hope, in a disparaging sense, but I would be very much in favour of a reduction of the number of lay people who take part in the actual administrative processes. I would like to see smaller and fewer committees.

If that's so, how would you get public opinion to bear immediately on educational policy-making? Could officials represent public opinion as well as councillors?
I believe that a CEO and other officers can be said to represent the community much more than any one individual councillor or indeed, very often, a group of councillors. A CEO knows his area, knows its educational and other needs much better than any individual lay councillor is likely to do.

What impact do councillors have, in fact, on policy-making?
I don't believe that councillors, on the whole, have great impact on policy-making. Many councillors act as a brake on policy-making, or they dilute a policy for the wrong reasons. Most of them are much more interested in the minutiae than in policy. And I believe, too, that councillors are unable from the very nature of their work, and the very nature of the system, to be policy-makers. Planning of the kind we'd like is not easy in the system which we operate, because of the way expenditure is controlled – annual watertight estimates – and because of elections. Therefore, we act in a pragmatic way. It is, I believe, the officers who make policy, in the sense of recommending it. It's the council, of course, who make it in the sense of seeing that it will be made to work and providing the resources for it and taking the responsibility for it.

The logic of this would be that education should be a national service, with local agents of a national ministry. Is that what you are suggesting?
No, I wouldn't go as far as that. As I've said before, I believe in strong central government, but I believe that we need the local professional and lay knowledge and experience to make the system work properly.

CHAIRMEN

*What about chairmen? They seem, to the outsider, to occupy very strong
positions which separate them quite distinctively from the ordinary
councillor. Not quite a minister, but getting towards that sort of role. Is
this your experience?*

The chairman of an education committee should be a very significant
person in the community. The relationship between the CEO and
the chairman is a very sensitive one and must always be so. I like to
think that the CEO and the chairman are of equal standing, each
doing his own particular job. They are very much dependent on each
other.

*Are you really saying that there should be strong delegation to the CEO
not only to recommend policy, but to carry the system out vigorously
on his own initiative once the general policies have been agreed by the
committee?*

I don't see the point in having a strong and highly experienced CEO
with all his very good staff around him, if he is not given a very
considerable amount of delegated power and often in quite significant things. A good officer always knows the point at which the
committee takes over. The chairman should know much more than
any member of the committee, and it is the job of the officer to keep
him fully informed, even on matters on which the officer is exercising full responsibility. A strong officer needs a strong chairman.

*Could you say something about the way in which public opinion has
affected policies? I suspect that there has been a change in the power of
public opinion in recent years.*

I don't think that public opinion significantly affects the work and
policy of a good local education authority, which should, in fact, be
moulding public opinion. But the authority then needs the backing
of public opinion. The modern CEO is very much a public figure. He
influences public opinion to some extent, and he certainly must be
sensitive to it.

PRESSURE GROUPS

*What about the pressure groups? Groups such as teachers' associations,
the local authority associations, the denominations and the voluntary
bodies. Do they have a powerful effect on decision-making in Devon?*

I believe that it's right that teachers should have a powerful influence
on decision-making and a good authority takes teachers into its
confidence. A good education officer brings teachers, members and
councillors much more closely together. It is important that the
teachers should be seen in the education office, as, for example,

members of working parties or playing their part in policy discussions. It is very important that at frequent intervals the CEO should see representatives of the teachers' associations, and also at intervals, perhaps not so frequently, the chairman and the vice-chairman or other members of the committee must take the responsibility of being deeply involved. Just to give one example, we make a point at some of our meetings with the representatives of the teachers' associations of having discussions about how the estimates are being built up and what priorities they would like to see within the funds available.

FREEDOM OF THE SCHOOLS

Let's turn to the schools. Are they really autonomous? Or is it just that they have a great degree of freedom or discretion within prescribed limits? If there are prescribed limits, who prescribes them? Is it the CEO's role?
Traditionally, the schools of this country are said to be free. We never examine exactly what we mean by it. But I think what it means is that, within reasonable limits, the headmaster and his staff are free to run the school as they think best, and to have the sort of curriculum they think best. But it would be absurd to say that they are autonomous in the sense that they can do just as they like. There are prescribed limits within which they work; for example, financial limits. These are prescribed by the authorities.

There are traditional limits as to what they teach and how they teach it. There is constant communication between the CEO and the teachers, and the CEO is aware, through the advisory staff, of the way in which a school is developing. He can use his influence, often unofficially, often informally, in order to encourage developments or to prescribe some limits to development.

You have said that you prescribe limits in as much as the financial allocations to schools come through you. You have also talked about the freedom of the schools in curriculum, and so on, but are you accountable for making sure that standards are at least of a minimum quality? For example, if a school is known to be going downhill, would the committee expect you to take action?
Of course I'm responsible, and I accept that responsibility. The difficulty here is to decide when a school is going downhill, if it is, and at what speed it's going downhill. And you'd be surprised how difficult it is to get agreement among, say, half a dozen visitors to a school about the health of that school about which you are doubtful. But I *am* concerned, and it must be one of my major concerns, about the health of each individual school. If the advice to me comes in

from a number of quarters that there is something wrong with the school, that it's off-balance, that the headmaster is not exercising proper leadership, that there is dissension, or that there are noticeable weaknesses, then I must intervene. In most cases, I intervene through senior administrative colleagues or through advisers. If it's a case of a man clearly not doing his job, being incompetent, or doing it very badly, I intervene personally. This is one of the most difficult jobs of a CEO. Teachers have nearly as much security of tenure as a parson and to get rid of a bad teacher is really one of the most difficult things in this country. I have been able to persuade some bad teachers or teachers who are obviously unsuitable to resign without any fuss. If, however, they refuse to do so, the agreed procedure is invoked, and it is a very unpleasant, time-taking business. It has to be done. If I didn't do this sort of thing, I would think I was failing in my duty.

Could we now turn to the role of the head? The schools are reckoned to be free although not autonomous, as you've just said. Does this mean that the head is effectively a prime-manager in the education service? Do they run their schools strongly?

I get very confused about the use of the words 'manager' or 'management' in relation to schools. And I get even more concerned when I hear heads glibly using the words. I believe – and always have believed – that the head of a school should be the first among equals. I do not believe in the hierarchical principle either in an education office, or in a school. But this means that we have got to have a body of assistant teachers who are deeply involved in the running of the school and accept greater responsibility than many of them are allowed, and sometimes, I'm afraid, will accept, even when it is offered to them. The head still has to be the leader and even now very little is done to prepare them for leadership of a school, whether large or small.

GOVERNING BODIES

What about governing and managing bodies? What do they do and what should they do?

The governing bodies, of course, will tell you they do nothing. Nothing worth while. Actually, if a governing body operates as I hope it does, then it has considerable influence. It's the agent of the LEA in that area. It's got to support the headmaster. But it's also got to be ready to tell the education authority that things are not perhaps as they should be. And above all, I think, a governing body exercises very considerable power if it is allowed to take part in the appointment of staff. I would like to see these governing bodies of schools having more authority. It, perhaps, could best be done by involving them more in the allocation of funds. The time could come when schools will be given a block allocation, though it would have to be subject to general policy decisions. A head and his governors would, for example, be given freedom to decide whether to use the money for a part-time assistant teacher or for an ancillary helper. But here some teachers would probably be a bit suspicious because, over recent years, many of them have been given considerable control over the funds allocated to the schools. One thing I feel strongly is that governing bodies should not be political – there should not be political appointments to them. I don't think it's right that an education committee should form governing bodies mainly from its own members. Every single school should have its own hand-picked body of people from within the community to act as a governing body, including representatives of parents and teachers.

ROLE OF PARENTS

Could we talk about the role of parents in the educational process? There are the formalised Parent–Teacher Associations. But more generally, what part do parents play in your schools?

Parents are becoming less afraid of school authority than they were. They are getting more involved in the life of the school through their associations or through getting to know individual teachers. In a more formal way, in my authority, a determined effort was made after the last election to get a parent on every single managing body and governing body and we succeeded with the exception of a very few. Some heads at first didn't like it – they thought it would mean interference from parents – but the majority of heads now welcome it and find among the parents probably their strongest allies.

ROLE OF THE CHIEF EDUCATION OFFICER

Could we turn back now to the CEO running this vast system? How far is he a leader or a moulder of public opinion in his county, or, more generally, on a national level?

I said earlier on that I believed the chairman of the education com- mittee and the CEO are bound to help to mould and lead public opinion as regards education. It was only after the idea of compre- hensive schools was explained to parents by CEOs and their colleagues, in terms of particular schools, that it began to be under- stood and that there then came the great pressure for them. So without appearing to put the CEO in too elevated a role, I do believe that in his own area he will mould public opinion if he is credible. He will be believed by teachers and others if he is seen to be sensitive, knowledgeable and ready and able to listen. The CEO should have time and freedom to sit back and question accepted practices and assumptions. Take sixth forms, for example. We still talk of sixth forms as though they were the pearl of the English educational system. It could be argued that they are, in fact, becoming one of the most over-rated institutions in this country. And the CEO should say so, if he feels it to be so.

What comes out very strongly from this is the way in which a local authority officer such as yourself takes a leadership role, is concerned with developing the service, with assessing its impact and changing it where necessary. Now, this is a bit different from the popular view of the local government official who is thought to be defensive, self-preservationist, protecting an existing position?
I have, I hope, a proper regard for the democratic processes, a proper respect for elected committees, but I do believe that of all the people engaged in government, whether it's national or local, it's the officers who are the people who have very few personal axes to grind. The majority of them are deeply devoted to the work they are doing and tremendously hard-working. I have little patience with those who accuse a strong officer, or an officer who is acting strongly, of being bureaucratic or of empire-building. If, indeed, he is empire-building in education, it is empire-building for children.

Could you give one example of how a CEO actually implements a policy or makes a change in the quality of the service for which he is responsible? How, for example, do you close a small village school?
We're closing them occasionally now. It isn't a negative policy; they are being closed, because they're uneconomical, educationally and financially. A small, two-teacher school costs about two or three times as much per head to run as a larger school. Whatever people say, these small schools educationally can be too costly, the quality of work not as good or as sharp as it should be. So we have a quite positive policy of setting up area schools. We normally choose a village that is already strong or is likely to grow, and there we build a school which serves not only the village itself, but a number of surrounding smaller villages. To give one example, we closed a year or two ago in one area six schools and put them into one. We knew that this particular village was likely to grow, we knew that it was going to have a new school, we knew that the villages and hamlets round about were most unlikely, according to all the information we had at that time, to grow and that the school buildings were obsolete. We, therefore, set about sounding local opinion. Then we came to the education committee with the proposal that we should develop an area school – a six-into-one school – and the education com-

mittee, which had long ago agreed that very small schools should in time close, supported the proposal. And then it became more official. It was made known through the press and then there were the formal visits to the managing bodies with one or two members of the committee with us. Then there were the meetings with the parents, then the whole proposal came back to the education committee and had to go through the county council and then to the department.

Claire Pratt

Hillingdon

Claire Pratt spent five years teaching in a public school, followed by nine years lecturing in a teacher training college. The college was destroyed by bombs in 1942, and as Vice-Principal, she was much involved in the organisation of temporary accommodation. She became an administrative assistant in the Norfolk education office in 1944 and within eighteen months every officer senior to her had retired or left the county. She remained as a senior assistant education officer until 1949, when she was appointed Education Officer of the Excepted District of Hayes and Harlington in Middlesex. In 1964 she was appointed CEO of the newly formed London Borough of Hillingdon from which post she retired in 1971. Claire Pratt died shortly afterwards.

BACKGROUND

I had a very strict upper-middle class, Irish Protestant background. We came over to England when I was about 3½ and I went to numerous schools because my parents were very restless. One was Winchester County Grammar School from which I went to London University on a Drapers' Scholarship. I then went on to teach in a Drapers' Company school in North Wales. It was a public school and I was there for five years, teaching maths and biology. I then went as a maths lecturer on the staff of a training college in Norwich, now one of the large well-known colleges. I stayed to become Vice-Principal.

From the training college I moved into the Norfolk education office. I had decided by that time that administration was what I wanted to do. I had already spent some of my holiday periods in the education office, because at that time it was difficult to travel and I couldn't get home to Ireland. I was helped a great deal by Gordon Bessey* who was pleased that someone should take an interest in the administration of the county. I was very much in two minds, because I was offered a headship of a school when I was going for an interview for the administrative assistant's job on the next day. And I accepted the much lower-paid job of administrative assistant. Although it seemed obvious that the sensible thing was to accept the headship, my instinct revolted. So I decided just to be guided by my instinct.

* At that time, Deputy Education Officer in Norfolk, later CEO for Cumberland.

BECOMING AN ADMINISTRATOR

Some would say that you wanted the power?
Really? Turn down a headship? The most powerful job in the world as
far as controlling people is concerned?

Can you see from this distance what it was that attracted you?
Yes. I didn't have any revolutionary aims. One of the things that
excited me very much about the 1944 Act was the idea of 'parity of
esteem'. One of the things that had hurt me, going into schools as a
lecturer and a supervisor of student teachers in elementary schools
after teaching in a public school, was this difference. I kept saying,
'Why can't they call all schools for senior pupils secondary schools
and take the consequences?' I had been educated in an ordinary
grammar school, so I knew a bit about maintained schools. I was
astounded on studying the White Paper that preceded the Bill to see
how my idea had taken hold! I wanted to be in on the clearing up of
the elementary schools, and particularly at that time, the senior
elementary schools, and I was also very concerned about and interested in primary schools. I went into the Norfolk education office as
an assistant to prepare the Norfolk development plan under the
1944 Act. I had to settle down and work out a scheme for secondary
education in Norfolk. I was also involved in setting up a system of
divisional administration. There was a CEO, two AEOs and two
county inspectors. We were the only teaching professionals in the
office, and within eighteen months of my arrival, they had all gone!
The CEO had retired, so had the two county inspectors and the two
AEOs had got other jobs. By that time, they had appointed Oswald
Bell as chief and Lincoln Ralphs as AEO, and Oswald Bell had me
promoted to AEO also. So I had to come off the development plan
and take over the administration of the schools more generally, and
without much experience at all, I had to run the schools section of
the Norfolk office with all the new legislation under the 1944 Act.

How long were you in Norfolk?
From 1944 to 1949.

What happened then?
I came to Hayes and Harlington as the Divisional Education Officer
for one of the Middlesex Excepted Districts. A very great friend of
mine was appointed as DEO in Gillingham, Kent, at the same time.
We were the only two women DEOs.

Could you say whether you have roots in the Hillingdon area?
I developed very close relationships with every section of the community in Hayes. I was there from 1949 to 1964. When I first came,

there were only sixteen schools. By the time Hillingdon borough was formed, there were thirty-four schools in Hayes. I knew the heads and teachers extremely well.

When I was appointed to Hillingdon, the most important first thing was to get the people in the education service to work together as one borough. This was a tremendous undertaking. Central government assumes that reorganisation happens very easily, but the two parts of the new borough had been very different. To win the confidence of the people I hadn't dealt with before, was the first thing, and there was naturally some resistance at that stage to be overcome; they were used to a different approach.

How do you see the CEO's own job in this sort of changing situation?
The job of the CEO is to run as good an education service as he can within the policies laid down by the education committee. The main elements of his own job will depend a bit on what he chooses to do himself. I regarded one of my main jobs as the getting together as a team the people who were doing the job in the field. This is really more than just the teachers. I have always felt it was extremely important to me to know the heads of the schools. But it extended further than the teachers. It also extended to the advisers and other staff who worked more directly under me.

CHANGES IN THE JOB

Is it possible to assess changes in the job during the period when you were CEO?
Of course, some changes in the job occurred because of changes in the council. The council that set up the borough remained in power for three years and then changed completely, and consequently the job changed at that point because the objectives of the committee changed somewhat. There have been other changes, too, in the relationships between the CEO and the other chief officers of the council.

We found that in the boroughs we were going to have a great deal more contact and interplay between the council departments than perhaps some of us had envisaged when we were thinking about the job. Gradually, the boroughs have been appointing Directors of Management Services who have become more and more involved in the deployment of staff within the departments. For example, I had never operated a typing pool and this was a new aspect of life to some of us older CEOs. We were used to organising our own administration but now there was more outside influence, with the approval of the establishment committee, on the running of the administration within the department. As you probably know, in

Hillingdon, there is an approved plan whereby certain central departments, like the town clerk's department, the borough treasurer's department, the management services department, and so on, shall, in due course, distribute certain members of their staff among the different departments. And I, personally, would have welcomed this, because I maintained that they would soon become part of the education service staff.

I suppose, putting a generous construction on this changing role, this is making education part of overall unitary services for the people of Hillingdon?
Yes, it is, and I do accept the fact that we were simply a part of the rate-borne services and that we must not live in splendid isolation. I did not want to live in splendid isolation, although sometimes the breaking out of the splendid isolation was extremely painful.

CHANGES IN LOCAL GOVERNMENT

You experienced, then, changes in management techniques in local government. How did they seem to you as the head of the largest of the services within your area?
During my time as CEO, 'management' as a technique with a theory, and a rapidly changing and developing vocabulary, came into considerable prominence, and senior local government officers were required to study and put into practice these techniques. As I have indicated frequently, I have always felt that economical and efficient administration is essential in order to release creative energy, and resources, for the improvement of the service, and I was therefore interested in, and sympathetic to, the introduction of any techniques which would lend themselves to this end. As I studied the 'new' theories, however, I found myself uneasy, first, because they seemed to take no account whatever of the end-product – the quality of the service offered to the public. In fact, when I put this point to a management expert who was inquiring into certain administrative processes, he stated that the quality of the end-product was quite irrelevant to management investigations. Secondly, I found that the 'new' vocabulary when analysed described processes that any good administrator should already be operating, for example, 'target budgeting', the careful preparation of an annual budget related to intended achievements during the year in question.

One other change of role which I welcome very much is that teachers are being brought much more into the organisation of the education service. We have always consulted teachers on a great many aspects of the service – buildings, changes to be made, anything that we could possibly bring them in to consult about – and this is growing and has grown in Hillingdon and is much more recognised by the committees than it used to be. Teachers are brought into consultation both through consultative committees, which is the formal setup for consultation between the committee and the teachers, but also in every possible way in anything that affects the service, and I welcome this.

Could we ask about the impact of personal style on the sort of work that you did as CEO? Can you think of obvious variations of what you did and wanted to do, and what other equally reputable practitioners did?
I think I went round the schools a great deal more than some CEOs because I have felt this to be so important. It is part of my way of personal contact.

THE CHIEF EDUCATION OFFICER'S JOB

To what extent does the CEO feel that he or she is accountable for the whole range of things, even though not concerned directly with all of them herself?
My instinctive answer is absolutely, completely. I would say that the CEO is completely accountable. If things are going smoothly, nobody asks for anybody to be accountable, but accountability arises when things go wrong. And I would say that the CEO should be completely accountable and, therefore, must have confidence in the staff to whom these various aspects of the job are delegated, must give a lead to the staff, and must be responsible for what is going on.

So you were responsible, and felt responsible, for the whole range of activities which the education committee covered. Which of them did you select as things that you thought the CEO should pay particular attention to?
I think one of the most important things that the CEO must do is the appointment of senior staff – all senior staff. He must be involved in the appointment of heads of schools, principals of colleges, perhaps deputy heads and principals, his own senior administrative staff, and he must keep in touch with them and establish communication with them after appointment. Another thing which I think the CEO should be involved in is the design of buildings. Right from the beginning, you must analyse what buildings are for, going pretty far back into educational philosophy.

I also think the CEO has always got to be involved in and personally responsible for the budget. You've got to establish, especially in times of financial stringency, priorities, and this means that the CEO must be involved.

To what extent do you feel you were able to exert leadership? You were, presumably, able to appoint the staff you wanted?

There are always certain constraints on the appointment of staff above a certain level. This means that the CEO does not, in fact, appoint the staff himself over a certain level, and it means that you don't always necessarily appoint the person that you want. There is committee involvement, and you can go so far, but in the end the committee involvement in senior appointments and the big allocations and divisions of the budget mean that the CEO isn't a completely free agent in any field.

AND AUTHORITY

Could you give an indication as to how influential the CEO is?

He has certain areas of complete influence. Take the area of teacher appointment. The committee is involved in the appointment of heads and deputy heads, but the CEO is there and it is usual for his advice to be taken seriously, even if it is not always followed. Below that level, the CEO is completely responsible for the appointment of assistant teachers, and he can either do it himself, or delegate it. In choosing the person to whom he delegates he, again, asserts his influence. As far as the budget is concerned, the CEO is very much concerned in its formulation. When it is settled, there are large spheres in which the CEO has authority to spend within the budget, and so by the way in which he operates this or delegates that, he will exert considerable influence.

DEVELOPMENT

Could we pursue this by asking whether there was any point at which you could look at the historic commitment and move towards the realignment of resources as against new researches, new policy developments?

Certainly, we looked at the historical commitments and changed the standards. Whether you could exactly describe it as a realignment, I'm not sure, because we didn't have an overall sum to work to, but we did look regularly at our historic commitments to see whether they were necessary, adequate and being properly deployed.

COUNCILLORS

It's said in such research as the Maud Committee on management that councillors aren't particularly good transmitters of public opinion both by virtue of the sort of people they are, and the amount of energy they put into the system.

It is in the good relationship between a CEO and a committee that the most interesting part of the dialogue comes about. The CEO's first reaction may be that something that is suggested by the committee is completely impossible in the light of good educational theory. But if you try to look at the thing from the point of view of the committee members, you can generally see some way of reconciling their view with what you feel to be the real needs of the educational service.

That might be quite legitimate. It might be that the political consider-ations ought to outweigh the good educational ones?
Yes, it may be, and one must be a bit humble about this. I think you've got to accept the fact that you can't always be right. Even if it is simply the will of the committee that something else should rule out the particular thing that you think to be important, you simply must accept this.

CHAIRMEN

Are there particular points about relationships with chairmen?
I think it is extremely important that there should be a good working relationship between the chief officer and the chairman and that they should be able to disagree in private. They should have suf-ficient respect for each other's point of view to be able to come to a reasonable agreement before the thing comes before the committee or the teaching body, or whatever. There are of course always times when this can't happen – when you disagree completely, and the CEO must loyally support his chairman's view, and give no inkling that he doesn't agree with it.

PARTY RULE

Speaking about central government, Harold Wilson once remarked that whoever is in office, the Whigs are always in power. By which he meant the civil service always runs the country. Did different parties, in fact, make much difference to the educational policies in Hilling-don?
Yes. They made a difference in big policies because the comprehensive issue was with us during the whole time I was in Hillingdon, and the speed at which the parties were prepared to put into operation plans for comprehensive reorganisation differed very greatly from party to party and this affected a great deal of our thinking with regard to the secondary schools. When, for example, we wanted to extend a building, it was important to know whether it was going to become comprehensive in the near future. On the general day-to-day running of things and on the planning and operation of the non-controversial things, I wouldn't say that it did.

Taking a different point of view on this now, the education department has to concern itself with long-range development. Against this you had three different councils. Is there a disharmony?

There isn't a disharmony. It did complicate life. For example, the first council had decided to allow children to remain in primary schools up to the age of twelve and, consequently, we were planning our primary schools on this basis. The next council decided that they would retain 11 as the age of transfer, and this meant an immediate cancellation of certain plans for primary school extension, and the transfer of building development into the secondary schools without a clear conception of when these schools would become comprehensive. Changes of council can result in abortive work.

PRESSURE GROUPS

We've talked about councillors and chairmen; what about the development of the informal pressure groups, CASE and STOPP and ACE and all of these?

I find it difficult to answer this one simply because I have always got on so well with all the different people with whom I had to work. There were parents' pressure groups at the time that the council was going forward with a more rapid scheme for comprehensive reorganisation. The pressure from that group was to retain grammar schools. We accepted this as an expression of a section of public opinion.

The sheer growth of interest and activity. Was that something that struck you?

Definitely. The growth of parental interest has increased enormously since my early days, when I used to go round urging schools to start parent–teacher associations. Now, of course, parents are vocal and have a much better idea of what they want and this is a result of our having educated them better.

CENTRAL GOVERNMENT

Could you distinguish for us the relationships between central government and local government in decision-making on education and the main agents concerned in this process?

The HMIs regard themselves as purely advisory and wouldn't say that they had any power to impose anything, and I think it sensible to make use of the expertise of this body of men and women. I have always had very good and friendly relationships with them.

We also had discussions with the DES on big schemes like comprehensivisation. Here, of course, we were, more than in any other field, conscious of political undertones. Relationships with the officers of the DES generally were very good indeed. They were as helpful as they could be. Another sphere of contact was when and if parental complaints ever got as far as the DES. There they were 99½ per cent on our side – having heard our reasons for doing what we did. There was always the other ½ per cent when they might inform us that we had acted unreasonably – it only happened once to me. I was 'directed'* once about a child going to a particular school when we had in fact acted perfectly reasonably, I was furious.

CONSTRAINTS

If one went through the decisions that you and the committee had to make in any one year, one would find that there is a whole web of constraints laid down by the law which the department makes through the parliamentary machine. Statutory instruments, circulars and administrative memoranda, for example; things like restrictions on nursery education, ages and stages of education, building programmes, flow of rate support grants. Would it be fair to say that there were frameworks within which there were discretions of local authority that powerfully affected the style, the level, the quality of the educational process which really were within the local authority's hands?
Oh yes. Within the national constraints they really didn't interfere. The style and standard of the education service were entirely in the hands of the local authority. The DES doesn't tell you how many teachers you can employ, for example.

One is always being told about the encroaching constraints of central government. Do you agree with this?
This was, of course, said when the block grant† was introduced but it doesn't, in fact, constrain you in any way on what you do spend on education. Certainly, you are constrained as far as your major projects are concerned, such as building a whole new school or greatly extending a school. We are also more constrained nowadays on minor works. But on other things, on the real stuff of education within the buildings, there are no constraints. The authority can spend as much as it likes on equipment (except fixed equipment), various categories of staff, clerical assistants, welfare assistants; and it can send teachers on as many in-service training courses as it wants to.

* Under section 68 of the Education Act 1944.
† The general grant was introduced in 1958 and replaced grants specifically tied to local authorities' expenditure on individual services. It aimed to make local authorities freer to decide how to spend but also made it more difficult for education committees to be certain of their share of resources.

What pressure was there on you from outside to innovate?
Let's take the administrative side. If I weren't innovating all the time and exploring and trying to make things as good as they could be, there are so many other controls in local government, for example, management services, telling me how I ought to deploy my staff. And I've got to have good answers. There's always financial control, as well. But even on teaching innovations, I have to be . . . I know that if my in-service training programme was not good, HMIs would impose their perception of how it ought to be. But I knew what my teachers wanted because I brought them into the planning. And that seems to be the best way to innovate.

Two things seem to come out of this. First, a CEO is concerned with development and innovation of the system for its own sake. As a profesional with a responsibility both as a teacher and as someone representing the community, he needs to ensure that there is development. The second point is the dimension concerned with what some would call bureaucratic norms, and what I would prefer to think of as administrative values, such as consistency, equity, adequate balance, or judgement – the values that are largely concerned with control in administration.
You should add economy. It is important to remember that one is responsible to the ratepayers.

Is the interpretation of 'value to the ratepayer' something you yourself have created in your own head?
I suppose I could only assess value to the ratepayer in terms of my own values. It may not be what they want at all. But just going a bit further on the issue of value and use of resources, I did toward the end of my time work through a period of considerable constraint on spending. There was in the borough a chief officer's budget committee in which I had to consider the whole spending of the budget, not just on education. If I had been tempted to be extravagant for my own service, this budget committee made one conscious of the need to deploy resources throughout the whole borough services effectively and not just in one's own service.

The third element of the administrator's role might be that he is not only there to control a system which is already in being, and to develop it and its policies, but he is really there to enable others to develop teaching and other activities. It would follow from this that the CEO is really an enabler of the head and his teachers to get on with the work. Is that a real third dimension of the administrator's role?
We try to make sure that a good teacher is in front of pupils and in the right and appropriate building, and with the right and appropriate equipment. And if one had to sum up what one is really there for, it is to ensure that education takes place.

As an administrator, aren't you really rather removed from that process? Even a headmaster is somewhat removed from the firing-line. So although this might be an ideal, when it came to your day-to-day work, didn't you feel that you really couldn't cope directly with the development and improvement of the educational processes themselves?

No, because I was concerned with things that contributed very directly to these ends. You say that even a head can't do it. Well, all right, even a head can't go in and take the class. But he is ensuring that the right teacher is handling the right child, the right way, most of the time. And he'll deal with breakdowns in the system and in the people concerned in it. And one of the most important jobs of the CEO is to make sure that the right teachers are in the right schools. But this is more complicated than it might seem. Because when trying to match teachers to schools or head teachers to schools, you always have in the forefront of your mind the educational developments that *you* want to see take place. There has to be someone outside the institution plodding along and helping the less good schools to become better. To help them take and accept what is relevant from the example of the good schools. This is an important function of the outside person. Some schools will be good in their own right because of the personalities running them. Others could be much better if they would only learn from the good ones. This is something that you can do. The way in which I would assert authority over a head teacher is that, first of all, I would work with the head through persuasion.

RELATIONS WITH HEADS

You seem to be saying that you were in a position directly to monitor and to some extent modify the power, the authority of the head. Were there some areas in which you had this power more directly than others? Were there some areas in which he could do what he liked?

That is a difficult one. To have the power, and to exercise it, are two such different things. I think the only occasions on which one would exercise it would be on questions affecting the welfare of pupils. If he was doing something which you felt to be wrong with a pupil, or threatening to throw a pupil out, or saying that he wouldn't have a certain pupil, you would tell him and exercise your power. Or exercise your power over treatment of a certain member of staff. I can't imagine other circumstances less urgent where you would.

If you thought a head was running a bad school, what then?
Send him on a course first.

Then when he comes back and is still three feet thick?
I have had to deal with this. One tries to introduce to him the idea that
there are other ways of doing things by getting him to visit other
schools where the desirable things are going on, and if he still will not
or cannot see it, you then try to strengthen him by building up his
staff – this is not an easy exercise because it is not easy for staff to
carry out reforms without leadership – but it can improve the head.
If you keep on and on at this kind of thing, he goes. I couldn't give
him the sack. It is a long and painful process. I could initiate it but it
has to go through committees, governing bodies, and so on.

*I would guess that the head is the most powerful role in the system. That
is to say, he is head of an institution the style of which is very much in
his own hands. And does this imply that heads do have managerial
authority over their assistant teachers? What are the evidences of this?*
Yes, appointment varies between authorities. The heads don't
'appoint' their staff, but any CEO with sense allows the head to pick
his staff, and the CEO advises him if he thinks this necessary but
allows him his say, because he has got to work with them. He deploys
them without interference. He timetables them.

*On this assumption one would find wide variations in style, quality,
expectations in schools which you are CEO of. Does it follow that
the institutions varied enormously in your area because of the
individuality of the heads?*
I think they do vary in character. I don't think they necessarily vary in
the standard of what they achieve. The head is subject to a constant
bombardment of advice, prodding, suggestion, staff threatening to
leave, because they are not being allowed to do what the chap down
the road does, and so on, so that he has insidious constraints but not
overt ones.

GOVERNORS

Could I go on and ask about the role of the governing bodies?
I am a bit bothered by the role of the governing bodies. I think they
have a very small role indeed in Hillingdon. In Norfolk, because of
the large geographical area, they had a much bigger role, since they
were the local people who knew the school, supported the head.
Perhaps the chairman would be a member of the education committee and could speak for that school. In a small borough like
Hillingdon, it seems to me that they have very little power and the
chairman is simply an additional support for the head, which is
splendid and what he should be, but you don't set up a governing
body just to provide the 'friends' who support the head when he
needs supporting.

PARENTS AND PRESS

We have the Plowden research about the association between parental attitude and performance; so plainly this is a key issue. Can you say something about the role they were playing in your schools in your time?

This is so general. Every parent has a different role. All I can say is that I think that parents in one way contribute more towards the education of their children than they used to do, perhaps because they are better educated themselves but also because of the fact that they are more outgoing than they used to be, and so mothers, for example, learn more about what other people's children do. They are more knowledgeable and more ambitious. This has grown even in the time I was in the borough. They are not always rightly ambitious for their children but ambition is something to start on. All I can say is that although it causes endless difficulties, and they can be a pain in the neck, I welcome it because the only way in which education can improve is for the parents to want it to improve. And in many ways it is adding material to educational resources. So many parents now are working for the schools in numerous ways. Doing things for the schools that they never dreamed of doing before.

You have already said you are not in charge of curriculum. Curriculum is decided largely by heads and governors. You can't really hire and fire teachers, or indeed staff. So that you are constrained in various ways from creating change in authority. Nevertheless, you do see yourself as an innovator. Can you give us some examples, in that case, and what areas you really thought you could innovate and how you go about it?

I suppose that one of the important things is that, amid all these constraints, you must choose an area that you can influence and work through that. Because one of the great things about the education service is the way things spread through it. And if I could quote one area of innovation, for example, I would quote the change in the teaching of maths, which has happened in recent years and which has been brought about by, in the first instance, discussion, consultation and co-operation between the HMIs and myself and my advisers, the running of various courses in the borough, the setting up of a maths centre and the staffing of the courses by HMIs who are particularly interested in the development of new maths in the schools. This has had, in my opinion, absolutely electrifying results in the schools. The teaching of maths has changed, as a result of all these things, in a way that I think is very gratifying and astonishingly quick. It has been spread by the teachers who have been on the courses talking to other teachers, by the teachers who have visited the maths centre, seen the exhibitions and listened to the person talking whom we put in charge down there, and by local advisers spreading the gospel through the schools – that is one of the ways in which we can bring about innovation.

Yes. But you weren't able to say to the schools 'You must do modern maths'. You provided the facilities for them to do modern maths?
Yes, we encouraged them and bullied them into going to the courses, and going to the maths centre and finding out what was done, and so on, and made it attractive to them.

But if a school had said, 'Look, we are opposed to modern maths', you wouldn't have been in a position to impose, would you?
I wouldn't have imposed. Whether I would have been in a position to impose is another matter. I have the greatest possible respect for a young head whom we appointed to a school which needed a facelift, and by dint of exhortation and example, by taking classes himself, he was able to persuade all members of his staff, except one, to change over to much more modern methods. But the one member of staff stuck and said that she could not teach in any other way than in the way she had taught all her life, and he let her continue. And I thought it was absolutely splendid that he didn't destroy her confidence, he didn't do anything about it, he didn't apologise for her, he just let her continue in her way of good but thoroughly old-fashioned teaching. Well, I wouldn't impose on a head any more than he imposed on that member of staff.

George Taylor

Leeds

George Taylor was educated at elementary and secondary schools in
Salford and at the universities of Manchester and London. He later
entered Gray's Inn, where he read for the Bar. After fourteen years as
a teacher, he spent eight years as a headmaster. He then became Chief
Inspector and Deputy Director of Education for Leeds for six years
before becoming Chief Education Officer. He held this position for
fifteen years before retiring. He was a member of the Executive
Committee of the Association of Education Committees for ten years,
president of the Association of Chief Education Officers in 1957–8,
and of the Modern Language Assocation in 1965–6. He has been
chairman of the Consultative Committee to Nuffield Foundation
Modern Languages Project and the Schools Council Primary School
French Project.

BACKGROUND

I was born in Salford. My family were working class. My father was an
assistant in a Co-Operative store. Shortly after I was born, he became a
branch manager and he remained a branch manager in the Co-Op
Society in Salford until he retired. I was the only child and my parents
were interested in my education from the beginning. They encouraged
me to read and to play chess. I went to the local secondary school,
where I did comparatively well. My parents were anxious that I should
go as far as I could in my education. I won a scholarship to Manchester
University, where I read history. Subsequently, I trained for teaching
and at the same time I was doing research for my MA, which I carried
on with after I started teaching. The research was on the Industrial
Revolution – most of the thesis was published in 1924.

You left university having done your research. You trained as a teacher.
  What kind of a teacher?
A secondary school teacher. I left the university in 1922, when it was
  extremely difficult to find a post. A number of my contemporaries
  were out of work for quite a long time. I took a post in a little private
  school – a boarding school – and spent two years there.
    When, after two years, I went to London, George Unwin suggested

that I should approach his friend, R. H. Tawney,* and I became a disciple of Tawney, who has influenced me very much all my life. I was appointed to Edmonton Latymer School and, although a history specialist there, I was asked to teach additional subjects – Latin, English and French.

I became a student under R. H. Tawney at the Institute of Historical Research. My research was on the sequestration of royalist estates during the Civil War, from 1642. I tried to discover the effects of this large transfer of land on the people. In order to tackle this work, I had to read a good deal of law – Maitland, for example – and I became very interested in law. I decided to suspend my research and read for the Bar.

Just about this time Tawney published his seminal book, Secondary Education for All. *You said he was a great influence. What sort of influence was that particularly?*
It had an effect on my outlook towards children and particularly towards the able underprivileged children. For example, I tried to ensure that school camps were available to children who would not have been able to afford them.

Tawney was at this time very involved with the whole 'equality scene'. Was this something that you were actively involved in?
I've never been connected with politics, but Tawney's general view on equality influenced my approach to life. You may, in fact, recall that after I retired I collaborated in writing a book dealing with regional and local inequalities in educational opportunity. It opens with a quotation from Tawney's *Equality*.

I went on after twelve years at Latymer to be headmaster of Cockburn High School in Leeds, a co-educational school of about 800 which catered almost exclusively for the working-class children of South Leeds. I would think that only 10 per cent, probably less, parents of its pupils were middle class. They both served the same type of community and I didn't try to get a post in a more elite area. It's a simplification to assume that all maintained secondary schools before 1944 were solidly middle class, although it might be true of the secondary population as whole.

ADMINISTRATION

I had been headmaster for eight years when the 1944 Education Act was passed. I thought this was now going to be an exciting time,

* Professor of Economic History, University of London, and author of *Secondary Education for All* (1922) and *Equality* (1931) and many major works on British economic and social history.

offering an opportunity to play a part in shaping education. The post of Chief Inspector of Leeds was advertised, I applied and became Chief Inspector. It was an interesting time. One of the first jobs that I felt I had to do was to carry out the Hadow Report* reorganisation, because I realised that less than half of the Leeds school population were attending secondary schools – they attended all-age schools. Only a few members of the education committee were interested in reorganisation and the Director of Education, following the tradition of Dr James Graham, one of his predecessors, was actively opposed to it. The schemes were not prepared by the administrative staff, but in the inspectors' section, mostly by myself. Consequently, I had to defend my proposals in committee and to carry them out. Although they were accepted, lack of suitable buildings made progress slow. I did this from 1945 and I carried on until I became Chief Education Officer in 1950. For two years I was Chief Inspector, and for the other three years or more I was Deputy. You see, I'm not a typical CEO. I entered administration at the age of 44. And so half my life was spent in the schools, and half in the office. I'm not representative at all.

So, then, the positive reasons for being an administrator are what? What does one see in the job?
A wider scope for one's activities, I think, basically. Obviously, as the 1944 Act came in a great task was going to fall on the administration; in the first place, the raising of the school-leaving age. You will remember that I said earlier that I had been influenced by Tawney, particularly by his concept of secondary education for all. The differences between elementary and secondary education were enormous. When I became Chief Inspector, I tried to persuade the heads of the elementary schools to not merely think in terms of having an additional year,† but of recasting the whole syllabus, the whole curriculum of the school, so that they could develop true secondary education for all.

OBJECTIVES

You mentioned the opportunities of the 1944 Act. Can you pinpoint any more specific things that you wanted to do within the broad framework that the Act now allowed you to do? Were there certain goals that you had yourself?

* Report on the Education of the Adolescent (1926), which recommended reorganisation of elementary schools into primary and secondary schools with a break at the age of 11.
† By section 34 of the 1944 Education Act, the 'compulsory school age' was raised to 15 in 1947.

Yes. I couldn't accept the limitations of the elementary education provided for 80 per cent of the population. I believed that children could learn, could develop their potential in a variety of approaches to learning, and I encouraged the heads to think in those terms of developing literature in school, of introducing a modern language. You see, in the past, one of the distinctive features of a secondary school was that it included a modern language. The mere fact that a language was being introduced into what was an elementary school, I think encouraged the children to feel that they were now in the secondary sphere.

You were saying earlier that you were not a typical CEO. Could you just specify what is not typical and say what you think is typical?
Well, the career structure normally for an administrator is to teach for five to ten years. It's rather exceptional for a man to go into administration with more than ten years' experience. It's difficult for him, of course, to enter at an appropriate level after ten years. I went in, you see, in an unusual way as a CI and later as a Deputy. I never served as an administrative assistant, or as an assistant education officer.

Do you think CEOs are divisible into the educational-innovator type or the managerial keep-the-ship-moving type? Is that a fair typology?
No, I don't think so. You'll find, of course, on the one hand, Lionel Russell,* who is the complete professional expert in administration, who regards his job as seeing that the machinery works efficiently, as testing all schemes thoroughly. He is, I suppose, the control administrator *par excellence*. At the other extreme is Alec Clegg.† I don't know if you've read Hogan's book, *Beyond the Classroom* (incidentally, Jim Hogan‡ had the remarkable experience of moving from administration under Russell to become deputy to Clegg). In this book he says his new chief was not interested in administration, except in so far as he thought it would advance his educational ideas and his programmes of reform. The dichotomy is not real in his case. I don't think my friend Sir Alec Clegg would mind my saying that he attends as few subcommittees as possible. In the different conditions of a county borough I felt I had to attend virtually all subcommittees. I spent a great deal of time in committee work, but I didn't lose my contact with the schools. Whenever I was free, I used to go into the schools. I found that by going into the schools, I could learn what was going on very much better than just consulting advisers. But there

* Sir Lionel Russell, former CEO for Birmingham.
† Sir Alec Clegg, former CEO for the West Riding.
‡ J. M. Hogan, former Deputy Education Officer for the West Riding.

was no distinction between attending meetings or visiting schools. It all led to the same purpose.

But where do they put the emphasis? You said when you had time you would go to the schools. That is to say, if you had to choose between a meeting and visiting a school?

I chose the meeting, because it was more important to me to ensure that the right decisions were made and that the educational resources were most appropriately used. I regard that part of the CEO's work as being more important than, shall we say, being an educational crusader. I don't think I could have been efficient as an administrator without knowing what was going on in the schools, and knowing where resources ought to be devoted fully. There are two kinds of management: the control or regulating, seeing that it doesn't become rusty, and the other is dynamic. And I would prefer to regard my job as being not a controller, but infusing or directing the machine to new enterprises.

But there is a difficulty here. A 'well-run machine' suggests equilibrium, whereas change in education suggests disequilibrium, to some extent. I would have thought that to that extent change was not all that welcome to somebody who was much concerned with administration?

It certainly wasn't welcome to some of the former and more authoritarian CEOs – or, as they were more aptly termed, 'directors' of education; a few actively resisted it. My approach – and that of my contemporaries – towards change was completely different. We were, I think, ahead of our committees in our desires to effect change but we realised that we must carry them with us. It was for that reason that I placed a high priority on maintaining good relationships between the committee and myself.

CHAIRMEN

At the same time educational or other change implies that one is perceiving a gap between present performance and future objectives, future goals. So that there is in a sense a continuing disequilibrium upon which one is building new policies. What are the elements of the CEO's job? Could you just say roughly what the job was?

It's important I think to have a demarcation of the CEO's role and that of the elected member. Quite early on in my career, the youth officer came to me after a subcommittee meeting that I'd been unable to attend and the chairman of this committee had very considerable influence in the party. So people approached him with great caution. The youth officer came to me and said: 'At the end of the meeting the chairman of the subcommittee asked me to remain behind. A decision had been reached that a letter should be sent to the DES, complaining about lack of support. The chairman asked me to give you this letter. He wanted it sent. Give this to your chief – this is what I am sending.'

I rang up the chairman of the education committee and said: 'I'm proposing to send for the chairman of the service of youth sub-committee and try to establish demarcation of responsibility. As CEO, it is my role to write to the DES. I am sure you will agree that it is my responsibility to deal with decisions of the committee and all correspondence arising from them.'

I then sent for the chairman, I invited him to come and see me. I didn't tell him why. When he came in, I said, 'It was very kind of you to help me, particularly as I wasn't able to attend the meeting, but it is my responsibility to deal with correspondence.' He said, 'This is absurd. I'm chairman of the works committee. I go along every morning at nine o'clock. I open the letters and I tell the chief officer what replies he must make.'

So I said, 'Well, you wouldn't if you were chairman of the education committee, because I wouldn't tolerate it; if you ask him, he will confirm that he has never attempted to tell me how I should reply to a letter. And he's never looked at my correspondence.'

At first he seemed to be more astonished than annoyed and then he began to get angry. I explained that the difference between the work of the works department and the education department was immense. 'By the 1944 Act, the committee must employ a CEO; there is nothing in the law of the country to tell the works depart-ment to have a manager and if your party decides that you, as chairman, can run the department more efficiently than the manager, there is nothing to prevent that happening but it couldn't happen in education. If you are not satisfied with what I've told you, I would advise you to go to the town clerk and get his opinion.'

He said, 'I'm profoundly disturbed at what you've told me. I don't agree with you at all. I'm going to raise this in the party.' I said: 'By all means. That is the line I'm going to take. I can't accept dictator-ship from any individual member of the committee or from the chairman.' I heard no more about it.

This demarcs the two roles. But more positively, what did you see as the role of the chairman of the education committee? What could he do? He couldn't deal with the correspondence, what was his role? And his relationship with you?

First, I should say that the role of the chairman largely depends on his own conception of the role – the amount of time he is prepared to bring to it and not least his ability and experience. Although there is much variation among CEOs, the difference among chairmen and their approach to their job are obviously much greater. The chairing of committees is, perhaps, the least important aspect of their responsibilities. Just as the minister is responsible to Parliament and to the public for the work of his department, so is the chairman answerable to his group, the council, the public and the press, particularly the local press. He is spokesman, the front man. Again, like the minister, he fights for resources among chairmen of other committees. In order that my chairman could fulfil this role, I felt that he should have the opportunity to exercise his critical judgement on projects before they reached the committee stage. If the chairman is to retain his authority within his party, he must know everything of significance that is going on. I, therefore, thought that it was essential that my chairman should be informed of everything that he felt was important for this purpose, as well as what I thought he ought to know about the general running of schools, colleges and the department. We were in daily touch. My chairmen were very generous in devoting time to education. I need hardly add that successful working of the service demands complete confidence and trust between chairman and CEO. I enjoyed that confidence.

Could you say more about the role of the chairman?
It is important for there to be differentiation between the role of the chairman and the CEO. In my view, the chairman should not communicate directly with schools, colleges, and so on, but once policy is decided, he should leave it to officials going through the CEO to make policies known and understood, and to ensure that they are implemented. This in no way undermines the democratic aspects of the system. Policies were for the committee and their chairman to make, but equally for efficient functioning as well as for the professional self-respect of officers, it was important that this differentiation should be sustained. The CEO must carry out the policies of committees and show no political bias in implementation – otherwise, there could be no trust. I would, for example, discuss how I would write to the DES on a confidential matter. I would sometimes send him a copy of a letter which I had sent to the DES. I was in daily touch with the chairman by telephone and he would frequently come in to see me. And I think this generally obtains. The chairman of an education committee, when Labour is in power locally, has a greater difficulty in controlling his party generally than the chairman of the Conservative Party. The Labour Party expect the chairman to know much more detail about management.

OFFICE ATTITUDES

Could you say something about the office-staff attitudes towards their work?

Yes. It was important to ensure that education office-staff had the right attitudes to teachers, to parents and to students. What I tried to emphasise throughout was that we in the education office were servants of the schools – we were there to serve, not to control. Government officers should not tend to see their work as an end in itself, taking priority over educational considerations. And one might develop the necessity for this ethos and argue for retaining education as a separate entity within government, since one cannot expect this particular sensitivity on educational matters from other departments of the council as a whole. The thing that staff should realise is that they are there to serve the community. It isn't a common attitude in local government. There is a major difference between the other personal services and the education service, in as much as the personal services serve individuals directly, while the education service does so through institutions. That is a very important element of the CEO's job. To see that his office has the right attitude. I remember Bill Alexander saying that you can tell in five minutes of setting foot in an office what the attitude of the office is. A third element is the CEO's relationships with teachers and staff in colleges. Another element, and we've already referred to it, is that the CEO should precipitate innovation. If you want some samples of my own attempts to innovate, I will mention some areas in which I tried to promote change.

In my early days as CEO resources of money, materials and manpower were limited. Revitalising music in schools was not costly in any way, so I started in this field, by forming a quartet of professional musicians to visit schools, encouraging music festivals and persuading the education committee to provide orchestral concerts during school-time. The teachers responded enthusiastically and I left it to them. In about 1960 the interest of teachers, and of the musical public and the support of the committee, led to the setting up of the Leeds Music Centre, a very flourishing institution.

DEVELOPMENT

This development was, in a sense, a minor change compared with the establishment of a college of education for mature students. I felt very strongly in the early 1950s about two things – the shortage of teachers, which was one of my major problems, and the fact that there were a lot of people around who ought to have a second opportunity. And I was very much in favour of providing means of retraining by setting up a college for mature entrants to the teaching profession. And that was the origin of the James Graham College of Leeds. I had considerable difficulties. The only day-college in the country was at Manchester. It was a women's college only. I thought men were entitled to the same opportunities. The Leeds Institute of Education was rather hostile to a college (of this nature) being set up. They had been told that many of the entrants to the Manchester College were young people, of 18, 19, or 20, who couldn't get into a residential college and, furthermore, the whole concept of day-training for primary teaching was not welcomed by the Institute. At first the DES were far from enthusiastic, fearing that there was little likelihood of a continuing source of recruits of older men and women wishing to become teachers. With a restricted budget, the DES were reluctant to commit their resources and agreed only because a disused school building became available. Like me, the education committee saw the proposal as a valuable way of reducing the local teacher shortage and gave full support (finance was not a hurdle here, owing to the pooling of teacher training expenditure), as did all my colleagues in the West Riding. This sounds like a success story. I'd like to mention an example where I failed in my attempts to influence streaming. Impressed by the then admittedly meagre arguments against streaming in primary schools, in the late 1950s, I addressed a meeting of primary school heads on the subject. I suggested that at least there was a case for experiment in non-streaming. But at that time, no one took it up.

RELATIONS WITH HEADS

Why didn't you feel, as the authority's chief officer, that you could not impress this policy? Why not? They were employed by your authority, they were managed by the authority. Why couldn't you do this?
Partly because I was a former headmaster myself. I would be reluctant to be in a position of an officer trying to enforce my conception of education on them. All I would do was to set out the case, try to persuade them, and if they didn't accept my advice, to accept the decision.

There are components that we might note here. One component is that the committee represents the electorate, to put it at its highest, and this is one set of norms. The second set of norms is that of a developmental liberal chief administrator with his view of what ought to happen, as well as of what's feasible. The third set of norms is those of the professionals running what we have described as the prime institution – the schools. We are discussing a triangle of forces, not necessarily all in conflict, but certainly in some cases in difficult relationships with each other.

There was no evidence seventeen years ago that destreaming would work at all. And I merely said that there was a case for experiment. I didn't press it, I didn't recommend it. I said, merely, 'This is worth looking at, it may well be that we are not developing the potential of all our children.' This has been one of the significant changes in opinion.

THE DEPARTMENT OF EDUCATION AND SCIENCE

Another aspect of the CEO's role is to maintain satisfactory relations – harmonious relations – with the DES. I look back upon my contact with the DES with gratitude. I got understanding and sympathy from my dealings with territorial officers and with senior officers. On further education, for example, I made contact with Freddy Bray.* When I became CEO, the College of Technology was scattered in nineteen buildings. One of my first priorities in dealing with the DES was trying to get a new building. It was so obvious that Leeds, a great industrial city, needed adequate facilities for further education, and those facilities obviously couldn't exist in the major building, which dated back to about 1850. I went up and discussed the matter with Fred Bray.

I kept the chairman in my confidence, of course. I returned triumphantly. He had said, 'Right, I can find you a first instalment of half a million'. I thought this was splendid. My chairman thought it was a great achievement. But when he reported to his party, they said that building a technical college would interfere with housing. Housing was their first priority. Party policy in many Labour-controlled councils was decided by 'the group'. I had no contact with the group, of course, being an officer, and the project was turned down. I had to tell Freddy Bray that unfortunately Leeds was not prepared to take up the offer of half a million pounds. You can imagine how furious he was, because the DES had lost half a million pounds – a tenth of the further education programme. So my standing at the DES dropped, because I had been unable to get this through. Two years later, the Conservatives came into power. The first thing I did was to tell the new chairman of the education committee what had happened and asked him if he thought he could get the Conservative Party to agree to the building of a technical college. He said, 'I will guarantee that my party will accept anything that you suggest'. I said: 'I'm not very hopeful because of my previous failure, but I'll do what I can.' So I went up and saw Bray again – I got a very cold reception from him. He said: 'Well, all right, we can't let you have what you had before. All I've got available now is £350,000 and

* Under Secretary, Further Education Branch, Ministry of Education, 1946–56.

make a start on that, if you can guarantee committee backing.' I said I was confident of committee support. We started building in 1954 and Lord Attlee came along, five years later, to open the first instalment of what is now the Leeds Polytechnic.

STYLE

What was the impact of your own personal style on the way in which the work was done?
As far as subcommittee meetings were concerned, I thought it was my job to brief the chairman fully beforehand, to provide explanatory material to the committee and answer questions. Otherwise, I effaced myself during discussions. To individual councillors, I was always available to explain the committee's policy. A lot of them came to see me to raise questions, following a visit to a school. I was also accessible to all heads and principals but I could not offer accessibility direct to teachers and parents. They had to go through an AEO. Then within the office, I believed in delegation to heads of department, but I had to watch that departments didn't become isolated from one another.

CHANGES IN ROLE

How did your role change during your career period?
As I have already made clear, the role of the CEO is complex. I don't know that I was aware of significant changes at the time. But on reflection, I realise that in the first part of the period, I was more involved personally in internal problems; during the second part, I was more concerned with consultation, innovation, relationships with other civic departments, and I worked less in isolation from these departments. First of all, the internal problems of my early years: the greatest was teacher shortage. So acute was the shortage in Leeds, which is not a teacher-producing area, that I felt obliged to supervise and encourage teacher recruitment, to streamline procedures for interviewing and appointment and to introduce various means of attracting teachers. From the long-term angle, from 1952, I encouraged the introduction of GCE courses in secondary modern schools accompanied by arrangements for transfer to sixth forms of grammar schools at the age of 16. In due course, teacher recruitment from this source was significant; more important, GCE courses provided opportunities for non-selected children and so removed from many parents the anxiety of the 11-plus tests.

OTHER DEPARTMENTS

In the second part of the period, I was more involved in matters outside the education department itself – particularly with other corporation departments. This was partly an effect of the government's policies, leading to the introduction of the general grant.* It became more difficult to get money for education after 1958. Up till then, I'd been able to say, when we discussed estimates, particularly for any new developments, 'The DES are going to provide a percentage grant for this'. After 1957, I had to fight every time.

Then there were claims by other departments, which I felt infringed the freedom of the schools. Claims by the works department to maintain the fabric and plant of the schools. They wanted to do it directly. They suggested that all the requests for alterations, down to repair of windows, should go direct to them. As the amount of money was limited, I felt that the education office ought to control this, because we knew what expenditure would be most profitable; for example, provision of a particular type of blackboard, provision of hardboard on walls could make a significant educational difference.

There was a tendency in corporation departments for one or the other to have a go at taking over functions from the education department. There were, particularly after general grant, more requests from the treasurer to look into educational expense, to examine the details of it. I had to meet such queries as 'Why can't the public library take over all responsibilities for the provision of school libraries? They can get books more cheaply.' 'Wouldn't school baths and playing fields be more generally available, if they were run by other departments?' I tried to resist what I called intervention by other departments, because I felt that their intervention would lead to less educational efficiency.

The climate of opinion is different today: at the time I'm talking of, heads would have resented the use of their playing fields and baths, and from my point of view, the proposals were in the nature of a takeover rather than a merger or a co-operative. Maud and Mallaby and the Sports Council have changed our ideas.

CHANGING OBJECTIVES

Shall I go on to more general changes? One constantly needed to review one's role in the postwar society, which was changing at an unprecedented rate. The objectives of schools and colleges between the wars were largely unquestioned, because the rate of general social change was not obvious. In the 1950s technological developments, progress in communication, more women economically active, a more

* This was the product of the 1958 Local Government Act, which substituted general local authority grants for specific service-related percentage grants.

mobile society, all these were at work, particularly in Leeds, and the breakdown of the old sanctions of the family and school, the prosperity of young people, the increasing sophistication of children, these too made their impact. Perhaps the most striking changes were, first, the virtual disappearance of religious issues, which had dominated education from 1902 down to the 1944 Act. In my period, denominational issues virtually ceased to exist.

The second overwhelming change in my time has been a new public interest in education development. This in itself led to a major change – the increasing incursion of politics in education. With the growing volume of educational expenditure, it was a nonsense to expect that decisions could be other than political. This involved the CEO in political conflicts within his own committee, between his committee and the DES, particularly when the committee and the government were of different political parties. The next most important change was the growing demand for the education service to take on wider responsibilities for promoting social justice. By this, I mean the 'strong'* definition of the concept – equality of opportunity – and the assumption that education appropriately organised would resolve social ills. This affected the CEO, in that he felt that more was expected of his service in the promotion of social justice than it could achieve because of other social ills. Organisational change is only the beginning of the social changes desired. On the other hand, the concept of positive discrimination following Plowden helped him to overcome the pressures of elected representatives for uniformity of treatment for all matters within the discretion of the committee. It became possible to say openly that some schools were in greater need of resources than others. This was almost impossible in 1950.†

The methods of financing higher education, pooling, mandatory awards‡ – together with mounting debt charges – made the CEO and his committee the payer of bills over which they had no control. And the pressure upon him to economise increased.

CONSTRAINTS

What constraints did you have to work within?
I suppose an obvious starting point, here, is the local authority's obligation to conform to national policy – in other words, to keep in step with the DES, to digest and interpret to the committee statutory instruments and official circulars.

---

* Anthony Crosland, *The Conservative Enemy* (London: Jonathan Cape, 1962).
† *Children and their Primary Schools* (London: HMSO, 1963); chapter 5 contains proposals for 'positive discrimination' – educational priority areas.
‡ For higher education courses.

Sometimes the DES imposed constraints not altogether backed by statute. Take building, for example. There has never been any statutory basis for the annual building programmes. Although control of capital expenditure was necessary since the government used building programmes as a financial regulator, their approval year by year – and often late in the relevant year – impeded local planning and was a serious constraint.

The 'roofs over heads' policy effectively removed long-term planning and discretion from LEAs, as also did the insistence by the DES that primary schools must either be one- or two-form, entry. Natural catchment areas and new estates just did not conform to this rigidity in the size of schools.

Other constraints imposed by statute, though not connected with building, I found could be quietly evaded. For example, we admitted to grammar schools outstandingly able children below the age of 10 years and 6 months – the lower limit allowed by the Act. We admitted children to nursery school for either mornings, or afternoons, although the current regulations required that children should attend for two sessions each day.

One of the most frustrating things about central government was the lack of collaboration between one government department and another. For example, there was no possibility of linking housing with education – we would have liked to include a small primary (especially infant) school within a large block of flats, in such a way that the school could be converted into flats if the need for the school lessened. There was, however, no machinery for such collaboration. In any case, in my view, approval for a new housing estate would have carried automatic approval for a new primary school.

To turn to local constraints, there was great hostility to *virement*, which I tried to introduce into the education department. Also to the carry-forward of any unspent resources – schools could not, for example, save up for an expensive item of equipment which they wished to purchase. Therefore, the schools and the office spent late in the year frantically, and not necessarily wisely, on materials and equipment which could be delivered by 1 April. Equally there was fear of overspending on repairs, which meant all maintenance work virtually ceased from the beginning of February until the beginning of the next financial year.

RELATIONS WITH THE DEPARTMENT OF EDUCATION AND SCIENCE

Could you now say what you consider to be the difference between local and central government decision-making?
Yes. At the centre, decision-making is broader – and longer-term yet subject to sudden variations, because capital expenditure is used as a

financial regulator. Also, decisions can be taken which present authorities with no alternative but paying the bill, for example, mandatory awards for higher education. Sudden variations make nonsense of local planning. For example, the Leeds programme on minor works for improvement – especially the replacement of outside lavatories and the provision of hot water – was frustrated by the cutback in the building programme, which meant that capital for minor works had to be used for the provision of essential classrooms.

I would say that LEAs have not got the wide area of discretion that they had at the turn of the century. Bradford was able to develop its nursery schools, and Leeds built grammar schools before there was any demand for them.

Could you say who really develops a school system? Does it come from the committee or from officials, or whom?
When the late Victor Wiseman* was first appointed deputy chairman of the education committee, he said to me that the greatest surprise he had was to find that all development, all impetus to innovation and change, came from within the office. He expected to find it coming from the members. As far as the purely educational aspect of education is concerned, the traditional source of progress is the work of gifted and inspired teachers. This will always be so. But at a time when change is taking place so rapidly, large-scale improvement can be reinforced only through organisations which promote development, such as the Schools Council, the teachers' centres and the Nuffield Foundation. They have facilitated profound changes in curriculum – in science, mathematics and French.

COUNCILLORS

Could you say what is the role of councillors in policy-making?
I've already quoted one example of the power of the Labour group to stop the rebuilding of the Leeds College of Technology. There was similar successful opposition in my first year to my proposal for GCE in secondary modern schools. It was agreed that there should be no examinations in secondary modern schools. I took the opposite view, that examinations being part of the structure, there could be no parity of esteem in a situation in which one school took an examination and one didn't. The Conservative Party, when they came into power two years later, approved the proposal.

It is, of course, necessary for officers to base their decisions on committee policy. And on known attitudes of committee. This is a useful check by democracy. I don't want you to think that I am

* Later Professor of Government at the University of Exeter.

opposed to the structure because I am being critical on some of the effects of it. Overall, I think the education committee plays a vital part in preventing the grinding of bureaucratic axes.

That is their negative role. What about their positive role? Don't they represent the people?

They represent the view of the people who are politically active in their ward and in their party. They were influenced by trades councils, the trades unions and ward meetings. They are political animals, they move along the political line which is, after all, the concern of a small element in the population. On the other hand, they are useful as ombudsmen, particularly for the inarticulate, who are reluctant to approach the education office. Councillors tend to take one view when they are in education committees, and another when they are in finance committees – they have two faces worn with their two different sorts of hats.

PRESSURE GROUPS

So far we've talked about officers, committees and chairmen. What about the wider political environment in which they move? The pressure groups, for example?

The main pressure groups in my time were the governing bodies of secondary schools, who were pressing the claims of their own schools. The more middle class the school, the greater the pressure. Pressure for comprehensive schools came from middle-class parents anxious that their children might not get selective education and, therefore, wanting to do away with the 11-plus examination.

RELATIONS WITH SCHOOLS

Could we now turn to relations with schools? They are said to be 'free' or even 'autonomous'. Are they?

Is it possible that schools can be free or autonomous, when political thinking in this country is based on checks and balances? Moreover, this freedom is under challenge not so much by the local authorities, as by public opinion. Parents and others have become more aware of the need for social justice, and this is usually interpreted as more uniformity – that what one school does, should obtain in others. Parents find it difficult to accept that a CEO will not intervene in internal organisation of the school.

But could he not intervene, even if the school were known to be very bad?

He can only intervene, in my view, by sending his advisory staff in to try to influence the policies of the school. Also by encouraging the teachers to go on in-service courses.

He couldn't get rid of a bad head or teacher?
That is, in my view, one of the great weaknesses of the educational system: the impossibility of sacking incompetent teachers. I had a number of teachers whose incompetence was well known – some of them graduates. All I could do was to unload them on the schools and say, 'Well, we won't count this against your establishment'. Even then the heads were reluctant to take them, they had become notorious. They ought to have been got rid of. And, in the same way, it was impossible to get rid of a lazy or incompetent head teacher. I think it is one of the great weaknesses in our system. A doctor – at least a GP – who is incompetent will lose his patients, but with an incompetent teacher there is nothing to be done. Though I did succeed in persuading a few bad ones to resign their posts. I always had the nagging thought that I should have been very unhappy if my own children were in their charge.

RELATIONS IN THE SCHOOLS

What about the head within his school?
Do they manage assistant teachers? What do we mean by manage? Well, fifteen years ago I would have judged a head teacher by his ability to persuade the staff to adopt a common policy, to improve teacher relationships, and by his approach to the curriculum. Clearly, to achieve this, he had to consult with and consider staff views. But having made a decision and laid down policy, I would have expected this decision to be complied with. In this sense, the head managed teachers.

In primary schools the head is a working member of a team for teaching and he is fully involved in curriculum development. With frequent changes in staff, the head is the linkman, the person who keeps up to date and trains his staff to conform with the school's approach. He is also the link with parents, not necessarily in any formal way, but he should be readily available and ready to give advice on a variety of matters not necessarily educational. In some schools the welfare work forms a major part of his role. What he should also include in his role, and rarely does, is to keep parents informed of curricular objectives, developments and changes. How well he can do this does depend to some extent on the educational level of the parents.

With a secondary school, the role is quite different. He will be *primus inter pares* in relation to heads of department. Through that, he will achieve a common policy for his pupils and curriculum. But he cannot avoid final responsibility for the school as a whole. Parents and elected representatives regard this as the position. This need not conflict with delegation of responsibility to his colleagues in charge of the various sections of the school. What then is his role? He is, I suppose, a leader of educational opinion. He must educate employers, so that they will respect his opinion on pupils. Schools are selective agents of employment and the head's view of the overall work of the child should be greater than that of any external examination. A useful study which should be made is the role of the heads of department and other senior members of staff. The hierarchical system which has grown up in the last ten years has arisen from changes in the salary structure, which was unplanned in relation to the running of schools.

PARENTS

What place do you give parents in the schools?
This is difficult. They don't have common interests which would make it easy for them to have an institutionalised say in the running of schools. They are interested, naturally enough, in their own children only.

I would be the last person to suggest that parents are no more than a necessary evil, but equally I am not sure that they are sufficiently disinterested or in possession of an overall view to make a contribution to planning for schools as agents of change.

What role would you give governing bodies?
I don't think the role of governing bodies has been sufficiently thought out during the last fifty years. I feel sure that the authors of the 1944 Act never stopped to think about it.

As far as the county boroughs are concerned, nobody of any standing serves because of the limited responsibilities given to them. This is inevitable. Policy and finance must be settled by the elected body. Planning for the place of a particular school in the system belongs to the same body. And as I said earlier, the general public expects a certain uniformity in internal policy of schools. This, in any case, is a matter for the head teacher and staff. There is nothing whatever in articles of government that governors can do to make a bad school into a good one. There is little an LEA can do, though they can avoid making bad appointments. Unless the governors are very perceptive, they don't know whether a school is good or bad. Most head teachers have the governors in their pockets.

I find it difficult to see what is the future role of governors. In as much as they are democratic institutions I am sympathetic with them, but in practice I find it very difficult to see what their role is.

INTERVIEWS HELD IN 1980

Fred Adams

South Glamorgan

Fred Adams was educated at Trinity College, Cambridge. After eight years teaching in a Quaker boarding school and with the Workers' Educational Association he entered educational administration in Monmouthshire in 1951. He became Deputy Director of Education in both Wigan and West Bromwich and then moved to Birmingham as Assistant Education Officer in 1963. He became Director of Education for the county borough of Bradford in 1967. Following local government reorganisation in 1974, he became Director of Education for the new county of South Glamorgan. He is a former president of the Society of Education Officers.

BACKGROUND

Mine was a fairly conventional pattern. I decided at an early stage that I had set my sights on being Director of Education. That was when I was at Cambridge. It may have been rather ambitious but that was the aim. I came from a teaching background, and to that extent, it was more or less assumed by the family that I would go into teaching. I went to Trinity, Cambridge. The first real teaching experience was at Ackworth School. Then I was diverted from becoming Director of Education by reading Richard Livingstone's book.* I felt there was so much in what he said about the right time to learn is in adult life, together with the fact that I was worried about going through life as a boarding-school master with a horizon limited very much by a very small community. I went into the WEA as an organising tutor, thinking I would come to terms with realities. In fact, in a sense, this may not be a true commentary on the WEA but I think it was then, and in the areas where I worked, it was exchanging one kind of elitism for another. I worked in Blackpool and the Fylde. The folk we got as our students tended to be civil servants, a few boarding-house keepers during their close season, teachers, clerks, and so on. The real working class didn't seem to exist in Blackpool, or to come along to the classes. After about two and a half years there, I decided to return to what I had previously set my sights on, educational administration.

* R. Livingstone, *The Future in Education* (Cambridge: Cambridge University Press, 1941).

You said you set your sights on being a director. Was there something particular that led you to believe at a very early stage that this was the thing that you wanted to do?

I have always been very interested, and this showed itself in the kind of options I took for my degree, in government and the mechanics of government. Educational administration has given me the opportunity to get an enormous amount of fulfilment from working with a purpose, which I think education does in whichever capacity you work, but together with close involvement in making policy and the administration of policy. That satisfies my dual interests in education and government. I think also I would have to say quite candidly that there is a strong element of ambition in this. At its best, it is a sense of feeling that you are making some impact in an important area of public life but also there is a wide spectrum of activity in which you are personally involved. Ambition is a motive of varying respectability. You can put it nicely, or you can say it's just a power-complex. I think inevitably a desire to be near to the centre of power was part of the motive.

After your experience in the WEA, you moved into educational administration. How did that come about?

It was what I wanted to do. I started off in what was the County of Monmouthshire – which I think were two of the most exhilarating years of my whole career. I loved it and, in a sense, it was a good time and a good place to be in. We were gradually emerging from the postwar difficulties and starting this period of expansion. I worked under an absolutely first-rate chief, who had a very powerful influence in my approach to administration altogether. That was Charles Gittens, who subsequently left the local authority and became professor of education at Swansea, and was the chairman of the Gittens Committee which produced a kind of Welsh Plowden. My job was an excellent introduction to administration. There were two of us and we had approximately half the county each, with all the managing bodies, all the governing bodies, and the district youth and further education committees, in the context of people who were very democratically minded – what Taylor said in 1978 could have taught them nothing. It was a very fascinating experience to have had.

You were there for two and a half years. From there you moved on?

I moved to Wigan for three years as deputy director and then to West Bromwich in the same capacity. I went from deputy in West Bromwich to Assistant Education Officer in Birmingham, which – although it meant second-tier officer to third tier – was quite a substantial promotion. And if you put those two bits of experience together, they were complementary in that West Bromwich was a small authority with some very enlightened people. The Director, Joe Turner, and one or two members of his committee, really ran the show in the way you can do in a small authority. Going to Birmingham was totally different. All the administrative niceties had to be observed there, and one got the impression that an enormous amount of one's energies were directed to keeping the machine going. The degree of perfection that we worked to was part of the tradition and the attitude of Lionel Russell and his meticulous care. Lionel Russell told me when I was appointed that one of the tasks which I would have to give some priority to was ending a feeling of isolation which schools in that very large area must feel. I think that it fitted in so well with my own thoughts about my job and my role that it seemed something which has influenced all my thinking subsequently.

How long were you at Birmingham before the Bradford post came along?
Four years. It was the only post I applied for when I was in Birmingham. I thought it was probably going to be a stroke of fortune if I ever became a Chief Education Officer. I started in Bradford, in January 1967, and I thought I was there for life. But this didn't prove so.

I know that you moved to South Glamorgan in 1974. How did that come about?
Bradford were going, under reorganisation, to become a metropolitan district with about 40 per cent coming in from the West Riding, and a series of events led to my not being appointed to the New Bradford. The post went to Richard Knight, an AEO in the West Riding. I can only say that it was as near to breaking my heart as anything that has happened to me short of bereavement, because I had found Bradford, the old Bradford, such a marvellous place to work in with a tradition of extremely good relationships between committee and officers, committee and schools. I think I would have to say that I didn't fit particularly well into the corporate approach at Bradford. I think the chief executive thought I was too old, and as I was then over 50, I could understand that. I think also, to its credit, the West Riding wanted to ensure that its own traumatic experience of disappearing off the map altogether would not involve any disadvantage for its quite splendid officers, whom they were anxious to slot into the various jobs that came along.

You then had to decide whether to retire early or to seek another post. Why South Glamorgan?

There were very few posts nationally advertised then. So, South Glamorgan was the first that came along. I had been extremely happy when I had been in Monmouthshire. And to my quite genuine surprise, I got it. That was within three weeks of having lost the job at Bradford. It softened the blow. And this is one of the miracles of life. It opened up a whole range of activities that, had I stayed in Bradford, I would never have got anywhere near. I got involved as the representative for Wales on the executive of the Society of Education Officers, and I became President of the Society of Education Officers last year, which I don't think I would have ever done had I stayed in Bradford.

REORGANISATION

Can I turn to the issue of reorganisation now? Would you say something about the way in which the South Glamorgan council emerged?
I think all my fellow chief officers here would concur in this statement that we can identify those members who are Cardiff-oriented, those members who are county-oriented. Attitudes die very slowly, and it is not at all unusual to hear people in the education committee talk about education in this city. They haven't adjusted. It is probably more understandable when you think that, in terms of population, Cardiff is probably about 70 per cent and it is the hub – the capital city. The Vale of Glamorgan, clearly, is the junior partner in all this. The task of trying to start new traditions and new attitudes has been quite substantial. The other task has been to try to avoid people in the Vale of Glamorgan thinking that this is a takeover by the City of Cardiff. It has been a great opportunity. I came here and took over the shadow authority on 1 November prior to reorganisation. So, in a sense, I had no operational responsibilities for five months.

You appear to be suggesting that Cardiff people saw reorganisation as an opportunity to expand their own empire, rather than resenting losing their autonomy in the way that, perhaps, Bristol did?
It was a confused situation and there was a curious combination of both attitudes. I think it was felt by some, including some officers in the education department at Cardiff, that this was no more than a boundary expansion.

What about the people from Glamorgan? Did they feel some resentment about this? Would they have preferred the status quo?
I am sure they would. You got this curious move on the part of Mid-Glamorgan and South Glamorgan to try to combine, and the first thing the two county councils did at their opening meetings before reorganisation when they were still shadows, was to pass

a resolution urging the secretary of state to amalgamate. The secretary of state turned it down. As you can imagine, the original proposal had been a West Glamorgan based on Swansea, and an East Glamorgan based on Cardiff. I think it is true that the Cardiff people would have liked the City of Cardiff to have been kept out altogether. My interpretation of the situation is that there is nobody who would want to go back to the old Glamorgan. There would be those people who are city council-oriented, who would like to see the city get its education powers back, but that is not particularly marked. At the time of Peter Shore's proposals for organic change, there was probably more support here in both political parties for keeping South Glamorgan intact, rather than to get involved in any further change at that juncture. There is a fair amount of pride in what South Glamorgan has achieved and, in a sense, that has established its identity.

CORPORATE MANAGEMENT

For many authorities, corporate management came as part and parcel of reorganisation. Was that the case in South Glamorgan?
Welsh authorities generally have not been so corporate management-minded as a number of English authorities. South Glamorgan appointed a Chief Executive, who was not just a replica of the old clerk to the county council or town clerk, but was the chief officer with the ultimate control and the ultimate responsibility for advising the county council. They defined those chief officers who would be members of a management team, and I think that has worked reasonably well. Our meetings gave us an opportunity to get to know one another and establish a fairly high level of corporate under-standing. But the fact that the length and frequency of our meetings were deliberately limited made it necessary that we wouldn't waste time and energy on some sort of ideological conformity to corporate management. Where I have some anxiety, is where third- or fourth-or fifth-tier officers from other departments want, perhaps, to assert a role for themselves in the education department. I don't find from the Chief Executive himself any problem. He happily takes the view that a specialist officer is appointed and it is his job to get on with running the service. There is a fair amount of practical co-operation with other departments, though it is interesting that the actual term 'corporate management', by Chief Executive decree, is never used in the authority. It gives the wrong image of the authority.

Who is represented on the policy committee and how does it relate to the main service committees?
The policy committee includes, in addition to representatives from the

opposition party, the chairmen and some of the deputy chairmen of the main committees. I can only think of one issue where the policy committee has overridden the education committee and that was in the very early days when the education committee decided it wanted to be represented on the AEC and the policy committee determined otherwise. But few education issues ever go to the policy committee.

Can I just follow up that example? A large number of authorities like South Glamorgan contributed to the demise of the AEC. Why did the education committee want to stay in the AEC and why did the policy committee decide otherwise?
I don't know. I think there were officers and members who felt that the AEC had a unique role in being the only body representing all education committees.

Issues which go to policy committee from the education committee are those in which another department is involved, for example, social services, or on major issues of acquisition of property. I don't find the policy committee intrudes to any extent. I usually make a point of either going myself, or the deputy goes, to the pre-meeting of the policy committee as that gives me a picture of what is going on and what the more influential members of the council are thinking. It rarely happens that there is anything of great significance for me to be present at the policy committee itself.

Is the impact on your role then minimal, so that you are able to carry on as the principal adviser to the authority on educational matters. You would seek advice from the Chief Executive and others rather than having that imposed on you?
I would say that was a very accurate statement. What causes some CEOs problems is the function of the personnel committee. We have managed here to ensure that as far as the teachers and college lecturers are concerned, this is a matter which doesn't involve the personnel committee. That doesn't mean to say that there are not issues where it is invaluable to have the advice of the personnel officer or his representative. On such things as the health and safety regulations and negotiations on conditions of service, we would want the help of the personnel officer. But he comes as an invited colleague rather than as a person who is in charge of the personnel side of the teaching force.

So you have an essentially professional relationship. What about non-teaching staff working in your schools and other educational establishments?
They have to be approved by the personnel committee, which is not unreasonable because there is a possibility of movement into other

departments of the county council. I would accept entirely that when you are talking about clerical and secretarial and administrative duties, there should be one common yardstick for all the county council's employees. Teachers are a different breed, and the relationship between the chief officer, the committee and the teachers is different in kind from the relationship that exists among administrators and clerical staff.

There are two other areas I would like to explore. One concerns the revenue budget. How do the policy committee and the education committee, and the chief officers team and the Director of Education, link into the budgetary process?
Right from the start here, we have had a system which has certain advantages and certain dangers, namely, the idea of global allocations. What worried me from the start, and continues to worry me, is the real risk that you are looking at one dimension only; you are looking at what the county council can afford to make available. If you are looking at resources only, then the risk is that you are not going to pay any regard to the level or the needs of the service. I think this is something which is of concern. The other aspect which worries me is that there is a danger, too, that having determined what your global allocation is going to be by reference to resources available, the finance committee may then look at where within that global sum you can be cut further. So, we have found ourselves in practice ending up with a rather more modest allocation than the one which we originally started out with. But for the most part, it is an education-minded authority anyway, and that goes for both parties. So, I don't encounter much of the hostility that sometimes is engendered by the largest-spending committee.

So, for example, has your pupil-teacher ratio been affected?
We improved it modestly in September 1974. We have maintained it by the skin of our teeth ever since, with a minimal improvement in September 1980.

Once the global sum for education has been determined by these processes, has the education committee discretion as to whether it is spent on one portion of your budget or another portion?
Until about three months ago, it had virtually unrestricted virement. All we had to do was to report any virement which the committee decided on to the treasurer, who reported it – no more than that – to the finance committee. Now, any virement is going to be subject to the approval of the finance committee. That doesn't mean to say that in practice the opportunity for virement will be any the less, but we just haven't got that ease of virement which existed before. But,

perhaps, I can elaborate on another aspect, and that is the tendency for important negotiation among members to take place outside the committees altogether. You can find that the chairman and deputy chairman will talk to the leader, and because of a general atmosphere of sympathy for education, for improving education, undertakings may be given there much more readily. That is the positive side, and very often the way can be prepared for some improvement by negotiations among the politicians themselves before the matter comes to committee. The unfortunate aspect of all this is an increasing tendency for decisions to be taken and reversed outside a committee. This has endless dangers. I think it may well arise from the current sensitivity to popular opinion and to pressure groups.

What part does the policy committee play in determining your capital spending, by comparison with your own committee?
This has posed a real difficulty for the policy committee, since much of education capital expenditure is determined by reference to national factors and not just local priorities. The dilemma is a real one for a council that wants to determine its spending according to how it sees its own priorities, while, for example, the expenditure on educational building, with its revenue implications for future years, is largely determined by central government. A council may draw up its own five-year capital programme which may not, in the event, prove to be enough to cover all the new projects for which justification may be made. In practice, of course, due regard in drawing up a capital programme has to be given to what can realistically be anticipated will be included in forthcoming building programmes, and so far no major difficulties have arisen.

So once a project was within the DES key sector programme, you were able to go through with it?
Yes.

COUNCILLORS

To what extent are decisions made by council members rather than by you and your professional colleagues?
I think it is true of Wales, and it is certainly true here, that the members, however enlightened they may be, are most anxious that decisions of policy are kept in their own hands. There is this firm understanding that policy is made by the members. They don't deny, I think, that in the policy-making process there is a place for the officer, the officer's advice must be given. I would hold this as an important part of my freedom to give advice, the best advice I can

give. It might nevertheless be necessary on occasion to exercise some judgement or discretion as to the appropriate time to give it, but I would not feel it right merely to provide the sort of advice, comment, or information that the chairman or his party might find most acceptable. They require and mostly expect a valid professional statement from their officers.

So, in policy formulation as opposed to policy determination, you would expect to have a fairly substantial role?
You have always got to have regard to what they are likely to accept. There is a fair measure of consensus, or at least in my experience there has been, on major educational issues, except possibly comprehensive reorganisation. The wiser folk of either party on the education committee will have a fair degree of understanding.

You don't detect any breakdown of consensus over the last decade or so?
There is a fair amount of shadow-boxing in the county council. They have got to be seen to be taking a different line. But when you come to the question of policy formulation in those preliminary discussions, good sense prevails. It happened when Labour was in control and it happens now. They bring in their political opponents on informal working groups, and so on. This is a tremendous asset. If you are working in an authority where there is likely to be political change, it makes good sense in the interests of continuity not only of my job, but of what the public can expect, if major policy decisions are based upon a bipartisan approach. It happens here. The two most pressing issues for us are the development of Welsh language education and the rationalisation of our 16–19-year-olds in the context of falling rolls. And in both those policies, although there have been peripheral differences and on occasions people have had to be seen in public taking a line, there is fundamental agreement which is of enormous value.

The policy committee has representatives of both parties on it, whereas in some authorities only the majority party is represented. Does that lead to decisions effectively being taken in the majority party caucus rather than in the policy committee?
On any major step, they will reach a decision in the group and then you will know in advance what at the end of the day will come out of it.

Is it possible for change to occur, or for argument to be influential, once issues reach the policy committee?
The mechanism can work to produce greater indecision than if it were done openly. Let me give you a case in point. There was an issue as to whether or not we should build a new comprehensive school at a

time of falling rolls. And there were various arguments that made it highly desirable in this neighbourhood that there should be. On the other hand, the resources argument and the possible effect on another school of falling rolls were quite serious. There was a series of reversals of decisions which, I suspect, resulted less from reasoned argument in committees than from differences of outlook, and indeed of conviction on the part of different individuals, which were worked out within their own party deliberations.

One of the potential problems in decision-making effectively taking place in party groups is that the moment of decision occurs without officer advice. Has this been a problem for you?
No. I wouldn't be afraid, in this authority, of their producing some cataclysmic decision taken in the group without my knowing.

Do you feel that your relationship with the education chairman is the central one as it has been traditionally within the education service?
I think it is central. I can't think of any argument which would indicate any change in that. It is a delicate situation. There can be a risk of chairman domination where he might try to usurp the administrative role, but equally there can be the risk of not seeing enough of your chairman, so that in those political arenas which you have been talking about, he might not be sufficiently aware of the issues and the professional advice that is relevant to those issues.

It may mean that not enough information is coming to member level prior to the committee. But you don't seem unduly concerned about that.
No, I am not. I think what did concern me was a situation which arose about four years ago, where we had discussions with the teachers on various issues, and as a result, reached a fair amount of agreement with the teachers. When it got to committee, we were never sure that the agreement we had reached with the teachers would be acceptable to members. The teachers wanted a greater involvement of members, so that there could be some measure of political will and not just officer intentions. It worried me at the time, but I don't think it need have done because even in that situation, I detected a certain advantage. If somebody from the operational level can indicate the detrimental effect that a particular measure may have for the service, or their particular aspect of the service, that's good. It would be more effective than advice.

The teachers' unions wished to be involved at a member level. Is that confined to the education committee, or were they seeking to involve other members?

For the most part, it is solely education committee members. What you said has applied rather more in the field of higher education. The Institute of Higher Education was set up through the amalgamation of four colleges as a consequence of central government more or less dictating to us that we would have to do this. That was a very major and expensive operation, with a highly paid principal, all of which rather alarmed members understandably and involved the then leader of the council and the Chief Executive. There has been a tendency from those early days for people in the field of higher education to want to address themselves to the leader of the council or the Chief Executive, rather than to the education committee. Happily, that hasn't been encouraged by the Chief Executive. But there are dangers that people might have a hunch that the centre of gravity of power has moved from the education office to county headquarters.

At one time, the post of education chairman was seen as perhaps the most important political post after the leadership of the council. Would you say that was still so, or has it been downgraded with the emergence of policy committees?
One would have to say that marginally it has been downgraded. The mere fact that there is a committee which can override the education committee is indicative of that. Also, the existence of a Chief Executive with a greater amount of responsibility than the clerk of the county council. One would have to face the fact that we are not the pre-eminent people that we used to be. Nevertheless, there is a very real status for education, for the education chairman and indeed for the Director of Education.

CENTRAL GOVERNMENT

Do you believe that central government has more influence in relation to the local education service than it had a decade ago, or less?
I think, perhaps, more. First and foremost, in regard to resources, for example, the way that the Department of the Environment can and does attempt to control local authority expenditure in a way that never happened up to about three years ago. Another aspect is the concern, which may be justifiable, for standards. I see no diminution of what I suppose Jim Callaghan in his Ruskin speech triggered off, namely, that the secretary of state has some responsibility for the level and quality of education which is being provided. There are two conflicting tendencies. The modern vogue for participation and letting the neighbourhood, the parents and the employer make an important contribution in determining what goes on in school. On the other hand, the central government are saying uniformity of

standards, uniformity of provision, core curriculum, and so on, must happen. How do you reconcile letting the governing bodies, if Taylor was fully implemented, go their own way, with the role of central government in ensuring uniformity of provision and standards? There is a great risk that between those two millstones the local authority is going to be squeezed out altogether.

Has the emphasis on standards led to a stronger role for the HM Inspectorate in South Glamorgan?
In practice, no. Coming to Wales, the feeling I got was that the Inspectorate here played a more positive role than they did in England. An inspector might take it upon himself to more or less direct how a head should organise a school.

Do you find any problems of overlap between your own advisory service and HMIs? Sheila Browne, at the Fookes Committee, said that the local advisory service looked at individual schools and standards within a local authority context, whereas the HMI did so within the national context and, therefore, there was a distinct contribution. Would you go along with that?
Yes. I would go a little further and say that the HMI have a much fuller programme of in-service training for themselves. They can keep up to date. There can be a process of cross-fertilisation much more fully than in the case of local authority advisers. They are a resource which I think a local authority can ill-afford to do without.

RELATIONS WITH HEADS

What is the nature of the relationship that you have as director with the heads of both schools and colleges?
I can't very well wish to direct them. It would be impertinent for someone who left the classroom thirty years ago to think that he could tell a school how it should do its job. Nevertheless, I have certain advantages which may be of use in that I see the whole educational scene. So, when I arrive at a judgement, it is on the basis of knowing competing claims, for example, in regard to resources. I would expect the head to manage the school, to determine in consultation with his governors, parental opinion, and so on, what he provides in that school within the broad framework that the committee would expect or lay down. I would expect my role to be one of making available to him such support as he needed. As a last resort, I am aware – as I think the heads are aware – that a real problem which goes beyond the confines of a school and which can't be handled at that level, is a matter for the local authority, which in the first instance means me.

Does there come a point when, as Director, you have to go in and sort a problem out?
In the majority of cases that I could envisage, I wouldn't, myself, do that. Where it is a question of poor teaching, poor discipline, or bad relations with parents, I would expect the advisers to take this on board in the first instance. My contact with heads would be more likely to be on a more general quasi-policy issue.

If heads really don't respond to that and continue in a direction which you consider undesirable, is there a further step that you would take?
There is an escalation of action. It might be necessary to get a team of advisers to go in and advise the head on timetable and curriculum and organisation. If that advice were ignored, then there would be a case for some further intervention. Hypothetically, what I would do in the first instance would be to go out with the advisers to the school. If then warning and exhortation had had no effect, I would have to start the agreed disciplinary procedures.

Has the problem of schools' contraction changed the essential nature of the relationship that you have with heads? Does the focus move towards the centre, away from individual institutions?
I don't think it has changed the relationship. I would pose the problem, as I see it, as somewhat different. They are worried about how their schools are going to continue to function with declining numbers. They know also that, where numbers have fallen, every summer term we have to work out a redeployment of those staff for whom there will be no further job in the schools that they are at. This year, for example, thirty-five primary and thirty-five secondary teachers will be redeployed. This is a process which goes remarkably smoothly, largely because we have got the good will of the teachers who jointly drew up with us a code of procedure.

When there is redeployment the ability of the head to select his own staff is reduced, and you and your colleagues have a much more powerful role in teacher selection. Is that worrying to heads?
Yes, for the best of motives, since if they can choose the teacher themselves after advertisement, they are more likely to get the best person; but if they are going to have to take somebody from another school, there is always that suspicion that the person who has been identified for redeployment is not going to be your star member of staff. It is a worry I sympathise with.

GOVERNING BODIES

Can we move on to governing bodies? Do they have a fair amount of

*authority in South Glamorgan or are they really rather subordinate to
the education committee?*

We put on every governing body teacher representation, parent
representation, co-opted members, and for schools with sixth forms,
we had student representation. The servicing, I thought, was important in that we have tried to maintain, and I think so far we have
succeeded, a fairly responsible level of professional representation
from the office; and I asked the advisers to take a share in attending
governing and managing bodies. The presence of an adviser was
intended to encourage some kind of educational debate or debate on
educational policy the county council were initiating. It still happens
that some heads are frightened of discussing education in their
governing bodies. Rather than have queries about their organisation, they would much prefer the office to be pilloried for not
having provided a rapid repair for the dripping tap. The head of one
school had, I thought, done extraordinarily well and used a very
detailed report on his very complex organisation, and I doubt
whether there were more than a few governors present who either
understood it, or were in the least bit interested.

That has been said of members of education committees as well.

Yes, indeed. If we are going to expect a greater educational contribution from the governors, then we have got to use a governing body
as a forum for public education.

*One view might be that the governing body can only carve out a stronger
role for itself at the expense of either the LEA, or the head and the
staff. Is it possible to get a strong role that doesn't infringe the rights of
either of these groups?*

I don't want a strong role. I am a reactionary, here. I want them to be
influential. I want them to be supportive. Much depends on the way
the head uses his governing body and communicates with them. I
want them to be communicators, to be the agency through which the
community it serves will understand what the county council is doing
and the constraints it is working under. Equally, they can be a
mouthpiece through which the needs of the locality can be brought
to the notice of the authority. But I would strongly resist a governing
body which saw itself as really determining the daily operations of
the school. And I wouldn't wish them to have freedom to pursue
policies which might be in conflict with the wider requirements and
priorities of the county council.

*Have there been occasions when governing bodies have either produced
a change in policy, or had an influence on the direction of policy?*

On any issue affecting a school's future, consultation with all the interests involved is regarded as essential, and governors are among the first to be consulted. For example, in making provision for Welsh bilingual schools (that is, schools where the medium of instruction is the Welsh language), certain schools have had to be reorganised, and the reactions of governors, as well as those of staff and parents, have been a major factor in determining how the strategy should be implemented. I anticipate also that in steps likely to be pursued in rationalising the provision for the 16–19-year-olds, the views and attitudes of governing bodies will play a crucial part, though in the last resort it will be how the council views the overall requirements that will be decisive.

PRESSURE GROUPS

How much influence do pressure groups of all kinds have on policy formulation?
I am not very keen on the thought that policy is made as a result of who cries the loudest, and we have tried very hard to project the idea that policy, the distribution of resources, goes according to the merits of the case, rather than who makes the loudest noise. In my view, the officer's credibility stands or falls by the extent to which he can be seen to be making judgements as to the merits of the case, rather than to the degree of warmth generated by a particular faction.

The concept of the 'silent majority' has been sullied somewhat, but that is presumably what you are getting at?
The line we have taken is that we will consult, and in consulting, it is not just a perfunctory exercise. We guarantee that all those arguments which are used by any group we consult will be carefully weighted. At the end of the day, the success of the measure is going to depend enormously on its level of acceptability by those who are going to be affected by it. But, equally, one has to say that consultation does not mean a guarantee that the party consulted is going to get its own way.

Members are inevitably going to be concerned about not only what is said, but who is saying it. Has that led to decisions being taken which had regard to community inevitabilities?
I referred earlier to the issue of whether or not a new comprehensive school should be proceeded with. Among the factors which produced changes in earlier decisions, there may well have been some regard paid to the relative strength of pressure groups for and against the proposal.

Are teachers' unions involved and brought into decision-making?

They are brought in a lot. It might be that they would wish to have a talk and sometimes we might take initiatives. That is one way, the totally informal *ad hoc* consultation. Another form would be where we would set up a working group for a particular issue. But the more formal mode of discussion is the joint advisory committee on which teachers and education committee members sit to deliberate on any issue which any teachers' union or ourselves wish to get teacher opinion on. We worked out the redeployment issue by *ad hoc* discussions between the assistant directors and the teaching unions and produced a code of practice there.

There appear to be many avenues available for teachers to bring their view to bear. I suppose the litmus test is the acceptability of the decisions and the sort of adverse reaction that you might have had?
The official unions see the committee and its officers as their supporters, and we certainly see them as ours. Where a lack of co-operation has occurred – and I can think of one or two instances of this – this has not been on a union or organised teacher basis, but has been the staff of a school being difficult over a particular issue.

CONTRACTION

Do you feel that it is a very much more difficult business managing a contracting service than it was, perhaps back in Bradford, managing an expanding service? What are the problems?
First and foremost, the question of morale. If everything is expanding, everybody is looking to improvement, and it creates in the minds of the people running the institutions the stimulus of challenge, but in the right sort of atmosphere. The reverse is the case when you see your school shrinking, wondering whether you are going to keep the better members of your staff, whether you are going to be able to provide music, for example, on your timetable next year. As far as education officers are concerned, I find it very worrying that the people who are coming into the service relatively new over the past five years or so have had no encouragement to be innovative because anything which can be deemed to be growth is ruled out. All their ingenuity is exercised towards a salvage operation, towards trying to maintain what they have got; and I have a horrible feeling that, in another decade, or even less than that, it is going to have a very bad effect, if all of us who are working, planning, injecting our own expertise such as it is, are concentrating on purely maintaining the *status quo* as our most lofty aspiration. What is going to happen to the service as a whole? Is it not going to get into an atmosphere of stagnation?

One aspect of contraction is the problem of young teachers faced with limited promotion prospects. Is that a problem here?
Yes, this concerns us very much. In primary schools, because of contracting numbers, and because of strong union feeling, we have had to confine our recruitment of heads and deputies to the existing pool of teachers. Over and over again, we are trawling the same limited pool to get our heads and deputy heads. By virtue of the falling numbers and little recruitment from outside, we are not getting younger people. We are concerned about the effect on the quality of the education which we are providing, precisely because of this lack of any injection. We are trying to get round it by making it easier for people to go out on early retirement, and in that way, we are making vacancies for new blood. In the secondary field it is not so alarming. All our posts are nationally advertised, so we have a national field to recruit from.

ACCOUNTABILITY

As Director of Education, to whom are you accountable?
If I say the county council, I am stating a legal position. Of course, the county council as such won't know very much about what is going on here. I am accountable to the education committee and I feel a certain amount of accountability to the Chief Executive. He is my superior officer and the chief adviser to the council. He has the good sense, however, to regard me as the education expert within his team.

How much does that differ from your previous experience working with a town clerk?
I accept that virtually whatever development or expansion or project one department proposes, will have certain implications or repercussions on others. I think, nevertheless, that the idea that we are all of us there to comment on one another's service to produce a corporate strategy is in practice a nonsense. In the light of all the professional advice that is available to them the politicians are going to have to determine their own priorities. You can waste an endless amount of time imagining that you are facilitating corporate development, when I really couldn't comment seriously on whether there should be a link road with the M4 and I wouldn't expect the Director of Environment and Planning to be able to determine whether French should be part of the core curriculum.

Is the accountability of the educational institutions mediated through you as Chief Education Officer?

The schools are in a difficult role, in that operationally they are accountable to me. But also a wise head will ensure that what is going on in his school is made known to his governing body. In the last resort where it becomes a matter of disciplinary action, the county council through its disciplinary procedures is involved.

If the heads were asked 'Who is your boss?', do you think the response would be 'The Director' or would it be something else?
I suspect that many heads would see their governors or chairmen, where she/he is particularly interested and active, as representing in part at least the authority to which the head is responsible. Operationally, however, I think that heads would see themselves as running their own schools, but that if they encountered serious problems and needed support or advice, the Director of Education (or his representative) would be the person to approach. In the event, too, of failure in performance, the Director of Education would be expected to take any necessary action.

ROLE OF THE DIRECTOR OF EDUCATION

What do you feel is the Chief Education Officer's distinct contribution to the education service, and how do you see the role developing in the next decade?
I do see myself as from the education world with a much closer affinity with teachers than with any other profession. I see my role as trying to inject the humanising element which I think is inherent in an educational attitude in the public service, and I hope that a Chief Education Officer, first and foremost, is a person who understands people, whether it is councillors or his fellow officers, or people in the schools and colleges that he is working with. I hope he is there to stimulate ideas, and not just there to intervene when the crises arise. I suppose I do subscribe to the view that I am a traditionalist. However, I should be surprised if you find a Chief Education Officer anywhere who is cast in the somewhat authoritarian mould of past generations. If the idea of some of the practitioners of corporate management ever got a hold, that you don't need to be an educationist, that you only need to be a manager, I think that would be a disaster. But you can see a certain logic in seeing all your professional advice coming from an advisory staff and the boys behind the desk being the administrators. However, I can't see a quality service being administered unless it is by administrators who have a feel for the service. And know precisely what those people are doing.

Do you think the day of the non-professional CEO is far away?
I think it is further away now than it was ten years ago. There is a
recognition that, if you are dealing with schools and teachers, you
want to know the language of teachers and the realities of the
classroom. It is not enough for me to be advised by an adviser on
the curriculum unless I know something about the objectives of
curriculum and the means to achieve it. I shall rely an enormous
amount on his expertise but I must know more than hearsay, if I am
going to administer an education service, or more importantly
perhaps interpret that to the politicians who are going to control
policy.

Robert Aitken

Coventry

Robert Aitken entered educational administration in Peterborough at the age of 15. He later graduated from Nottingham University and taught for five years in Hertfordshire primary and secondary schools. He entered educational administration in Southgate, Middlesex, in 1959 and then moved to Newcastle upon Tyne as Assistant Director of Education in 1960. He became Deputy Chief Education Officer in Kingston upon Thames in 1965 and was appointed Director of Education for Coventry in 1969.

BACKGROUND

I left school at 15 and went to work in the Peterborough education office as a clerk. I had no qualifications, but a boss who was interested in helping people. That was Leslie Tait, who had come from Newcastle. He had worked his way up from a lad, and I was lucky enough to be taken under his wing. I matriculated while I was working in his office. I then went and did my national service at the end of the war, and from there went to Nottingham University, where I took a history degree and teacher's certificate. I then began teaching in Hertfordshire, first, in a secondary modern school, and then a Church of England primary school. While I was there, I did my MA by research on the development of education in Hitchin, which is a surprisingly rich area for nineteenth-century educational development, with a lot of Quaker influence. I then went into one of the divisional executive offices in Middlesex, then became Assistant Director for Schools in Newcastle upon Tyne, in a way thereby repaying some of the debt I owed to Leslie Tait. I became deputy in Kingston upon Thames, and Director of Education in Coventry in 1969.

Did you see teaching as a route to administration right from the start?
Yes. Leslie Tait told me that, if you want to get on, you have to graduate and you have to have teaching experience. Had teaching so enthralled me that I wanted to stay in and become a head, I no doubt would have stayed. But I was bitten by the administration bug and I enjoyed it. I think I would not have been happy painting on the canvas at school level; I need a bigger brush and a broader canvas. It is a very challenging, intriguing, constantly changing role. You are

servicing a whole community, you're involved in some ways with national development, but basically it's a job that is about the quality of life and the improvement of the quality of life. It's pretty meaty stuff. The other thing is, of course, that the continual variety, the daily variety, is fascinating and stimulating, too.

You express it in dynamic terms. Do you see the CEO's role as dynamic, positive, active, rather than regulative and static?
I see the role as offering leadership, stimulation, some direction in the service for a whole area. And in one means or another, assisting that development.

Is that approach still valid in the political and economic climate of the 1980s?
Yes. Certainly, even more so. Just take the example of falling rolls. We face a decade where the larger part of falling rolls is yet to happen. We've got to move from twenty-five years of expansion, with all the natural stimuli and challenge and change and opportunity that that offered, to a period of constriction, contraction, limitation on developments, closure of schools, members of staff getting stuck at intermediary levels in their career because opportunities are fewer. The natural result of all that will be sapping of morale, sapping of creative energy, because there is seemingly much less outlet for it. A staffroom that is shut in and is feeling some lack of confidence will reflect that in the education of children. We've got to try to avoid that.

How as a CEO can you overcome that feeling of depression and demoralisation among teachers?
I think we have to develop the management skills, the personal skills of our senior colleagues, both in the education office and among advisory teams, but also among heads, deputies, heads of departments. This is something we haven't really paid much attention to in the education service. There is very very little training for management. It is being realised that more is needed but so far very little is done.

REORGANISATION

What was the impact on Coventry arising from reorganisation and the loss of some services to the new West Midlands county council?
The main impact resulted from the change from county borough status to metropolitan district status. Education was untouched. Social services untouched. Housing function untouched. The main difference was that we lost the Medical Officer of Health function to the

AHA and buses, police, fire and ambulance to the metropolitan county level, and some overall strategic planning functions. Water went out to the regional water authority. All that has unfortunately weakened Coventry as a functional local government unit. It was stronger as an all-purpose county borough. Secondly, it has unfortunately left education in the position of being an even-bigger cuckoo in a smaller nest. The tendency is that education is seen as having an abundance of resources and power. There is, therefore, a natural view that when there are problems and cuts, the first carcass for the meal is the education service, because it is the biggest. I think the quality of some of the other departments, the quality of officers, possibly the quality of members, has suffered, too.

You say that reorganisation weakened Coventry as a local government unit. Do you believe that all-purpose authorities would have been a better outcome of reorganisation in 1974 than a two-tier system?
Yes, I think I do. As long as the areas they are dealing with are not too big. Coventry is a compact, manageable size. We could go a bit bigger than 336,000 but it works as a unit, we are in touch with one another. I don't think it would be helpful to go to a vast size. How you manage the education service in Strathclyde, defeats me. I wouldn't want to work in that situation. But yes, the all-purpose authority I find has a dynamism and gets things done, because you are all there working closely at it together.

You said earlier that education is perhaps the carcass that the crows turn to first. Has the education service come under greater pressure in Coventry than other services with the cuts that all authorities have been facing?
No, it would be unfair to say that. I was postulating that I think we come under greater pressure by the circumstances of being a metropolitan district but the actual incidence of policy and financial constraint have not unfairly or particularly weighed against education here. That is, I think, partly because there is a strong tradition for, and a strong respect for, education.

You suggested earlier that you have at least as good quality in your officers in the education department as in other services?
I can only be straight about this. I am proud of the quality of officers I have been able to work with in the education service in Coventry. I think we are as good, if not better, than any other department in the city. But so we ought to be, mind you. We pack a hefty punch. If you include the advisory services and psychologists, you're talking about a group of about sixty. All our senior professionals are graduates with teaching experience, and we have an array of talent and

different disciplines which collectively are a pretty powerful system in themselves.

CORPORATE MANAGEMENT

For many authorities reorganisation, along with the Bains Report which just predated it, was a catalyst for the development of corporate management. Was that the case in Coventry?

You have to remember Coventry was badly damaged during the war. It doubled in size during 1945–70, so huge capital investment programmes took place and the city developed styles of co-operative working between committees, between departments, under the pace and force of the enormous amount they had to do. Then in 1969 when the former town clerk was retiring, they appointed a Chief Executive; corporate management, in the style that we now know it, began in Coventry then and, indeed, went beyond most of what is being practised in the country. The new Chief Executive was formerly the city treasurer. He had the opportunity, therefore, immediately to appoint a new treasurer and a new Director of Education, because my predecessor retired at about the same time, and a new city solicitor, or city secretary as we say. He had the opportunity immediately to create a team. He, with the backing of the management team, then began to introduce programme budgeting. Coventry had always been a bit unusual in its budgeting, in that it did more than a one-year roll on. They were budgeting for three to five years. We went then into programme budgeting in a fairly full way, to the extent of setting objectives for every activity or main service of the council and rerouting the budget to fit programmes, rather than departments or committees.

In 1969 Coventry had a Chief Executive, a new treasurer, a new secretary and yourself as the new Director of Education. What sort of working methods and relationships did you evolve?

We had formal chief officer meetings as a full group once a week, which you were expected to attend, and informal chief officer get-togethers every morning in the Chief Executive's office. Usually, informal and short. I think that he did that deliberately, partly to institute and consolidate group working. Then we also all had the opportunity to attend the policy advisory committee, a requirement that I more or less insisted on when I was appointed. If you are going to have a Cabinet of members, which is what a policy committee is, then I think the head of a major service must ensure that he is at that table giving advice, and not only contributing to, but listening to and therefore reading and understanding, the steps towards the formulation of policy.

What was the relationship between the Chief Executive and the other chief officers? Was it a managerial relationship or was he primus inter pares?

It was clearly a managerial relationship. He was the head of the chief officer team and had, and was expected to have, some powers of requirement or direction. The exception was and had to be in the professional disciplines of an individual chief officer. The Chief Executive couldn't tell the city engineer how to build bridges or what thickness of steel he needed. That was his responsibility which nobody could take away from him. Similarly, advice on education was my responsibility. Each programme that was instituted was backed by an interdisciplinary team of officers from all the departments that might be involved or wanted to be involved. A chief officer was chairman of those programme area teams, at least initially. The education team included representatives from treasurers, solicitors, personnel, engineers, architects, social services, medical officers, virtually the whole gamut. The chief officer of an individual department had a responsibility to see the contributions his department made were in the terms which he would support. It had a stimulating effect, initially, and worked well for a while.

Was the education programme team chaired by you or one of your representatives, rather than an officer from the Chief Executive's department?

Oh yes, that was so from the beginning, and I think this was a recognition of realities by the Chief Executive. He didn't set up his own department. His approach was to use the existing departments and their chiefs as part of the common purpose. Where it really began to come apart at the seams was that it was very much an officer machine, an officer approach. I said it was quite stimulating at the beginning, and it was, but it began to go a bit sour when all this vigorous officer work – setting objectives, analysing priorities and suggesting programmes to support those objectives – when that work began not to be recognised by the politicians, who would come along with an illogical programme of their own which didn't meet all these lovely considerations. I think there was a tendency on the part of that Chief Executive to think that scientific management meant that you could measure virtually any problem and, through the process of measurement and analysis, you would get answers as well as a determination of priorities.

Politics is about pleasing a whole host of individuals. It ends up really with a gut feeling as to what you can get away with and what you can't get away with. It's not logical and it doesn't fit tidy, refined, measured processes. Measurement can tell you that there is, say, an

area of the city where there is a concentration of problems, depri-
vation, old people, pollution, whatever you like. But the political
insight may be that it is not a very distinct or urgent focal point, it can
afford to wait, because there are more insistent problems facing a
politician which he must answer if he is going to have any credence.

That's the gravy-pot you are stirring and you've got to make sense
of it. My reading of our experience was that very sustained scientific
management could not quite come to grips with the political situation. Or you can put it round the other way and say that the
politicians couldn't come to grips with the logic of this powerful
machine.

What is the role of the policy committee in Coventry?
Probably stemming from Coventry's wartime history, there was a
    tradition of an inner Cabinet of senior members, so it was an
    evolutionary process to produce a policy committee, or policy
    advisory committee as it is called here. Traditionally, this is com-
    posed of the senior members of the party in power and, therefore,
    also the chairmen of the major committees. I've sometimes
    wondered what the position would be if ever the chairman of the
    education committee was not a member of the policy committee.
    But it's never happened in the nearly eleven years that I have been
    here. Not all chief officers are supported in that way, in that their
    chairman is also a member of the inner policy group. It happens to be
    so in education. Usually, two or three other members of the policy
    committee are also on the education committee. They may have
    been in the past chairmen of the education committee. So, for one
    reason or another, the education experience and voice there has
    been represented. That is not to say that they have always performed
    well: it is useful that I am there, too!

*Is the role of the education committee weaker than it was before the
    development of the corporate approach in Coventry, or by com-
    parison with authorities that have adopted corporate management less
    wholeheartedly than Coventry?*
Before I had experience of the system in Coventry, I might well have
    said that it was leaving the education committee weaker, but in
    practice, the position of individual committees is respected and,
    indeed, committees do on occasions make direct representation to
    the policy committee because they feel or have felt they are being
    done down in some way, or another committee is getting better
    treatment. So, certainly, in Coventry there are pretty open rights on
    this sort of thing. I find that compared with a number of authorities I
    have worked in, there is more delegation to the committees by the
    council and by committees to officers.

Can we look now at some major processes as a test of how structures work? You mentioned earlier the importance of investment to the postwar reconstruction of the city. What is the capital budgeting process in Coventry?

That's a well chosen example, if I may say so. The policy advisory committee controls and allocates the whole capital programme for the whole council and for all committees. Immediately, colleagues elsewhere may say that that must be a weakening of the education committee's position. I don't think it is, because the education committee is in a position to promote capital schemes and ideas to the policy committee and, in any case, the DES capital building programme is an important determinant of the education capital programme in Coventry, so there are influences and checks and balances.

Does the policy advisory committee attempt to buck the education expenditure which is at least ostensibly committed to spending on certain types of education project through the key sector mechanism?

I've never experienced that bucking. The mood of Coventry has been to use their capital programmes to the hilt, and they have usually gone looking for ways of doing more. So, in effect, there haven't been any great problems. The cloud on the horizon, of course, is the Local Government Bill which is now proceeding through Parliament, which looks as if it will throw block capital allocations to a local council without determination of how much for housing, how much for education, how much for social services. So, there may be more pressure, more scrapping locally over programmes – but that is what more freedom to local government is about, apparently!

It is very interesting that you see that as a cloud on the horizon because arguably it is consistent with the development of the corporate approach in local authorities.

In theory, it is the way it ought to go. But remember the government is taking away with the other hand what it is giving, because it is slapping very rigid controls on the amount of capital development or spending that a council can undertake. Whereas in the past a council had more freedom to do more capital work from revenue contributions, or by selling some assets like land and developing its capital potential in that sort of way, it would now seem that the government is bent on a very much more rigid system. So you have freedom to scrap among yourselves about a much more limited amount of resource. That's the cloud on the horizon.

What are the roles of the policy advisory committee and the education committee, in the determination of the revenue budget?

We have a fairly developed system here, which you could almost call continuous budgeting. The process starts with the policy committee in June setting guidelines for the preparation of forward spending programmes, usually on a five-year forward basis. At that point, the policy committee will be advised by all its chief officers, so education advice is included. The policy committee will also be advised of public expenditure White Paper policies, government and economic trends in terms of spending and policies, and will be advised on the trend for the local economy and the capacity that the average household has to pay a level of rates. The policy committee will then issue guidelines. Those guidelines are usually in a broad form. Will you test out three levels of programme, for example? This may be 1–2 per cent above or below the current level of spending, or in a time of severe constraint, it may be all levels would be that of minus. The guidance may be different for different committees.

One of the criticisms that has been made of corporate management is that the central committee is unable to differentiate among its policies and imposes a general increase or decrease in spending, rather than really determining its priorities by saying we want more of this and less of that.

That's not true of Coventry. It may be, at this early stage, the testing out of guideline strategies may be applied to all committees but later on a differential application will emerge in tune with political priorities. The next stage is for those guidelines to be tested out by each service committee. That process rolls through usually until October, when there is a further report back, a consolidated report from all committees on that position. There is also political consideration going on outside the formal council constitution. What happens then is dependent on the circumstances. In the last year or two we have been in great difficulties. The government has been wrestling with the economy and has been unable to give early enough guidance, so it leaves a local authority in limbo round about October, waiting for the Rate Support Grant settlements and where that's going to go before they can amend or confirm the guidance that they have given. But we usually end up in about December with confirmation of programmes. These are then in Coventry put out to the public for comment before the end of January, when they are finally confirmed. The December business is important, because it gives an indication to the politicians as to whether the guidelines are pinching the shoes of individual services too much and, therefore, need easing. It is then that you get the fight, for example, as to whether nursery education should be accepted or cut. The politicians, with some fairly fierce help sometimes from their officers, come to an adjudged settlement.

If the education committee has to make a substantial reduction in its budget, would it be for the education committee to determine where the axe should fall?

For the education committee, but on occasions the policy committee has said that it is not to touch certain aspects. It may be there has already been determination of this within the party. In the past we have often had an early indication that the pupil–teacher ratio and per capita allowances for equipment and materials spending were not to be cut. Last year we didn't have that and, in fact, both are being reduced a little. May I add one other important thing? The education committee will, in that process, carry out fairly extensive consultation with the unions.

Coventry is in a minority in having only majority party members on its policy committee. Does that mean that the informal and secret party caucuses which are thought to determine policy elsewhere come out more into the open in Coventry?

Yes, it is one party. I believe that it makes sense and is realistic. I believe it does bring out the caucus or the otherwise secret considerations more into the open to share with the council's officers. That is not to say that, on occasions, a debate is not stopped with typically the words, 'Well, I think we shall have to take this to another place'. And that means that it will go for debate and for determination to the party group. We all know this, we all acknowledge it and it works. It leads me on to say one other thing. I believe this is healthy. One of the things that I like about Coventry is the very close involvement there is between officers and members. I've worked in authorities elsewhere where there has been a very clear dividing line, and I was even told in one authority that I wasn't to speak unless I was spoken to in a committee. You don't get that here.

You are suggesting that the eventual decision-making on key issues is going to be better informed than would otherwise be the case?

Precisely. I have never been prevented from speaking at policy committee. Either on an education topic, or on a broader one, because I count it as part of my duty as a corporate chief officer to contribute to the city's affairs generally and not only and narrowly on education. This has always been welcomed.

What are the roles of the personnel department and your own department in the appointment of both teaching and non-teaching staff?

This is an interesting and somewhat fraught area, particularly in some other authorities. Corporate management has led in some authorities to the establishment of very powerful personnel departments. I think that has been one of the seeds of discontent and problems in a number of other cases. I think Avon is one of them. Perhaps typically, Coventry avoids the worst extremes of either position. There is a manpower services unit within the city secretary's department. We have a personnel and administration committee which is by constitution responsible for all staffing and personnel matters, conditions of service, as well as grading, and so on. In practice, that committee and the manpower services division operate across the board for all council services for all staff, except teachers. But again, in practice, the manpower services division works through each of the departments, so I have a personnel officer on my staff in my department, who is also responsible to the head of manpower services. We work together in that way. Teachers are the responsibility of the education committee and of the education department. Conditions of service and the interpretation of them are the education committee's province, in so far as they are not delegated to me. That is the position which we enjoy and I defend. Just occasionally, questions are raised as to why are teachers different, why is education different. I do not believe that I could help in the management of the service and of schools, and neither could head teachers, if the professional side of it was not within the compass of the education service. I think, of course, it is helped by the very dispersed nature of our administration and, of course, the rights of governing bodies, particularly of voluntary schools. It makes it enormously difficult for a personnel department, in fact, to put a blanket policy over it. I have found usually in the end it takes a monkey to deal with a monkey. My staff and I have been teachers and we know the tricks.

Coming back to non-teaching staff, is appointment of, say, clerical and welfare staff and technicians, in schools handled by people from the personnel department rather than your own staff?
They are usually involved but so also is my department. I think this is an area where we are not as good as we could be in Coventry. It is an area that chafes, not only with my department but with others, which I think we generally would like to improve. I would like to see more delegation to my department and the other departments within a framework of policy to get on with the appointments, regrading, and so on. There has to be an overall policy. It is right that there is an administration and personnel committee that will guide and control that. There are so many different conditions of service and people on similar gradings working in various departments. You can't let each go off willy-nilly into the sunset, following its own whim, because the council would have a half a dozen employees doing virtually the same work treated very differently. We must recognise it makes

sense to have a central policy but I would like to see more delegation. If we can manage all the intricacies on the teaching side, I am sure we can manage more on the non-teaching side. But that's really an internal argument.

You are saying that there is a need for consistency with other departments in respect of non-teaching staff, but there is a suspicion that non-teaching staff in schools do not earn salaries commensurate with the kind of responsibility they often take.

I would guess, speaking generally, that you are right. The approach to this through bureaucratic regulation tends to produce what you are saying. A school of a certain size gets the same non-teaching staff and grading as a school of a similar size. The differences of content and usage by the head, all the idiosyncrasies which make schools different from one another, tend not to be taken into account. There is a broader aspect to this. An institution such as a school tends to work like a large family. In practice, within the institution there is not that much difference between a teacher or a cook or a caretaker or a lab technician in the contribution that they make to the total ethos, 'climate' and forward movement of that institution. I think we do need to recognise managerially, therefore, that the head of the institution should have some flexibility, some delegated function, to be able to work his system in recognition of that and the contributions that individuals are making.

ILEA, of course, operates an alternative use of resources scheme. Would that sort of scheme give an opportunity for institutional flexibility?

Not necessarily in that way. I am projecting ideas forward, because we don't practice much of this in Coventry. I say that regretfully, and at the moment there are severe limitations on resources. It is not, perhaps, the time to expect to be able to go ahead. But even within the resources we have got, we need to try to encourage more open and more flexible use of them. For example, I believe that in a period of restraint, it is the right time to move forward to more democracy in the school staffrooms.

If resources are very limited, staff ought to be able to control what they consider to be essential to the job, rather than have that determined centrally.

Yes, but it is not always that easy because of the national controls on local government. To give you an example, we are paying out, nationally, in the region of £35 million a year on extra allowances to teachers in schools that serve priority areas, the social priority allowance. We have not been able for the last four or five years to

change the number of schools. We can only add a school, if we take
another one off the list. Most teachers would rather have the
opportunity to use that money in a different way and have it as a fund
for the school to use. And I would much rather we did it that way.
But we cannot, because we are stuck with a national scheme. One's
ideas for greater flexibility can be frustrated by these types of
external factors.

*In the context of corporate management do you still feel able to make an
individual impact on educational policy-making in Coventry?*
Oh yes, I should be very bothered if that were frustrated! I suppose we
all have our own interpretation, our own sense of identity as to what
the role of a CEO is. My view is that one is the senior professional in
the service, the senior adviser on education to the council for its
area. Your role is to judge the health of the service, the quality of it
and to help move it forward. You need to be judging what forward
trends and forward problems are likely and, therefore, to have some
early sense of what the responses should be. So, in that sense, too, I
think one needs to have a catalyst role, a role to stimulate and to
break out of moulds if that is necessary. There is a danger that you
can spend an enormous amount of time in meetings, in conforming
to a corporate system. The system itself tends more and more to
become bureaucratic. I am afraid my response is that if I have
educational priorities and problems I have got to attend to, then I
don't go to the corporate meeting. That is not to say we are not
represented. My deputy stands in and he has to go more often than I
go.

*Can you point to a particular initiative to illustrate your ability to make
an impact?*
I am not sure I can answer that question in that way. Certainly, I have
contributed or started ideas which have come to fruition. That is an
essential part of the role, but they have then been hammered into
shape on the anvil of professional and political debate. That is the
nature of things and the ideas get changed and improved in the
process. Some possible examples are: our teachers' centre, canal
boats, community education and our schemes for unemployed
school-leavers. But there are as many ideas that failed the anvil test!

CHAIRMEN AND COUNCILLORS

*In the past, the CEO – education committee chairman axis has been
regarded as the key relationship in the management of the education
service. Is that still the case in Coventry or has it been superseded by
other relationships at the political level?*

It is still very important. Certainly, as far as Coventry goes, both political parties leave a fair amount of political responsibility with the chairman for policy formulation for that service. So, on the politicians' side, they rest a fair amount of trust in their chairman. Therefore, it is very important to understand one's chairman, both as a person, and to understand the politics of the local scene through him initially. Having said that, it is also important to keep a wider intelligence. So one keeps in touch with the leader of the council and, indeed, maintains a reasonable relationship with the shadow chairman of the education committee and the shadow chairman of the opposition, because it may not be long before they are in power. That has been the pattern here. What you are building up is, in fact, an understanding which enables you to interpret what you can do or what you can't do, or what politicians can accept and what they cannot accept at any point in time. You are also building up trust, and that is very important. You must maintain the trust of your politicians, your chairman first and then the other members of the committee and of the party. You will always have your critics, but basically, if the politicians trust you and your staff, then they will listen more; your advice will be more effective and often then, in partnership with politicians, you can get things done. Sometimes, I find they have vague political prejudices which they want interpreting into detailed patterns of policy, and it is your role to do that and to say if this is impractical, offensive, or retrograde. By that process, stemming first from trust, you and your staff have influence, a greater influence. It can happen that you have a chairman who does not pack a clout inside the party. I had one who was a dear man, very committed to education but wasn't very articulate. That didn't matter when I was with him, because we had an understanding. Inside the party he often couldn't manage it. So you work with other members of his party to see that they supplement the chairman.

Do you detect any change in the type or level of decision being made at the political level rather than the officer level?
I've already said there is a fair amount of delegation to officers in Coventry. I would say in general the situation has stayed much the same. There has been a slight tendency since 1974, which is something of an expression of the corporate system, for so-called performance review committees to be set up which investigate a particular capital project or some other particular policy issue like repair and maintenance of buildings. This has partly been caused by the politicians not knowing quite how to handle an intractable problem or conflict of loyalties. But, also, it has been tinged with empire-building by the treasurer, in that he had not felt that the former scientific management of programme budgeting had been

replaced adequately in his terms, so that he has sought another way of putting a bite in. He might not agree with that interpretation, but I believe that is what the position is and we have had to counter it.

CENTRAL GOVERNMENT

Do you consider that the DES is more influential in relation to the local education service than it was, say, a decade ago?
I think less so. Events have proved it that way. If you take the issue of unemployment. The major programmes for this are being expressed through the Manpower Services Commission. The major programmes for training or retraining the workforce of the nation are being expressed through the Manpower Services Commission and the Industrial Training Board, through the Training Opportunities Scheme. The budget of the Manpower Services Commission is now about equivalent to the total budget for further education. And really much of that work is being done on an agency basis within the education service. It would be better done and more accountably done by the education service direct. We've been squeezed out in a major way. The DES has been too mild and lacking in impetus, dynamism and leadership, on this issue. I think it shows in other ways, too.

Do you think that the legislation that has come forward, say, the 1976 legislation on comprehensive education or the proposed 1980 legislation on the block grant, has limited or will limit the discretion of the local authorities and make the centre more powerful?
I think, in general, yes. That looks to be the case. I think it may well be the case with the 1980 legislation not only the Education Act, but the Local Government Bill, as it now is. It may not only enhance government's position, but also a centralist style within local government. It may enhance the roles of the central services of lawyers, clerks, treasurers and personnel people and possibly your technical officers. We may end up finding that they have more control.

HER MAJESTY'S INSPECTORATE

Another aspect of central influence on local education is, of course, HM Inspectorate. Do you detect any change in their role in relation to the local education service?
I think they are trying very hard. There is no doubt that HM Inspectorate waned in influence substantially in the 1960s and, indeed, their numbers were reduced considerably. Locally, that has meant that they withdrew from inspection, on a regular basis, of schools; they withdrew from that to a more intermediary position of

occasional monitoring and the development of an influence through major reports and courses. Latterly, since the time of the 'Great Debate', and under the present Senior Chief Inspector, they have been trying to get back on track. I think this is an honest endeavour to make a response to the fairly fundamental criticisms that were engendered before and at the time of the 'Great Debate'. Large resources were being devoted to education, yet the standards seemed to be slipping. So, yes, they are less influential. I think they are trying to make it up. I think that means they are also fighting their corner more in the DES, and power to their elbow! So, in a way, we are witnessing something of a power struggle going on. I would welcome, certainly in the DES, a greater influence from the Inspectorate. I think part of the wishy-washyness of the DES has been because they suppressed the Inspectorate. I don't agree by a long way with all the Inspectorate says and does, but on the whole, they are on our side, they are on the side of the children and the professionals.

Has the development of much stronger local advisory services led to overlapping advice from local advisers and HM Inspectorate, or are their roles complementary?
I think the roles are complementary, but I first of all remind you that it has been necessary in my view, and a lot of my colleagues' view, to develop the local advisory services, partly because of the withdrawal and reduction of HM Inspectorate. They no longer give a full inspection of schools every seven years, which is the sort of thing they were doing in the 1950s. HM Inspectors are just not available to give you detailed advice with detailed knowledge of schools. You must have it locally and, certainly, that was one of the arguments I used to develop the advisory services here. There are other reasons why you need strong advisory services.

Sheila Browne, in evidence to the Expenditure Subcommittee suggested that the withdrawal of HM Inspectorate, in so far as she conceded that point, was a response to the growth and development of local advisory services. Is this just a different perspective on the same development?
We all catch arguments to suit our case when we can and where we can. I think it's different expressions of similar developments. Another reason for the development of advisory services is because we are expected to be more accountable, and this trend will continue.

Do you believe that the DES should be leading the education service, and regardless of the answer to that, do you think it is actually doing so?

I think the DES in our country can only lead the education service in a very general way. They don't lead it in terms of the day-to-day work and quality and content. Indeed, I would strongly argue that most developments in this country since 1870 have come from local initiatives, which have then caught on in a wider sense. Often HM Inspectorate have a vital role in noticing, catching up, disseminating, promulgating. They are more like bees, cross-pollinating the flowers. The flowers grow at local level and are cultivated by such as we.

RELATIONS WITH HEADS

What is the nature of the relationship between you as CEO and the heads of the institutions in Coventry? Are they responsible to you? Do you manage them? Or are you there simply to advise, stimulate and provide resources?
This is a key question. The key relationship. One at which I have had to work and learn. At rock bottom, you are the head of the service and you are expected to be able to give directions. That is the position and I certainly would wish to honour it, so that for example if an institution is really failing, and if it is basically the fault of the head or he or she is the cause of it, then you do something about it. You seek the removal of the head in the final analysis. Your relationship very largely is one of senior colleagues working together, with respect, with trust, with understanding, and by that I mean understanding of each other's position, problems and needs and possibilities. I see it as part of my role to stimulate them, but that they have a similar position to me, to stimulate, to cajole, to encourage, to persuade me to use my position and influence in our common cause. So, I see it very much as a shared common professional purpose among respected colleagues.

Do you think their perspective is similar? Would they see you in the same light, as a professional colleague, but nevertheless acknowledging that in the final analysis they are accountable to you as well?
I think they probably would. It is something like a good marriage, a successful marriage – you have to work at it. When I first came to the area, the secondary heads were in sectional groups; they didn't meet together, and they had certain hierarchical views and stances. We worked at it over a long period but now I positively enjoy secondary heads' conferences, which we have together with my senior staff. They joke among themselves, they tease one another and me in my presence, and we have a very honest and I think fruitful, professional relationship. I am very proud of that because it is an achievement that I think has been born of gradual development of all those things I said, particularly trust.

The development of a good professional relationship is obviously valuable, but do you think it is likely to be especially important in a period of contraction and falling rolls? Particularly if one takes the view that these problems can be solved only on an authority-wide basis?

Oh yes. But, you see, if you have this sort of relationship of shared professionalism when you have these problems, you share them at an early stage. Let me give you an example. We are currently concerned about the size of our sixth forms, in that there are too many small teaching groups which are absorbing staffing resources which are needed in the younger part of the school. That's just one facet of this. We shared this problem with the heads. They themselves have come up with consortia groupings. They themselves have said there are certain subjects which don't fit, and they are leaving me to decide about those. In other words, they have worked it out to a certain level beyond which they know, and they have said, it requires decisions beyond them, by an arbiter if you like. Now, surely, it is much better to have got to that position through open discussion and recognition than to be forcing the issue and I think we are the stronger for it, all of us. I think falling rolls is proving to be a major challenge at many levels in the service and it will search out weak spots in management.

The issue of staff redeployment might be regarded as a particularly difficult consequence of falling rolls. Does it take away the right which heads formerly enjoyed, with their governing bodies, to make appointments and give that power to CEOs and their colleagues, and, if so, has the professional confidence and trust survived?

It hasn't meant a retreat from the previous position, which is a shared position. In secondary schools the appointment of staff is at governing body level, and then delegated to the head and Director of Education up to senior teacher level, when members of the governing body are engaged. But it does mean a greater recognition by heads of factors beyond their schools. We have shared the whole problem of a fairly sizeable reduction in staff for next September with our heads, and they all know what each one of them is facing and they have, therefore, been able to compare and assess whether the position is a fair one. They all know they have to lose staff and that there has got to be redeployment. And they know that if they don't play their bit in that game, then they will be blocked by some of their other colleagues. If they pass a weak member of staff without notice, then one of their colleagues will suffer, and it will reflect back on them. Some pretty straight exchanges have resulted but it is open and the professionalism is surviving.

GOVERNING BODIES

What is the role of governing bodies in Coventry? How much authority are they given?

Not a lot. We have two sorts of governing body. We have the governing bodies of our community colleges. Those governing bodies have a fair bit of authority, because they are also the governing committee for the community college association. The rest of our secondary schools have the more traditional position at the moment, and I think it would be the wish of my committee to make advances in that direction of probably offering more authority to those other governing bodies.

What sort of increases in authority will your committee want for governing bodies?

My views perhaps would not be popular with politicians and there is a certain tension about this. I think they would want to see more involvement of parents, more accountability of the head and the teaching profession for what is actually going on. I don't think they really are that committed to handing over control over resources and maybe they are realistic about this.

Teachers might feel that any increase in the authority of governing bodies ought to be at the expense of the local authority rather than professional discretion.

Yes, certainly. I think that this is why it could well be a matter for lively debate. We shall have to see. I have spent a fair amount of time explaining the CEO's role and I don't think you weaken your position by being more accountable.

Do you think that the governing body is bound to be squeezed between the power of the council and the institution as expressed through the head of the school?

It is a possibility, but I hope not. I think there is a real area of opportunity for the teaching profession to come out of the 'secret garden' and share the education of children with others, particularly with parents, but with the community and the leaders of the community. I think in the end it will lead to greater strength rather than weakness, I think it will enhance respect for the teaching profession. I think they are more likely to be accorded a status that they once had and seem somewhat to have lost.

INTEREST GROUPS

What is the role of teachers' unions and other interest groups in policy formulation?

The two main groups that have been influential in recent years are the teaching unions and the non-teaching unions, particularly manual workers. The practice in Coventry, as I said earlier, is through established consultative procedures. And that will usually mean that before a major decision is taken affecting their area, they will have a chance to be consulted and comment.

Is that cosmetic or a genuine feeling on the part of the committee that these groups have something to offer?

It varies at times and with the issues, but I think on the whole, there is a genuine wish for participation. On the other hand, there has been some reluctance on the part of particularly the teaching unions, to take the opportunity up fully. Now, in a way, you can understand that. If you are being asked to comment on, or rank in order of priority, a series of reductions in expenditure, and maybe reductions in standards, when you as a union are committed to improving the conditions of service and operation of your members, it is somewhat hostile. It is contradictory and, therefore, I think their reluctance is somewhat understandable. But again, you see, changing times require changes in operation, and I have noticed this year that the teachers' unions and the manual workers' unions are more prepared to take part in positive discussion about how strategies for containment can operate. This includes dialogues that have produced suggestions which have enabled some abatement of what otherwise would have to be done.

Can you give an example of something that was suggested by the unions, which avoided savings which might have been made in other areas?

We mentioned community education. We have four or five education project areas and we allocate a budget to each area in addition to what the schools in that area get. And a little bit of extra staffing. In the process of slightly reducing overall the pupil–teacher ratio, the teachers' unions said they would prefer that we abated the community education allocation slightly and reduce the extra budget instead. That was partially adopted.

CONTRACTION

Is it very difficult for you to persuade the layman that you can't cut education point for point as pupil numbers fall?

It is difficult but I find that if you build it up in a fairly simple manner, and explain in terms of the immediate and familiar, then it is not too bad. Let us take the example of a local primary school, where there are now differential sizes of groups in classes. Although that school has lost twenty-five children that only may mean three pupils per class, you still need the school, and the caretakers and the cleaners; it begins to be seen that you can't always relate every cost to the number of children. There are premises-related costs; there are child-related costs.

Is it more difficult and demanding to manage the service in a period of decline and contraction than in a period of expansion?
I once said to Alec Clegg that he had the rich golden times and our generation has got the greater difficulty for the reasons you pose. He hotly denied it, of course – all those problems of roofs over heads! I don't know that you can make a comparison. Every age has problems. It is challenging to meet the needs of the job, and if that means changing your style, developing new skills, then that's all part of the excitement, the stimulation of the challenge.

ACCOUNTABILITY

To whom is the Director of Education accountable?
Well, immediately in terms of one's employment, to the chairman of the education committee and the council of Coventry. In professional terms the children first, and the teaching profession second.

Are these accountabilities compatible or not?
Not always. One is seeking to make them as compatible as you can. You couldn't live in this job, if you were an out-and-out idealist who could never compromise on anything. It has to be a pragmatic approach and, therefore, it is a matter all the while of balancing interests and seeking the advantage towards an aim, towards a benefit, for a group whenever and wherever you see the opportunity to get it. You advance on one front or three fronts under one administration, and maybe you advance on three or four others when you have a different administration. Thereby, hopefully, you are keeping the general state of development moving.

Do you consider that an increased emphasis on accountability leads to a restriction of professional discretion?
There is tension but they have to co-exist. I think it goes back to things I have said earlier. Accountability is a form of questioning, it is the arrogant professional who thinks he should never be questioned, or never have pointed out that there are perhaps gaps or there are other ways of doing things. But on the other hand, being prevented from one's honest endeavour by others who are outside the profession, who claim to know better without the experience, is intolerable. One of the joys of being a professional teacher is that you have a fair

amount of freedom to practice in your own way. Success lies most likely with those who practise with commitment and zeal and confidence, because then there is likely to be an enthusiastic transmission between teachers and taught and things happen. There must be that sort of freedom but any profession ought to be big enough to be able to be held accountable.

ROLE OF THE DIRECTOR OF EDUCATION

What do you think is the director's distinct contribution to the education service and how do you see the role developing over the next decade?
I think the distinct contribution of the chief as opposed to the assistant directors in his office is that he is the forward-thinker, the appraiser of where the whole apparatus, the whole vehicle, is going. It is up to the chief to be reconnoitring the forward territory, the parts beyond the immediate horizon. And to be working on what the changes of priority and strategy should be in response to that map. On the question of the future, I would say CEOs certainly in the next five years, probably longer, are going to have to demonstrate more resolute leadership both within the service, and in securing and maintaining the position of the service in local government. We have difficult times ahead not just because of the economic crisis, which doesn't show signs yet of abating, but also we have to fight the creeping loss of confidence in the service and the whole psychological state that will be engendered by a position of falling rolls. But there are also opportunities. As we reduce the loading on the service at the young end, the school end, there is the opportunity to turn existing resources to other use. The critical contribution of the CEO in the 1980s could be the extent to which he is successful in retaining resources released by falling rolls and using them to make education accessible throughout the community. We still have a long way to go to achieve a truly comprehensive education service, offering life-long educational opportunities. There are encouraging signs that this is increasingly being demanded. My map beyond the horizon tells me that, with more leisure, less time spent in employment, earlier retirement, life-long education will be a reality in the next generation. Our challenge is to take the opportunity, to build the foundations, so that it can be achieved – or not to lose those opportunities.

Eric Briault

Inner London

Eric Briault was educated at Peterhouse College, Cambridge. After fourteen years teaching in secondary schools he joined the former London County Council as an inspector in 1948. He became Deputy Education Officer in 1956 and was appointed Education Officer in the Inner London Education Authority in 1971. He retired in 1977.

BACKGROUND

I was at school in Brighton and I had an open scholarship to Cambridge, where I read Part I history, having got a history scholarship, whereas I really wanted to read geography. I then read Part I geography in my third year. I came out at the time when the Geddes axe had fallen on the teaching profession. Hardly anyone at Cambridge considered training before teaching; in fact, it was regarded by some headmasters as a disadvantage to be trained in the Cambridge department anyway. I went straight into a job, which I thought myself fortunate to get. It was at Queen Elizabeth's Grammar School, Barnet, Hertfordshire. When I was appointed, I had a letter from Herts, saying they were sorry they couldn't appoint me because I had a first-class honours degree and they couldn't afford it. I started on the basic scale! Those were the days. I moved from Queen Elizabeth to Latymer Upper School in Hammersmith just before the war, and I taught altogether for fourteen years. I never really had any intention of going into educational administration. My ambition was to be a headmaster. However, shortly after the war, one of the people on the staff of the school drew my attention to an advertisement for an inspector of geography in the LCC and I applied for it and was appointed, much to my and everybody else's surprise.

Why did you apply for the inspection service rather than proceeding with your original idea of becoming a headmaster?
I think there were two factors of which the major one was that I was an extremely keen geography teacher and the person who held the post and had just retired was Leonard Brooks, who was nationally known in the world of geography as an outstanding figure, and any geographer would have been pleased to succeed Leonard Brooks, I think. It was an opportunity to go on with one's specialist subject in a

much wider sphere. That was the main reason. The other was that it began to be fairly clear that I would be unlikely to get a headship as I had been a conscientious objector during the war. I would get in for interviews for headships and then at the point when they said 'what did you do in the war?', and I said I was a conscientious objector, the shutters came clearly down. Very understandable.

A Turning point

Yes, well, I was the district inspector in Lambeth for seven years, dividing my time between general responsibility for all the schools in the Lambeth part of what was then the LCC and my responsibility for geography which was throughout the LCC area as a whole. I thought that someday I might, perhaps, aspire to the post of Chief Inspector, which did in fact fall vacant in 1955, I think it was. And I was unsuccessful. A man much senior to myself was appointed. I changed my district and went over to Chelsea and Fulham, a rather smaller district where I was appointed Staff Inspector for geography, so that I could devote more time to my specialist subject. Meanwhile, however, the planning of the first comprehensive schools was beginning in London and the then Chief Inspector, A.G. Hughes (Hughes and Hughes used to be a very famous book for teachers), set up a little working party and made me secretary of it. It was arranged for me to be seconded part-time from my inspector duties to the administration to be associated with the reorganisations linking up the opening of the new comprehensive schools, so that for around the period 1954–6 I became a bit involved with administration as a seconded inspector. After the chief inspectorship appointment which I hoped I might get, John Brown, who was then education officer, retired, and Bill Houghton, who was deputy, was appointed in his place. I had been working with Bill Houghton on the reorganisations, so I decided to apply for the deputy education officer job, not ever expecting to go into administration until these circumstances arose, and to my surprise and the annoyance of pure administrators, I was appointed. And then for the next fifteen years I was deputy to Bill Houghton.

EDUCATIONAL ADMINISTRATION

What were your main responsibilities as deputy?
Bill Houghton, knowing that I was quite inexperienced in administration proper, began by giving me a limited brief: one of which was very directly the planning of the accommodation requirements of the newly built comprehensive schools and the reorganisations associated with them, and the other was one that had always been the deputy's job in the LCC and continued into ILEA, that of being

responsible for the budget – for finance. In those days, of course, education under the LCC was competing for resources with other services in the LCC.

In preparing the estimates, each branch made its estimates; they came to me and then were sent on to the Comptroller (that is, the treasurer) and then each branch had a meeting with the assistant education officer, Carpenter (Assistant Comptroller) and myself, to settle what really did go into the estimates. And I found that some branches but not others were in the habit of inflating their estimates because they knew that Carpenter would cut them down, and this was the system. And I wouldn't have it. I said after I learned what they did that next year, I won't put to Carpenter any estimates that I can't absolutely stand by. My position will be that this is the money we've got to have. And on that basis I will argue your case, but not on the basis that you don't mind if we drop. Some of them didn't like it but as a result I established a relationship with Carpenter which was very fruitful, really. He realised that this was my line, if I said that's what it was, it really was. And things moved, the whole business of the estimates when I took over was an absolute nightmare. Meeting after meeting of frustrating argument over details, and so on, a terrible waste of time. But after a couple of years, we established a position that greatly reduced it, because Carpenter knew we were playing it straight. Gradually, more and more things came my way. It was partly a matter of heads of branches much older than myself who had been in post longer doing their own thing, and doing it better than I could have done it, but as they went and retired and new people came in, I found myself with more responsibility over a wider front. The scope of my responsibilities gradually spread until in the last two or three years when Bill Houghton, although we really didn't know it, was a sick man, I was doing a great deal, let's put it like that. You may remember that he died in office, actually. For a couple of years, he wasn't really able to stand up to all the pressures and take on as much as he had. He eventually did decide to retire before he was 65 and the post was advertised, by which time I was 59 and, well, one didn't know what would happen but I did, as you know, get the job. I had a broad conception of what I wanted to do, which really was embodied in the thing we published called *An Education Service for the Whole Community*. I thought to draw the service together to make the AEOs much more of a united team and to involve the members in the same concept, and I think the first three years of my time were really very fruitful in that respect. I took all the AEOs away for a residential conference in order to thrash out thinking. I took all the leading members away with the AEOs on a residential conference, and we went through the same sort of thinking that resulted in that publication which led, I think, to a great

deal of fruitful development of closer understanding and relationship with different branches of the service – which tended to be such
an enormous service and rather separate. People would say probably that I tried to do too much. I took the view that I needed to be
involved in, to know about and to agree to anything of importance in
any part of the service. A whole lot of stuff came up through the
machine that didn't involve policy that I got involved with, but
nothing of importance went by without my being involved in it. It
was very heavy going but, you see, there was no other generalist in
the place to do it.

What did you see as the main requirements of the job?
I think, first and foremost, a conception and understanding of the
    service as a whole and, therefore, the ability to appreciate the
    relationship of this or that particular proposal to the needs of the
    whole service. In such a large service the tendency towards frag-
    mentation which shows in any part of administration was that much
    greater, because there is so much expertise involved in the different
    parts. I could see that in terms of the broad budget requirements, in
    terms of the use of manpower, the involvement of the inspectorate,
    the use of resources, in terms of buildings, new ones or existing ones,
    it was my job to see the thing as a whole and to look for its
    relationships. I established, therefore, a co-ordinating committee
    which met regularly under my chairmanship, which gave both the
    inspectorate and the administration on all sides a chance to draw
    attention to a particular point of view about something in their
    sphere of influence. It was my job as chief officer to chair that kind of
    discussion, to see that all the points were taken into account. The
    second major responsibility, I felt, was to make sure that the
    committee, through reports that went up over my name, was
    properly and fully informed of all the important information they
    required, properly advised as to the implications of what they were
    being asked to do and given a proper recommendation. In other
    words, I saw the reports going up to committee as in the end my
    personal responsibility.

REORGANISATION IN LONDON

*At the time of the reorganisation in London, did the LCC want to retain
    its identity as far as possible, and did the officers have much oppor-
    tunity to influence the decision?*
I can't speak for the LCC, as a whole, really at all. But I recall very
    clearly the way in which the education department operated. We
    were involved, of course, in the preparation of evidence which was
    to be given by the LCC to the Royal Commission. We argued for the
    continuation of the education service with its particular pattern of

distributed administration, divisional organisation. When the report came out which proposed the breaking up of the LCC, and the breaking up of the education service, we couldn't as officers get directly involved but we were much involved in assisting, on the one hand, the members, and on the other hand, the teachers in the campaign which they mounted against the government proposals; and there was a tremendous upsurge expressed at the massive meetings of parents organised by the teachers against the proposals to break up the LCC education service. We didn't appear as officers on those platforms, but in unofficial or informal ways, we were much involved in the matter. The campaign made the government change its mind, one of the few examples of a success of this kind.

There was something of an alliance, then, between the professional and non-professional interests and also the politicians and administrators?

Yes, that's right. What Bill Houghton understood extremely well, and what it took me years to learn, was the importance of the right relationship between administrators and the teachers' professional associations. As I saw the teacher representatives behaving at official consultative meetings or in public or at the NUT conference, they often said things which I had little sympathy with. What I learned was that, if you got things right, those public utterances are really a kind of façade as often as not, and that the real agreement is reached across the table between people like Vic Shaw (then London NUT secretary) and Bill Houghton.

Looking back over the fifteen years since the creation of ILEA, do you think now that it was the right decision?

Yes, no doubt about it. The arguments for a unified service in the old LCC area are extremely powerful. It doesn't follow from that that ILEA has always done the right thing or always made the right decisions or is not capable of being extravagant. But, in principle, that's the right way to run London education, I have no doubt. After the first three years, you may remember, the Conservative Party, to everybody's surprise, actually captured the ILEA. In 1967 they were completely taken by surprise. For three years, therefore, Bill Houghton and I worked with the Tories. They brought in Chris Chataway, he wasn't elected of course, they made him an alderman to bring him in, and he was leader for the first half of those three years. And we worked with a group of youngish Conservatives, a number of whom are now in Parliament, and worked very well with them. I mention this to illustrate the point that they had no doubt at all, I am quite certain of that, that this was the way to run London education with no talk among them of breaking it up.

The arguments put forward by supporters of the Baker Report are partly financial and partly relate to the issue of accountability to the electorate. Do you think those points have substance or not?

Well, all the GLC members for inner London are directly elected and they constitute the majority of ILEA anyway, and that's no different therefore from what would be the situation if education were under the boroughs. It's true that the other thirteen are nominated by the boroughs but they come on to ILEA representing the individual borough, and it quickly becomes clear that they are highly conscious of how the behaviour of ILEA is going to look to the boroughs that sent them up. So that I have always found members of both sides very sensitive to the opinion of their electorate, and this is very true of the borough members as well as those directly represented. It looks a bit untidy and one could have direct elections as an alternative. The difference of course, and I can see this point, is that ILEA is not directly competing for resources with other services. I'm not sure that one can say that that has led ILEA to spend more than it would otherwise have spent. I think the position really is this, that some inner London boroughs, if they were responsible for education, would be more extravagant than ILEA, and others less.

The point about competing for resources has become rather stronger than it was a decade ago with the development of more integrated decision-making structures in other education authorities. Does this sharpen up the difference between ILEA and the other authorities?

Yes, it does. That's quite fair.

But not sufficiently to make you change your mind about the reorganisation of education in London?

No, because the arguments for a single service in the whole of the old LCC area are very strong. First of all, in terms of secondary schooling, the borough boundaries have little significance. Lots of children go to a school in another borough. The complications of trying to deal with falling rolls, to plan secondary education, to deal with admissions, without this free trade which the London Government Act laid down – imagine that in terms of the twelve boroughs – the administrative prospects are absolutely frightening. Now, if you go beyond that, think of London's responsibility for further and higher education. It's inconceivable that that should be run by twelve individual boroughs. Hardly any of the technical colleges, the further education colleges, let alone the polytechnics, are really borough-related. Then if you think of the overall services, the careers service, for example, you couldn't conceivably run a sensible careers service borough by borough, because so many youngsters are seeking jobs in London, not in Chelsea or Camberwell. The

Inspectorate, which plays a major part in development and standards in inner London, is able to advise right across the board. It's able to advise on further and higher education as well as schooling. Again, if you broke up the system, what would happen to the Inspectorate unless all the boroughs agreed to run it jointly? It's almost inconceivable.

One argument put forward by supporters of the plan is that education costs a lot of money per head in London in comparison with other cities. Is the ILEA service less expensive than twelve individual services would be?

You've got to separate two things, I think. First of all, is ILEA spending more than it need or should? Secondly, would it cost more if it were broken up? Now as to the first, it's bound in the end to be a matter of opinion as to how rich, how well staffed a service you think a great city with all its inner-city problems should have. It is true that the cost per head of primary and secondary education in ILEA is very high compared with most other areas. A great deal of the argument for that is in the nature of the circumstances and the problems of the inner city. But it is true that more resources are available to children and teachers in London than in other parts. And that's a matter of judgement on the part of the elected members that on the whole the people who have elected them will agree to that level of expenditure on education. I don't think you can prove that London has *got* to spend all that much. What you can show is that it has a rich education service as a result of spending that much. On the other hand, I have no doubt whatsoever that it would cost much more to run education by twelve boroughs than it does in ILEA unless standards were seriously worsened, and the argument for that is that the administrative costs would go up in my judgement by about 20 per cent straight away just to run the separate services. And the reason that I say that so confidently is that that is exactly what happened in Middlesex in 1964. The costs of administration, to nobody's benefit, compared with Middlesex went up by 20 per cent because every borough had got to establish its hierarchy and do its thing and do its budgets, so that more would have to be spent to sustain the service at its present level if it were broken up. It's true, then, that the individual boroughs could worsen services but to compensate for the additional cost they would have to reduce standards to a degree that would do harm. The other point is, and this is where Baker is of course completely up the pole, he got all his figures of child population wrong in the report. He was nearly 50 per cent out in some of the projections and a borough like Kensington and Chelsea by the second half of the 1980s would have so few children as to be absolutely ridiculous. Several boroughs are way down below the sort of level that Baker was talking about. Even so, there is a suggestion in the Baker Report of the possible borough combinations. Now, anything more absurd I can't imagine. Can you imagine Kensington and Chelsea under Tory control running a joint education service with Hammersmith under Labour control? Who decides what they spend?

Because it is to a large extent independent of the other parts of local government, ILEA could be regarded as a model by those who support the removal of the education service from local government. Do you think that the ILEA concept could be generalised over the whole country?

Provided those independent authorities were directly elected, yes. I've no use for the health service system, because it seems to me that the local administration of the health service is hampered by the fact that the members are not elected, they are only nominated. Given that there were direct elections, yes I think this would be good. However, I can't conceive either the local authority politicians or government giving up the pattern, the corporate pattern, now established, for which there are strong arguments. I am not saying they are absolutely wrong. Given a free choice, I think I would go for the independent education authorities.

COUNCILLORS AND CHAIRMEN

In the London context, free from the constraints of corporate management, was the education officer's key relationship at the political level with the chairman of ILEA?

Yes, the leader, technically. The chairman is a different figure. That's quite central to the successful operation of the whole system. Mind you, in such a big service with subcommittees doing so much of the work, the relationship with the chairman of the subcommittees is equally important. The leader had a co-ordinating committee on which all the subcommittee chairmen were represented, and that was there for taking corporate decisions with administrative colleagues arguing the case and submitting reports and issues to them. But a very great deal of the more detailed work was a matter of the relationship between the head of branch and the chairman of the subcommittee concerned.

The party caucus presumably met without officers?

Yes, that's a different meeting, what they called the group meeting. The meeting we had was with the leader, the deputy leader and the chairman of the subcommittees, and that was the crucial one from my point of view. They went from that to the group meeting where they would from time to time meet opposition and points of view that differed from the line they had taken with us. Part of my job, of course, was to make sure that they had all the necessary information to meet possible criticism from a long way further down to the left.

The testimony of CEOs in County Hall was that officers were able to have a strong influence on the direction of educational policy. Was it more difficult to have that kind of influence in London?

It varied a lot according to the area one was talking about. There was, in most of the period of my time as deputy, the political issue about comprehensive education between the two sides, and the political decision to proceed with comprehensive reorganisation was a party one and the officer's job was to translate that into practice. The fact that I happened to agree with it was fortunate but, in a way, neither here nor there.

The politicians in London have often been able and well-known people. Did this create problems for the education officer?

No, I don't think so. I think that ILEA, and the LCC before it, benefited from it. Not only the chairman, but other members of the committee, who really had national standing in education. Sir Harold Shearman was a member of the Robbins Committee and wrote the minority report, now Sir Harold had a national standing in education and Bill Houghton and I worked very closely with him. He was a marvellous chairman of the education committee. We gained from his wide knowledge. Now Margaret Cole is another example. She was chairman of the further education subcommittee for many years. Her knowledge of further education was quite remarkable. When I first became deputy, the man in charge of further education was equally experienced, a chap called Mavor, now Mavor and Margaret Cole worked together tremendously closely and Mavor benefited – I've heard him say this – from Margaret Cole's very great standing in this field. There have been others since. The more members know about it the more involved they are, because it means generally, certainly this was true of Harold Shearman, Margaret Cole and Chataway, they are not only prepared to listen to what you have to say and expect to be given all the necessary information and be properly advised, they expect to discuss it with you and argue it; and then at the end of the road, they are fully capable of carrying it through the party group, of handling the party discussion. With Sir Ashley, with his legal training and mind and his involvement and understanding, once you'd convinced him, once he'd made up his mind, he was a marvellous person to put it across. He could do it far better than I could ever have done.

So you were happy to work with strong and knowledgeable politicians even though some CEOs in the past might have preferred people who were malleable and would go along with their view?

I think those days must be past because of the changes that have taken place, and in particular, the very great power now of the group meeting when the officers are not present. If you go back to some of the heroes in the past, you are talking about a time when the decisions were actually made in the subcommittee or in the education committee when, and it was true in the early LCC days, subcommittees were not open to the public; the officers would argue their reports with the members of either side and the decision would be taken there in the subcommittee. But nowadays decisions are taken behind closed doors before the subcommittee ever meets, and if you are not there and you have got a weak chairman of committee, he's going to lose out to whoever it may be in the party group who on this particular issue knows a bit more about it or speaks more loudly. You've got to have strong politicians, these days.

Is one interpretation of what you are saying that officers have a relatively neutral role?

No, I don't take that view. I think, as Lord Morris said, to the British Educational Administration Society administration in local government, certainly in education, has on the whole been dynamic rather than only regulative. A great deal of the movement has come from officers and I am a great believer in dynamic administration, but one recognises that in seeking to shift education in the direction that one believes is right, one can only do it by convincing the people who in the end make the decisions. One mustn't delude oneself that one is really making the decisions oneself. If you have a view that such and such is the right course, you must give the facts, you must argue it and hope that you can carry them with you. But if you can't, then you can't.

You referred earlier to party group decisions and the need to brief the chairman. Can you point to any examples where the party caucus nevertheless overturned something that you and your chairman wanted, or did it always work smoothly?

It didn't always work smoothly, but I can't recall any instances of the thing being in the end overturned. What I can recall are occasions when things were postponed, when the leader's co-ordinating committee had taken their view and then ran into difficulties and would come back and say, 'Well, we decided not to take the report to the next committee', which meant they were saying to me, 'We haven't got it through yet'. I don't recall it being turned upside down in the end. One would occasionally be asked to alter a report to suit the politicians. This would sometimes come from the co-ordinating committee, it would occasionally come from the chairman of an individual subcommittee. The AEO would prepare a report and put it to the chairman for clearance – one had to get it cleared by the chairmen in the sense that they were not going to have it on their agenda unless they had cleared it, fair enough, that's right. Now, just very occasionally the chairman would say, 'I don't like that. Why did you say so and so?' And just occasionally, I was asked to alter a report before it went through the committees. And that I think is a real dilemma. I did alter a report where it was a matter of present-ation; then I felt it was not unreasonable to say 'can you present this a little differently?' Where I would have to say, 'No, I can't alter it', would be if I were asked to leave out material facts. I took the view that my responsibility through the report was not only to the majority party, but to the whole committee, and that material information relevant to the decision they had to take had to be available to the whole committee – both sides of it – and therefore I couldn't alter a report to omit something that might have influenced the decision. One of the subcommittees had a section making appointments, for example, to the administration or to the Inspec-torate. It was the officer's job to do the first round of interviews and to put up a shortlist for the committee to interview. A difficulty which occasionally arose was that the chairman of the subcommittee would say, 'I want the committee to see Mr so and so'. And I would say, 'We have interviewed him but he won't do! He's not up to the job'. And the chairman would say, 'Nevertheless, it's my sub-committee, we can see who we like and we're going to see this person and they will be put on the shortlist'. Now I took the line that, OK, you can do this, of course, but the subcommittee is going to know that you put this person on and not I.

How did you let them know?
By going to the appointing subcommittee, insisting on summing up and letting it appear there. The normal form return is signed by the education officer saying, 'I recommend the following should be interviewed by the committee'. I never got to the point of putting up a report saying, 'I recommend this and the chairman has recom-mended so and so'.

Nevertheless, I suppose to some extent it was compromising because your report included the name of this person and, although you distanced yourself from it later, you appeared to be associated with it at the report stage?
Yes. This was probably the most difficult aspect of this. I think I ought to mention that I have become aware of an increasing tendency on

the part of some leading members to want to be involved in the details of what I would call executive action. With earlier leaders of the committee, like Harold Shearman, James Young and Chris Chataway, the understanding was almost complete as to what decisions the politicians took and what action the administration took. Now, in my last two or three years at County Hall, there were instances, and I am not talking about Sir Ashley now, more about subcommittee chairmen, of members seeking to involve themselves more than I thought proper or necessary in what I thought was executive action. And this occurred because certain executive action gave rise to local repercussions which came their way as elected members for their locality. Perhaps it caused them embarrassment and they felt they should interfere rather more. A particular instance was over suspensions from schools, the heads having the power to suspend, and then follows a difficult process of involvement of governors and consideration of the reasons. Several awkward cases arose where governors took the view, and certainly local politicians took the view, that the head had acted arbitrarily and they were very strong in defence of the parents' rights on behalf of the child. We had a few awkward cases which led to a situation where a particular subcommittee chairman demanded to be told of every suspension of every child that took place. Now, I thought that was ridiculous. But that's the line he took. And that's an interference, I think, in executive action.

CENTRAL GOVERNMENT

Do you consider that Inner London had more influence than other authorities in central government policy-making?
One of the major changes that took place after ILEA had been set up was the decision that ILEA took to give up its special status and to join the AMA. In the LCC days, it was one of the bodies formally consulted by the DES. Whenever there was a committee or commission in education it was consulted. Whenever the Central Advisory Council for Education was constituted as with Newsom and Plowden, and so on, the LCC was always invited to give evidence just as the County Councils Association and the metropolitan authorities and the AEC were. And we were members of Burnham in our own right. So that in those days, right up to 1964, the first eight years of my deputyship, we were formally consulted and, therefore, we had a particular relationship with the DES through that means. When ILEA decided to join the AMA, we lost that particular position, not entirely, but we didn't get the formal invitations. We brought our influence to bear rather more indirectly through AMA. That was less effective. We continued, I think, to

have a pretty close relationship with officers at the DES, probably because of our size and our involvement with national affairs, and so on, but we lost the position we previously had.

Do you think that the Department has become more influential in relation to the local education service in recent years?
I don't observe an important change really. I know it's fashionable at the moment to talk about more centralisation. There are influences in that direction, I suppose the APU setup is an example. The DES has shown much more interest in the curriculum in the last year. I can't myself see that that interest amounts to, so far, any increased control over authorities. Perhaps it's a means of making local authorities more aware of their responsibilities for the curriculum and providing them with better advice, perhaps, than some of them have had. But I don't see any fundamental change really.

HER MAJESTY'S INSPECTORATE

Do you consider that there is overlap between the role of HMIs in London and the ILEA inspectorate, or are they complementary?
Well, first I want to say that I attach very great importance to strong local authority advisory or inspectorial services. It seems to me very important there should be a body of professional people who stand somewhat independent of politicians, administrators and the teachers, who are able to give professional advice in all those three directions, and I would want the inspectorate to be free to give advice and to have it on record, if necessary, even though it doesn't accord with what administration may be saying. I think that the strong inspectorate service is a source of strength to schools and colleges and a way of making sure that administration and politicians understand the truly educational and professional issues in the decisions they are taking. Now, I think that standards in institutions depend a very great deal upon the right influences from the inspectorate. It's difficult to quantify that but it occurs in a multitude of ways – the one extreme full inspections, and the other through the odd word of advice to the individual teacher. But it is critically important in maintaining standards, I have no doubt. I think that the sheer numerical strength of a local inspectorate as they are constituted even in London at the present time is none too great to do that direct advisory job, and that any support and help in the same tasks that comes from the HMI should be welcomed because there isn't enough to go round. The two inspectorates, as far as London is concerned, are complementary in the sense that the London inspectorate is very directly involved in advising the administration; it's involved in matters of promotion of teachers, in organisation of

schools, in the detailed working of the service, whereas the HMI is more removed from those direct relationships and able, therefore, to advise against the national background and to complement the perhaps more localised point of view of the inner London inspectorate. I think that the one helps the other. There were in the old days occasions of overlap, I think. For example, I can recall a time many years ago when probationary teachers were inspected both by HMI and by a London inspector. We soon got rid of that sort of nonsense. There was in my early days a full programme of HMI full inspections and LCC full inspections. We always co-ordinated those programmes, and even taking the two together, a school was never inspected more than about once in twenty years anyway.

There wasn't enough of it to go round in any case. I believe that in some authorities HMIs have been much more directly involved with administration, but this has never been the case in London. I don't suppose they are so involved now, and I would have thought that the current HMI role which is very much emphasising the kind of surveys that they have been doing is of very great importance to any authority, whether or not they have got a strong local inspectorate, because they can never have access to that wider picture which one needs to know.

Do you think there ought to be further changes in the HMI role in view of the strengthening of local inspection services?
I think that a full inspection is a very valuable exercise for the school, the teachers, managers and governors, and the administration. Really, I think the HMIs have withdrawn a bit too much. The tiny percentage of resources that goes into inspection, whether at national or at local level, pays for itself in my view in the standards and morale time and time again. When I sometimes come across this or that authority deciding to retain a large number of teachers despite falling rolls, or to improve its ratios quite substantially, and you count the cost of that, and that same authority refusing to appoint an adviser for religious education, let's say, because they can't afford it, to me that's absolute nonsense. My anxiety is that many authorities are insufficiently advised professionally, in matters which are now so much a matter of public interest, of standards, curriculum, and the like.

RELATIONS WITH HEADS

What is the nature of the relationship between the CEO and the heads of institutions? Did you see yourself as their manager in any sense?
I wouldn't use the word 'manager'. I would see them as having some degree of responsibility towards the CEO, and I would see my

responsibility to be in direct contact with as many of them as possible, and if I couldn't do that myself to make sure that my administrative and advisory arrangements made sure that there was somebody directly relating to them and advising and helping them and in a position to draw me in if necessary. It is obviously quite impossible for me to have personal contact with 1,200 head teachers. On the other hand, I felt it my duty to meet a number of them in their schools and to have some degree of contact and personal relationships with heads of further education colleges and polytechnics. In other cases, I had to make sure that other people had such contact and to know who those people were. If a member said to me, there was something happening at a particular school, or a college for that matter, I would know exactly who to go to to find out what was happening. I visited at least once, and sometimes more than once, every further education college, polytechnic and college of education, a very high proportion of the comprehensive second-ary schools, and certainly a month would not go by without my spending time in two or three primary schools, and I think all that is very important despite the enormous pressures of the committees and the writing of reports. It's got to be done, I think, to make sure that you are seen to be concerned about what is really happening in the places where the education is really taking place. You can administer, some people have said you have to administer, an enormous service from the desk. I didn't take that view. It put me in a position to become personally involved, as with further education reorganisation, as with the polytechnics. When the authority decided as a matter of policy that they would wish polytechnics to reduce the proportion of overseas students, I went personally to the governors' meetings because this was a highly sensitive matter. That would have been hopeless if that had been my first visit to the polytechnic just to go to that governors' meeting. I spent time in the polytechnic and got to know the principal and met him not only at County Hall at consultative meetings, but 'down there'. It gave me a base from which to help with that sensitive matter.

WILLIAM TYNDALE JUNIOR SCHOOL

Did that kind of activity in the field also help you to deal with the problems that inevitably crop up – the bad school, or the occasional head who appears to be going downhill? Or were they as difficult anyway?

Yes, I think it must have helped but the fair answer is that they were difficult anyway. When one got to a point of substantive criticism of a head or the conduct of his or her job, one was then into the whole disciplinary procedure which required my not getting involved. You

are in the business of formal inquiries which have got to be under-
taken through the agreed processes. When this point was reached, I
had to stand back out of it.

Did you make a point of seeing heads before that stage?
I did leave it to the Inspectorate. I didn't think my role in these
relationships was to get personally and actually involved in the
difficulties or problems. If I became aware of them, then it was my
job to put in train the necessary support or help or advice or
surveillance, but not to get involved in it. Supposing it came to my
knowledge that relationships between the head and the staff were
getting to the point of real trouble, what I would do then would be to
go to the Chief Inspector and say, look it seems as if difficulties are
there, will you arrange for an inspector or a small team of inspectors
to go in and find out what is happening and advise and keep me
informed, not to do it myself.

*Do you feel that the system at ILEA was strong enough to cope with this
kind of situation or was a problem like the William Tyndale school
going to arise regardless of the kind of monitoring done?*
I think that the only possible way of dealing with the Tyndale situation
is in principle the pattern that we had, that is to say, for professional
advice to be made available to the head, for the situation to be
watched through the local administration and the local inspectorate,
and for a decision to be taken at some point to move from support
and help to objective assessment and possible disciplinary action.
The kernel of the Tyndale problem would always, I think, be the
kernel of such a situation, and it is really, at what time do you move
from support and help to disciplinary action and who decides to
make the move. Don Rice of the district inspectorate sought to
adopt an advisory and supportive and helpful position in the hope of
so moving the situation as to avoid a final showdown. And looking
back, I think probably he and we went along that line just too long.
But it's a very hard thing to know just at what point you should say to
the head, look we've tried to help you, we're now going to stop trying
to help you and are going to come in and assess you objectively to see
whether you shall be disciplined. Now if for years you have been
working with the head and trying to stop him doing damn silly things
and trying to make him sensitive to parents views, it is very difficult
both to make that decision and to get it across and to make it soon
enough. We went on a bit too long and then in the end it had to
become a matter of public note and the inspection and the rest of it.

*The inspection system failed at Tyndale both at the local and national
level. Is there anything that could have prevented that happening?
Was there too much discretion with the inspectorate?*

Well, I think with hindsight, and I said something like this in a report to a committee, that probably a visitation should have taken place sooner. We shouldn't have left it to the individual inspector quite so long. The Chief Inspector should have arranged for Staff Inspector Primary to go in and carry out a visitation not resulting in a formal report, but in advice presented both to me and to the managers at a somewhat earlier stage.

GOVERNING BODIES

The managers were certainly active in the Tyndale inquiry. Is that symptomatic of a strong interest by governors and managers generally or was Tyndale an exception?
I think in a great many schools the managers and governors were pretty heavily involved with the way in which the school was being run, not interfering, but being kept fully in the picture, and their co-operation being sought in various directions. I can think of secondary schools where the governing body is at the present time playing a very positive part in such matters as admissions, the image of the school locally, the reaction to proposals for reorganisation and the rest of it. It varies a lot from one school to another but many more governing bodies are probably involved than is common.

One interesting development in inner London is the substantial degree of financial discretion accorded to schools. Would you describe that scheme and, in particular, say whether it was planned that governors should be involved?
Well, the whole Alternative Use of Resources scheme was my particular invention, based on greater discretion at school level in the use of resources. I planned and worked out that AUR scheme which, on the one hand, provided for basic resources of teaching and non-teaching staff which couldn't be varied, and then on the other, put into a single block the margin above that of what was capitation money plus further resources which could be used for either teaching, or non-teaching staff, as well as capitation items. And I think that's right, and I think the basic idea is right. I am not arguing for total budgeting being handed to the school. In times of expansion, this scheme was splendid. It worked extremely well when schools were still growing. I don't suppose the scheme is as popular now, in times of contraction, as it was in my time. I think the case still goes, for it added a tremendous amount to the opportunities an enterprising head had. For example, the staff of a particular comprehensive school could and did decide that they really wanted to do quite a proportion of their teaching with the use of non-personal learning resources – television, tape, videotape, the whole caboodle.

Henry Thornton School chose to put resources into not only a media resources officer, but support technician staff, and created a network within the school which enabled teachers to draw on audio-visual resources to a quite remarkable degree. They could do that because they could choose between having an extra one and a half teachers or an extra two and a half technicians. That's the way they decided to play it. And when we first gave the freedom, mind you, it was during a time of shortage of teachers it's true, we found that it did result in quite a switch in resources away from the employment of teachers. One of the most imaginative things that Mrs Thatcher did, to my knowledge, when she was secretary of state relates to this. We went, I remember, on one of these usual delegations to the DES to complain about our minor works allocation. I went with the members and gave illustrations to Mrs Thatcher about how this or that development was being frustrated, because to put a new plug on the wall was a charge on minor works. I said we have a scheme, and I described the AUR, and that the authority would be quite prepared to allow a school to make its own decisions to spend money on that plug out of this block money. It wouldn't involve any additional expense. And she said, that's interesting, you can write to me about that, and I wrote to her about it and she agreed, allowing 'mini-minor' improvements out of AUR to be not chargeable to the minor works allocation.

Once the decision was made to allow schools greater discretion, where did the decision-making power lie within the school?
The head's proposals for the use of the AUR had to reach the divisional office through a governors' meeting with the governors' approval, so they could have varied it. Generally, the governors accepted it.

Presumably there was provision for them to have some responsibility? Was it largely a dead letter as it is in most authorities?
Yes.

Do you think that governors ought to have a stronger role? Or did you feel that the head was the right person to make that kind of decision?
I am not in favour of an arbitrary series of decisions by the head teacher, myself. I think that while he clearly has got to co-ordinate the demands and eventually crystallise the proposals into intentions, he needs to do that in the light of consultation with at least his heads of departments. He needs to be able to convince his governing body that he has carried out that consultation and that the outcome of it makes sense in terms of the objectives that the school has to which the governors are party.

*Were pressure groups in London particularly active? How much impact
did they have on your role?*

First, I attached great importance to the formal consultative procedures and used them I think fully. Secondly, with key people,
whether teachers' associations or other bodies, I attached similarly
great importance to informal consultation. Then, thirdly, I always
thought it right to take notice of and in fact go to see particular
groups who wanted to make a point. I would always advise members
if they were asked or the leader to see, for example, representatives
of managing or governing bodies, or representatives of the parents,
or CASE*, or whatever it might be. I think these sort of people
should be given a hearing. What they said was some indication of
opinion locally, held by some people, and one, therefore, did not
disregard it. It doesn't follow that one did or could do what they
wanted. But one tried to take it into account. I was conscious of the
threat to some parts of the service, arising from extreme pressure
groups who were not, in my view, really representative. I found it
necessary to be cautious about the pressures brought to bear by
certain local teachers' groups within the total of the Inner London
Teachers' Association, because one was aware that some of these
small local associations within ILEA had been taken over by unrepresentative and extremist groups of people. Again, I followed the
policy of giving them a hearing, but one didn't take their view quite
so seriously except to the extent that one had to make sure that they
were not unduly influential when it came to the formal consultation
or local decisions.

*It is always possible, of course, for interest groups to influence
politicians and other decision-makers. Were there cases when they
influenced decisions in a way which, as a professional, you felt wasn't
really wise?*

The only instances I can think of are the kind of pressure groups of
parents and teachers who are fighting for the survival of a particular
school, where one's professional advice might be in direct opposition. They did occasionally prevail. I remember Bow, a so-called
comprehensive school in East London, which had come down to
about a two-form entry and we had a surplus of places, and it was a
very unpopular school. We issued section 13 notices to close it and a
great campaign to save it was mounted. That pressure succeeded to
the extent that the secretary of state didn't agree with the closure.
It's still going in some modest size. After it had been saved, a new
head was appointed and it took on a new lease of life for a time.

* Confederation for the Advancement of State Education.

It seems that however unpopular a school might be in practice the minute you try to close it . . .

. . . it suddenly becomes the most desirable.

CONTRACTION

I would like to discuss contraction because it had already become an issue in London during your period of office, and also because, as a result of your research, * *you are well placed to comment on the issue in general terms. How much does the problem of falling rolls affect the role of the education officer?*

You are talking about the extent to which an authority is going to be prepared to grasp some of the nettles and not just let the thing run. Certainly, many authorities now are beginning to consider the implications and to make plans to meet it, including closures of schools in some cases. The need to review the whole secondary school system over this decade will certainly lead to the administration being more involved with the schools. The other way in which it seems to me that power is likely to shift away from the individual institution, and indeed from the governing body, is over the contraction of staff levels and the redeployment that is necessarily going to follow. Nearly all authorities at the moment are talking about no redundancies. They will only hold that if they are able to redeploy. Quite a lot of redeployment is taking place in the primary sector, which is not too difficult. When you come to the secondary sector, redeployment involves placing a specialist in a different school, and it will be necessary if this is to be effective to take away from governors the power of choosing all their staff. Certainly, one authority has promulgated a document about redeployment which specifically laid it down that the authority will decide if necessary that such and such a teacher has to be sent to another school on the advice of the senior adviser and the advisory service. If that pattern is followed, the CEO is going to be in a position of actually, in the last resort, telling head A, you're going to lose that post and not fill that vacancy, and telling head B, you're going to have this chap. I think only a few authorities have put themselves in this position yet. If redeployment is to work through the decade, as it will have to do, that will increasingly become the case.

* Briault, E., and Smith, F., *Falling Rolls in Secondary Schools* (London: NFER, 1980).

ACCOUNTABILITY

To whom is the education officer accountable?
I contributed recently an article on the accountability of the Chief Education Officer to a book edited by John Lello.* As I recall, the main points I made in it were that the CEO is primarily answerable to the education committee and I mean by that, the whole committee, all its members. His reports must place all the relevant facts before the committee and his objective advice is tendered to it as a whole and to its subcommittees. Unlike Members of Parliament, all elected local education authority members traditionally have access to officers. But, in practice, the Chief Education Officer is largely accountable to the majority party, and in particular to the chairman of the education committee and the chairman of the subcommittees. In recent years, decisions have more and more been taken in the party group meeting which officers do not attend, thank goodness! But this means that the briefing of the chairman is all-important. The Chief Education Officer has a degree of answerability to the corporate management team but I don't take the view that he is directly answerable to the Chief Executive. Apart from County Hall responsibilities, one has a great responsibility for the general health and quality of the education service. One is accountable, if you like, to the customers. The local education authority's responsibility for the curriculum and for the conduct of the service has to be carried out directly and indirectly through the Chief Education Officer. It is this kind of accountability which gives local authority administration its dynamic quality, as well as its regulative function. To an extent, he has always been accountable to the learners – the pupils and students.
   The administration has a responsibility, as any good manager or director has, towards the employees, and I have always felt an important degree of accountability towards the teachers and the non-teaching staff. Another interesting aspect of accountability is his relations with governors and managers, which are to some degree parallel to those he has towards the education committee. In the end, the Chief Education Officer is the professional and his final accountability is in a sense to his own professional conscience.

Do you consider that heads of institutions were accountable primarily to you or were they accountable to committees or to governors?
Primarily accountable to the school in all its manifestations. They are accountable to the governors of the schools, they are accountable to the staff for their management of the total enterprise. But I think

* Lello, J., *Accountability in Education* (London: Ward Lock, 1979).

that they also have an accountability upwards from the institution for the health of the institution to the employing authority, and the manifestation of that employing authority I would think is the CEO rather than the politically elected members.

Do you think heads are very conscious of that accountability?
I do. It looks different for a voluntary school head, but speaking of county school heads, I think they were conscious of this. As a chance phrase, a number of heads would speak of me as 'the boss'. Not all, but one heard it too often not to feel that it did represent a feeling that I represented the authority for them and that they were accountable to the chief officer in some degree.

Was the eventual closure of William Tyndale Junior School and the amalgamation with the infants school the only way that the head could be curbed or was there, on reflection, another way of resolving the problem?
He didn't accept the definition I have given. He didn't regard me as his boss. Ellis had to be dismissed, whether or not there had been an amalgamation of the two schools, because he was shown in a disciplinary hearing to have failed to carry out his duties, so badly failed as for it to be irresponsible for the authority to leave him with that responsibility.

One of the ways in which he failed was in not acknowledging his accountability?
That's right. One of the major disciplinary defects that Ellis perpetrated, in my view, was his decision to close the school to prevent a full inspection. That was a major defiance of the proper responsibility to his employing authority, and his accountability. I did my best, personally on the phone to him on the day before (the Friday before it took place on the Monday) to make it clear to him that he had no right to close the school. It wasn't his school to close. When I had eventually to bring the disciplinary charges against him, that was central to the charge I was making. He took to himself the authority to close a school which wasn't his personal school to close, in spite of direct instructions from me as chief officer representing the authority.

ROLE OF THE DIRECTOR

What is the CEO's distinct contribution to the education service? Do you foresee any changes in the role of the CEO in the 1980s?
Well, I think his distinct contribution is as the leading professional concerned with education. He has a major responsibility for it being

a dynamic administration, that is, an administration intended to shift things in positive directions, in the direction of improvement of quality in the service and as a person, as distinct from his corporate capacity, to have a view of the whole service which can't be expected of most of his assistants, though it can perhaps be expected of the deputy. His other personal responsibility is the key relationship with the leader, or chairman, or whatever. Nobody can substitute for that. I would hope that the kind of relationship between the administration and the politicians which I described earlier might survive the pressures that now exist. I think it is in danger because of the caucus system and from the tendency of some members to want to get involved in administrative details, but I think by and large it probably survives. It seems to me of central importance to the future that there should be that understanding of the decision-making power of the elected members, the responsibilities of the administration to inform, advise and help them to make those decisions, and then the transfer back to the administration of the carrying out of the decisions. If only one can keep that pattern right, as I believe it is still right for most authorities, that is what I would like to see and that is what I think is correct.

Derrick Williams

Avon

Derrick Williams was educated at Cambridge University and taught in a grammar school and in adult education in Nigeria and Leicestershire. He gained administrative experience in Oxfordshire and West Suffolk and moved to Bristol as Assistant Education Officer in 1965. He became Deputy Education Officer in 1967. He was appointed Chief Education Officer for the new county of Avon in 1974. Derrick Williams left Avon in 1977 to become Director of the Gloucestershire Institute of Higher Education.

BACKGROUND

I was a working-class scholarship boy from a small country town in Shropshire, without any early ambitions towards a university education. I was encouraged and stimulated by an active and sympathetic headmaster who found time to teach, and went to Cambridge just as the war started. After an interruption for war service, I finished my degree and professional teacher training at Cambridge in 1949. I then took the conventional way into education by teaching at a grammar school in Rugby. After only a year, I found myself in West Africa at the newly established University College of Nigeria, doing adult education work there. I then came back and was appointed adult tutor at the first Leicestershire community college in Ashby-de-la-Zouch. From there, after two and a half years, I moved to Oxfordshire, doing very much the same job but on a wider area basis, and was responsible for the development of adult and community education in the northern half of the county. I suppose it was at that point that I developed an interest in administration. I went to West Suffolk as their first Assistant Education Officer, with a particular responsibility again for the development of adult and community education and further education. It was not until I got to Bristol in 1965 – there again, I was appointed as Assistant Education Officer for further education – that I began to realise the satisfaction to be had from a senior post in administration. It was the rapport that men like Harold Sylvester, who was then the CEO, and his deputy Hubert Thompson, had established with the teaching profession, and the skills they evidenced in presenting educational policies to the politicians, that made me realise what satisfactions they obtained from being in a position to influence the decisions of the local education authority. After less than two years as Assistant Education Officer in Bristol, I was appointed deputy when Harold Sylvester retired. Thompson succeeded Sylvester as CEO and I was appointed deputy which, of course, gave me very much wider responsibilities than the further education field in which I had been contained in the first part of my career. For some time, I confess, I think I would have been content to have ended my career as a deputy but perhaps inevitably the attractions of being at the centre of thought and influencing the decision-making led me to the ambition of becoming a Chief Education Officer, and the creation of Avon in 1972, which was about the time when I might have expected to find promotion, brought it about.

The Avon authority was carved out of Bristol and part of Somerset?
It was Bristol and Bath, which were self-contained local education authorities, part of Somerset and part of Gloucestershire – its urban area.

Why did you decide to apply for the chief's post in the newly created authority?
It was an exciting opportunity, a unique opportunity, of being in on the beginning of a new authority, based on Bristol, which had been a progressive authority with a total commitment to education.

One result of reorganisation would have been politicians coming in from four rather different county and urban authorities. What impact did that have on your job?
Not a noticeable one in the first instance because everyone was concerned to establish the basic mechanics of the new authority, and it was clear from the beginning that a corporate management system would be introduced. An Avon Joint Committee of the four participating authorities had been appointed early in 1972 and had commissioned management consultants to advise the new authority on its structure. The politicians from the four areas had their different expectations of the new administration, of course, but these were largely controlled by their party political organisations.

CORPORATE MANAGEMENT

What were the essential features of corporate management as it applied in Avon?
The establishment of central resource committees was the feature that was greatly emphasised. There was on the committee side a re-sources co-ordination committee (in other authorities it would be called a policy and resources committee), resources committees for

finance, personnel and land and buildings, and then what were called programme area committees for education, leisure, social services, planning, and the like.

What was the relationship between the different types of committee?
During my time there was a great deal of uncertainty and confusion as to the responsibilities of the committees, but there was a trend towards decisions being taken within the resource committees at the expense of the programme area committees, which bothered me.

What was the officer structure in Avon?
There were two groups of chief officers – resource officers such as the county treasurer, director of personnel services, director of estates services and a director of administration who was also the county solicitor; then the group of programme area officers – the Chief Education Officer, director of social services, county engineer, county planner, librarian, and so on. All chief officers were members of the Chief Officer Management Team, led by the Chief Executive, who had no departmental responsibility. Each programme area officer was supposedly the manager of his service and my own job specification held me responsible for ensuring that the resources available to education were deployed with maximum cost-effectiveness. But at the same time, the resource chief officers were also responsible for the use of resources, and it was a confusion of function which created considerable difficulties and was not resolved in my time in Avon. It's the feature of corporate management which most worries me, because it's extremely difficult in practice to define the respective responsibilities of resource and programme area officers and departments – perhaps, there shouldn't be separate departments – and corporate management ironically tends to disperse rather than unify managerial control. Obviously, because Avon was a new authority, its chief officers had to spend a lot of time on the establishment of the administrative structure. They had little time for corporate planning, which is the real justification for corporate management, and if there isn't a corporate plan there are no clear policies to work toward. I'm not suggesting that corporate plans come ready-made and they take a great deal of time and negotiation to prepare, but if a Chief Officer Management Team is neglecting that function, it gets over-concerned with administrative matters.

So the problem was that the officers were managing in a policy vacuum and you attribute some of the particular difficulties of Avon to that?
I felt that the resources officers, particularly, were tempted into claiming day-to-day management responsibilities in the programme

areas, rather than concerning themselves with the allocation of resources to the programme areas and their application to policies and objectives.

Was it possible for the problems you have identified to be tackled fundamentally within the education service or were they issues on which other departments and committees had a major influence?
Not in terms of proposing policy, but in terms of the application of policy, yes, other committees of the authority did have influence on educational issues. Perhaps I can illustrate that. The education committee might set its objectives in terms of its future building programme and have it authorised by the county council. But then the education committee would find that the land and buildings committee and resources co-ordination committee would intervene in the implementation of the programme. It was the land and buildings committee which accepted tenders for building projects, and decided the cash limits to be applied to each, without reference to the education committee. The total programme of building projects could be frustrated by a decision made by the land and buildings committee to accept a tender significantly above the estimated costs for one project.

Did you or your representative attend resource committees when decisions of that nature were being made?
We took care to attend, but in my time such committees still regarded education officers as responsible only to the education committee. The situation I have quoted was symptomatic of the difficulties in the authority of establishing a complex and sophisticated management system which had the intention of centralising the control of resources in the resources committees. In a corporate management system there has to be an extremely refined and detailed definition of the responsibilities and power of resource and programme area committees, respectively. It might be perhaps simpler in the case of an existing, ongoing, authority to convert to corporate management. Certainly, it is extremely difficult to introduce it to a new authority and very many of the difficulties I experienced were, I am sure, the results of the somewhat dogmatic application of corporate management theory without a regard for the realities of the situation.

You said earlier that the land and buildings committee may accept tenders to such an extent that the whole building programme would not be achieved in the programme year. Who would determine which projects were dropped from the programme?
In effect, it was simply the accident of which projects were first brought to design completion and tender by the architect and taken to

committee for approval. Later projects were not necessarily dropped but could not be implemented in the programme year and had to be deferred – at the risk of not getting into the next year's programme. Priorities would still be determined by the education committee but their achievement was undermined.

Another process that is normally regarded as symptomatic of how corporate management works is the revenue budget. How was the budget prepared in Avon?

Budgets for all the services were prepared in the treasurer's department and submitted to the finance committee, finally approved by the resources co-ordination committee and, in effect, passed to the education committee as its budget for the year. There were, of course, consultations between officers of the education department and the treasurer's department in the formulation of budget proposals. The education committee were not at that stage consulted, but were given their budgetary cash limits at the end of the process.

If there was disagreement between the treasurer's department and your department on aspects of the budget, how would that disagreement have been resolved?

It would be resolved in the cells of the finance committee and the resources co-ordination committee, not resolved in the education committee.

If the education committee thought it right to seek an improvement in pupil–teacher ratios, for example, and were willing to sacrifice some expenditure on, say, maintenance of buildings or capitation levels, would that have been a possible response from the education committee?

Only with difficulty. Once the budget was established, each of the resource committees would assume responsibility for its allocation. So that expenditure designed for the non-teaching staff of schools, for example, was the responsibility of the personnel committee. Expenditure designed for the maintenance and upkeep of buildings was the responsibility of the land and buildings committee. So the education committee's role was limited to representation to these committees.

If there was a vacancy for a clerical assistant in one of your schools, what would be the process for filling the vacancy?

The head would normally be allowed the discretion to make that appointment but approval for the establishment of a non-teaching post at a school or approval to fill a vacancy was at the discretion of the personnel committee, not the education committee. It was also the case that the personnel department became responsible for the supervision of the non-teaching staff in schools. A headmaster who had disciplinary problems, for instance with a caretaker or a cleaner, would do better to go to the personnel department, who controlled the conditions of service, the overall establishment and filling of vacancies of non-teaching staff in the schools, rather than approach the education department.

Were office-based supervisory staff, such as the supervisor of caretakers or school meals supervisor, located outside the education department?

It should have meant just that, at least in the case of the supervisor of caretakers. In fact, there was such a supervisor in the education department and his role was somewhat ambiguous, so too were the responsibilities of a small personnel section originally allowed in the structure of the education department. By 1976 the bid was being made to have the section, or most of it, transferred to the personnel department and responsible to the director of personnel services, even though they would remain accommodated in the education department's offices. This was part of a general move toward the centralisation of what were called support services in the resource departments which seemed to me to be splintering the management of the education service, and was confusing to the schools.

This suggests a blurred line of responsibility from the head back to the office, and on certain issues it would be to a department other than your own?

This was my major concern about Avon's version of corporate management. From the point of view of heads of schools, there were too many unco-ordinated managers. Heads of schools found themselves responsible to four or five chief officers and my own officers in the education department were left uncertain about their roles.

Was the management and appointment of teaching staff located within your department?

Yes, that was left with the education department.

Why do you think that is? In terms of consistency, that might also have been located within the personnel department?

I always feared that the time would come in Avon when the personnel department would be responsible for the county's establishment and the number of teachers in each school. It didn't happen. Perhaps you would regard it as the illogicality of the application of corporate management in Avon.

Was it a recognition of the power and influence of teachers' unions in Avon? Would they have taken the view that the professional education officer should be responsible for teaching staff?

They were aware of the possibility, of course, and would have opposed it, but it was never put to the test.

Have you any other comments about corporate management?

I appreciate the need for corporate planning and for a corporate outlook towards the generality of public services a local authority provides. And where corporate management is taken to mean the co-ordination of committees' functions and responsibilities, it too makes sense. But my experience of corporate management – or to be fair my experience of one developing version of it – is that it muddles and sometimes duplicates the respective roles and responsibilities of chief officers, particularly between resource officers and 'programme area' or 'service' officers. A CEO cannot be held responsible for the efficient management of the education service, if its resources, manpower, money and sites are each managed by a specialist chief officer. I don't contest the obvious concern of resource officers for the use by a service of its resources but that concern ought not to demand their day-to-day management, control and administration. Implicit, too, in this issue of responsibility for the use of resources is the *central* management of resources. Corporate management linked now to the current scarcity of resources tends to reduce the managerial discretion of heads and principals as well as education officers. And I am quite sure that resources are best managed at the place in which they are deployed.

Was your decision to move from Avon to your present post as Director of the Gloucestershire Institute of Higher Education a product of this situation in which the education service was managed to some extent from outside the education office?

Yes, I didn't feel that either I, or the education committee, could effectively manage the education service even though we had the nominal, indeed the statutory, responsibility. Too many cooks were stirring the broth. Despite my representations over the last twelve months of my time as a Chief Education Officer, I could see no prospect of any changes being made which would clarify the roles of either officers, or committees, in the management of the service.

REORGANISATION

Avon's four constituent authorities must have had different standards and levels of provision. How did you set about the task of producing a measure of equality among the institutions of the four former authorities?

I can't pretend that in the mere three years I was in Avon we achieved total equality of provision between the four parts of the local authority. There had been the hope that we could apply to all schools the most generous standards of staffing and capitation we had inherited, but Avon was born at a time when public expenditure was being reduced and we had to compromise. I think there was general agreement within the schools that uniformity was preferable to the continued existence of discrepancies between each of the four parts of the county. Clearly, staffing ratios and uniform capitation allowances were the key to the matter. We did achieve equality in those on a reasonable basis within the first two years.

Were there any other issues arising out of reorganisation that were of particular significance to you as CEO?

Another immediate concern was the rationalisation of further education. Avon inherited from Gloucestershire two technical colleges right on the boundaries of Bristol. From Somerset, we inherited two technical colleges – a substantial one based in Weston-super-Mare, and a smaller one. From Bath, there came into Avon a technical college. At the same time, you will remember, the rundown in teacher training was foreshadowed and Avon inherited Redland College of Education, and in Bath the College of Home Economics and Newton Park College of Education. So, the major tasks there were rationalising the provision of further education facilities between the technical colleges, and considering the future use of the colleges of education. Perhaps, I ought to mention in the list of colleges of education the voluntary college of St Matthias, as well. The advice given us by the DES was that Bristol Polytechnic should assume responsibility for all teacher training in the Bristol area, and this left us with the decision as to how the resources of Redland College and the voluntary college might be used. So, there was the need for a comprehensive reorganisation of further and higher education in response to national strategy immediately Avon came into existence.

One argument put forward for local government reorganisation was that larger authorities would enable rationalisation of provision for the post-compulsory sector. Does the Avon experience justify that view?

The creation of Avon could be justified in those terms. Bristol was the effective centre for higher and further education in the area, in any case, and it was comparatively easy in professional terms to propose the forms that rationalisation and reorganisation might take. Securing the political adoption of those proposals was a different matter, because there were a number of vested interests involved – not just institutional vested interests, but political ones. Inevitably in the early years of such an amalgam as Avon, there were local and area interests which wished to preserve their own facilities and these were always a stumbling block in achieving the political will to give effect to rationalisation schemes.

To what extent did councillors consider themselves to be Avon members, rather than, say, Bristol or Somerset people?
By the time I left Avon, there was a growing recognition of Avon's identity as a local authority, but you are right in suspecting that in the early years many, if not most, members remained loyal first to their local areas, particularly since the great majority of them had been senior councillors in their previous authorities. The Somerset faction particularly remained strong, it would be unfair to say insular, but certainly its members were primarily concerned with facilities in their own area. You can, perhaps, remember the strength of the 'Save our Somerset' campaign which preceded reorganisation.

COUNCILLORS

Do you consider that politics has intruded rather more strongly into the education service in the last decade?
No I don't think so. It's true of course that education has become more politically sensitive and obviously in such policy matters as secondary reorganisation, under which lie political philosophies, there would be a very considerable political interest. But I didn't find in Avon that there was a heightened political interest in the administration as such of the service. The councillors of modern authorities are far too busy to concern themselves with the detail of administration, unless it is going wrong somewhere.

In the past it was often assumed that the CEO's recommendations would be acted upon more often than not by the members. If that was ever true, is it less true now than it was, say, a decade ago?
I doubt that it was ever true, but if so, it is certainly not the case today. Now, with corporate management, the CEO is not regarded as the only adviser to the education authority and his authority with committees is dispersed among the chief officer group.

Are there particular types of decision that you would have taken in Bristol that have now moved beyond the officer level and become political or member decisions?
A number of decisions might now be taken by councillors – a result of

their anxiety to achieve tighter financial control – but not in order to exercise political control. I think, for example, of the sensitive decision as to whether or not particular staff vacancies in schools should be filled, where groups of members would take these decisions with budgetary considerations as much in their minds as educational ones.

Was your argument, which presumably was for the most part to fill the vacancy, generally accepted?
Yes, for the most part because my officers had done their own screening of the need to fill vacancies. But you had to argue for every case and be conscious of the financial implications.

CHAIRMEN

There was a time when the CEO–chairman of education axis was regarded as the central relationship at the political level. Is that still the case or are there other relationships which rival that one in importance?
The relationship with the chairman and the education committee is still absolutely essential, but it is weakening. The CEO is not responsible simply to the education committee, but to the council also. In corporate management systems other chief officers are as responsible to the education committee as the CEO. Within the relationship between a CEO and the full council, the relationship he develops with the chairman of the policy and resources committee is as essential to his functioning as his relationship with the chairman of the education committee. But there must be a close and confident relationship still with the chairman of the education committee. The CEO relies upon him to represent the education service within the policy-making group of the county council, whether this is a party caucus or a policy and resources committee, and he is often the ambassador of the education service to the general public. The more he knows about the education service, the better able he is to represent its interests.

Can it be postulated that the emergence of the apparatus of corporate management might lead to the post of chairman of the education committee being held by a less influential member than in the past?
Yes, I think there is that danger. It depends on the personality of the chairman but that itself is the result of the deliberate selection of the chairman of the education committee. The power caucus within the council is likely to be the chairman of the county council and the chairmen of the resource committees rather than the chairmen of the programme area committees.

There is a suspicion that education has weakened compared to other services in local government, partly because the chairman of the education committee does not always have the influence with the policy committee which he had when the education chairmanships were always central.

Yes, I share this suspicion, and I think the events preceding reorganisation prove it. If you remember, one of the early recommendations of the Bains Committee was that the education committee should lose its statutory status, and certainly many authorities, and I am generalising here, see the education committee, which takes up 70 per cent of the budget in many authorities, as too powerful, and have set out to distribute its functions among other committees of the authority just as they have dispersed the functions of the education department.

CENTRAL GOVERNMENT

Do you think that the DES is more or less influential in relation to the local education service than it was, say, a decade ago?

I regret that I think the DES is less influential. If we examine its record, for example, at the time of the creation of the new authorities, we find that it was not prepared to take a stand against those authorities which transferred the oversight of adult or youth and community services to a committee other than the education committee. It seemed not prepared to insist upon the observance of educational legislation which required that the statutory education committee of the authority should have the oversight of the whole of the education service.

The legislation that has come in the last decade might suggest that the centre is taking a stronger line. Examples might be the 1976 legislation in relation to comprehensive education or the 1980 Local Government Bill. Do those examples suggest a significant movement towards the centre?

There seems a trend towards centralisation on the part of the Department of the Environment, certainly, in terms of expenditure control overall, which must affect the education service; but I doubt that the DES is increasing its control or direction of LEAs, because it seems to me its own influence in central government is waning. It is quite unable to ensure that the educational components of Rate Support Grant are actually spent on the education service as the failure of Mrs Shirley Williams to develop the in-service training and retraining of teachers illustrated.

Did you find the DES helpful to the kind of initiatives you wanted to develop?

Yes, I've always found the DES officers both extremely helpful and, in fact, remarkably well informed about the local situation. The expertise they obtained via HM inspectors as to the need for buildings projects, particularly in the secondary and further education fields, was impressive. And I remember being greatly encouraged by their readiness to co-operate with Bristol in the development of its 'green fields' polytechnic. Personal and honest relationships with them are the key to the matter of course.

The building programme is an example of one of the department's stronger controls. You have suggested that they often cannot push a particular policy through, for example, on in-service training. Do you think the balance is about right?

I would think the balance is about right. It is for the department to provide national policies for the education service, and the secretary of state has a legal responsibility to supervise the application of those policies which is exercised mainly through the Inspectorate. I wouldn't want to see any greater detailed control exercised by the department. Interest nowadays in the content of the curriculum, for example, ought not to lead to centralist direction.

HER MAJESTY'S INSPECTORATE

Do you detect any change in the role of HM Inspectorate in the last decade?

There was a time when a lively inspector could influence the educational policies and decisions of an authority by working closely with the CEO. I have the impression that inspectors are no longer quite so influential, if only because the policy decisions of authorities are now taken in the deeper recesses of their committee structures and HMIs rarely carry authority with politicians and officers of other departments. However, they are still closely concerned with educational standards in individual institutions, and this is the most profitable role for them, although there is a danger there of different advice to the CEO from HM Inspectorate on the one hand, and from the well-developed advisory services of the new LEAs on the other. In practice, though, I think there is a very useful partnership being developed between HM Inspectors and LEA advisers, which provides a very considerable flow of advice about institutions coming into the CEO and his senior administrators who don't these days find it easy to get out to see for themselves.

204 / *Directors of Education*

Was the nature of the advice from HMIs at a different level from that of local advisers? How would you distinguish between the two sources of advice?
I think I'd make this distinction: whereas the advisory team of the LEA are bound to some extent to reflect the preoccupations and prejudices of the education department, inspectors are independent of that domestic view. So theirs is an independent wider assessment of the state of schools and colleges.

RELATIONS WITH HEADS

What was the nature of the relationship between you as CEO and the heads of schools and colleges?
I looked for as close a personal relationship as was possible, although clearly it was difficult in a large authority. Avon has 500 schools, so that it was physically impossible to be in contact regularly or even to visit all those 500 heads in their schools. I met them regularly at area group meetings and particularly during the first twelve months of my time as CEO spent a day each week visiting as many schools as I could. I've always believed that a CEO should be as far as possible the leader, adviser and confidante of headmasters, and I see the relationship between the CEO and his senior staff with heads as being the key to the effective and necessarily co-operative management of the education service. I think it is a relationship which the CEO neglects at his peril, except, as I say, that in a large authority it can't always be a continuing relationship. If it can't be achieved at a personal level between the CEO himself and the heads of schools, it must be achieved by senior officers on behalf of the CEO. In this respect, I think the post-1974 development of advisory teams has accentuated the importance of a chief adviser of senior rank, to build the bridges between the administration and the schools. My chief adviser occupied a second-tier place in the administrative hierarchy and was invaluable in this respect.

The delegation of authority to advisers suggests that you were not concerned to see a particular style of leadership in the schools, whereas perhaps other chiefs at other times have sought to promote a particular style.
Perhaps other CEOs in other times. In a large authority like Avon, I don't think you could realistically expect to impose a particular style of leadership upon a variety of educational institutions in a variety of different environments.

Do you believe also that heads of institutions are entitled to expect a large measure of autonomy or should discretion be within strong guidelines from the CEO and his team of officers?

I think of 'discretion' and responsibility rather than autonomy. For my part, I would argue strongly the need for clearly defined and delegated management responsibility and discretion to the head of a school or college. There have to be parameters within which managerial authority is exercised, but they should be drawn generously. The growing professionalism and expertise of modern heads and principals as managers must be recognised and makes for a more efficient and economical education service, I believe.

If you came across some cases of heads using their discretion in a way which you or your senior colleagues found to be unreasonable, what sort of action did you feel able to take?

I would prefer – indeed most use – the closest relationship which existed between the head concerned and a member of my staff. He or she would normally be a senior education officer or the chief adviser, or indeed, the area adviser, who is the man or woman expected to have detailed knowledge of the situation in the school and the personality of the head. But I would certainly regard the matter, in the first instance anyway, as an internal, professional problem between the department and the head of school. It would have to be a very serious issue, and the circumstances would have to be very extreme before governors or elected members were brought into the matter and formal disciplinary procedures invoked. I remember one instance where a head was under suspicion of embezzling money and in that case I interviewed the head and asked the authority's auditors to investigate the situation before it was raised with the governors. In all cases alleged abuses of responsibility would be thoroughly probed by a senior officer or adviser and formal disciplinary action would only be taken after consultation with governors and possibly the education committee.

What about assistant teachers? Were you happy to leave any monitoring of teaching standards to the head, or were there any occasions when you had to involve yourself directly?

No I didn't feel it necessary to involve myself directly, but certainly there were occasions when it was necessary to ask my chief adviser or a senior colleague to undertake an assessment of an individual teacher or a school or college. There, the general procedure was for the advisory team to follow almost the course of an HMI inspection of the school. The findings were then discussed with the head and only then discussed more widely if solutions were not found. By and large, the philosophy was a personal advisory relationship between the administration and the school concerned.

CONTRACTION

Was the problem of contraction beginning to make itself felt during your period of office in Avon?

It was, but not of course, as drastically as it since has. There are two dangers in coping with contraction, which is a demanding exercise – more so than the management of expansion. First, with all its stresses and strains, it stretches the confidence of the relationship which the CEO has been able to build up with heads and staffs of schools. Secondly, contraction encourages very much greater central control and the assumption by the centre of responsibilities which in more ordinary circumstances you would expect to be exercised by heads. With some schools at least, it becomes necessary for the authority to exercise a much closer supervision of intakes, and to intervene in staffing policies.

Did you also experience problems arising from the redeployment of staff?

Yes, this was quite a considerable problem in Avon and there were, of course, no easy solutions. My own was to have the total situation, and indeed the proposed strategy, discussed in detail with the teachers' organisations. There were particular difficulties in Avon, because redundancies consequent upon the decline of school rolls were occurring for the most part in Bristol and the urban area, whereas redeployment opportunities were available in the still-growing suburban areas. This often meant we could only offer new work at a distance of perhaps twenty miles.

What are the implications of that for the heads of receiving schools? It might be thought that the teachers who become available for re-deployment are not necessarily the ones that the exporting schools are most anxious to retain and therefore they might not be teachers the receiving school would have chosen if they had a free choice. Was that something that concerned you?

There was a need for central direction in the exercise. My officers had to arbitrate about the identification and reception by schools of redeployed staff. I believe this was done with some sensitivity, and certainly always with regard to the particular needs of the receiving school. My team of some twenty advisers and three or four education officers were spending a great deal of time and care on this.

Do these problems of contraction change the essential nature of the relationship between the CEO and the head?

I would regret that, coming back to what I said earlier, such issues can quickly affect the confident and personal relationship between head and CEO. The CEO tends to become the 'agent' of central controls which are imposed upon and reluctantly received by schools, in the interests of the authority's education service as a whole. One of the most encouraging developments in the management of the education service through the 1950s and 1960s was the increasing managerial responsibility and discretion which authorities, good authorities, were able to give to the schools, and I see those discretions as now being withdrawn. Moves towards central control of institutions, particularly within a corporate management environment, encourage the process of treating schools as if they were comparable with engineers depots. And there are other chief officers and departments in some authorities who regard heads and staffs of schools as if they were unskilled employees, not professionals.

GOVERNING BODIES

Did governing bodies have an important role in Avon?
We'd hoped they might in Avon, as sounding boards of public attitudes toward schools which we ourselves knew little about at first. We would have liked to give them some real responsibility but I don't think the committee system of local government has yet found a proper role for governing bodies of schools, even though in the case of further education a governing body can act almost as a subcommittee of the local authority. But in the case of the school governing bodies, they remain nominally representative of the local community, the community's interest in the school. They often find it difficult to relate their own interest in the school to the interests of the authority. They are a somewhat uncomfortable part of the system because so few functions are delegated to them.

You use the word 'nominal'. Do you feel that the interests of the head and his staff, and the rights of the authority, are just too powerful for the governing body ever to achieve a meaningful role?
I would agree with your comment in general terms. It seems to me that a body with local interests can't be expected to reflect the same concerns that the authority would have for the place and purpose of a school within its total provision. Nor does it seem to me that a governing body as it is usually composed can effectively supervise the work and direction of a school.

PRESSURE GROUPS

Do you consider that pressure groups are able to influence policy formulation?
Pressure groups have become more aggressive of late – I suspect

because of their difficulty in finding the real point of decision-making. There must always have been pressure groups. I'm equally sure that they must have operated more quietly, and I suspect more effectively before they were forced, in order to be heard, to shout their messages from the rooftops. Pressure groups should influence any administrator – or politician – but our decision-making processes seem actually to encourage their formation unnecessarily and they seem to have become essential to the declaration of interests. But they simplify the issues and often have a negative effect upon decision-making because of their aggression.

You are saying that pressure groups are sectional, and officers may perhaps have to take account of interests not vigorously pressed. Are you suggesting also that pressure groups are more vocal now because of a lessening of their influence?
I would expect any officer and responsible politician to recognise the sectional character of a pressure group and equally to give weight to interests, as you put it, not vigorously pressed. But yes, my main point is that the further away a group is from the real decision-makers, the more loudly it feels it must make its case – the more, too, it will go public with its concern.

Are you able to illustrate that point by an example from your own experience?
There was one particular situation which rapidly created a teachers' protest group. A blanket decision was taken within the authority, without consultation with the education committee, not to fill the vacancies which occurred regularly among the non-teaching staff of schools and colleges. The teachers' organisations baffled by the lack of understanding of the situation the decision revealed, reacted immediately with public protests and lobbies. It took some time to restore relationships and achieve a sensible policy of manpower economy. It was the manner in which the original decision was made and announced which polarised the issue.

One possible summary might be that if the education officers themselves are less able to influence policy-making and pressure groups and educational institutions are also unable to influence the policy process, what may occur is a situation where policy is really made by a rather small closed group, meeting in secret.
I think that gives the essence of the situation and some exponents of corporate management would justify it. Certainly, the Bains Committee argued the need for a central policy committee, if not a sort of Cabinet meeting in private. It is right at the heart of the corporate management principle that decisions should be taken in the know-

ledge of the necessity for policies right across the board of the local authority. You will find differences in its application: authorities where policy is decided comparatively openly within a policy and resources committee which may or may not, in fact, include members from the minority party; or where policy decisions will be taken by a caucus within the party in power and are rubber-stamped at the committee level. But whatever the method, the point is that policy-making is less open and consultative than the variety of educational interests, professional and public, expect.

ACCOUNTABILITY

To whom were you accountable as CEO?
I make a distinction between what I called my managerial accountability and my professional accountability. The first was to the county council, and I mean the county council as a whole (with, of course, the qualification that the party in power tended to require the accountability of the CEO to its policies). It was not a particularly unusual situation, and is similar to that of civil servants. I always held strongly that I had another accountability, 'professional' accountability, which I owed to the local community for the efficiency of the education service, and indeed to the county's force of teachers, for whom the CEO is leader. The essential relationship within the education service is between the administrators of the education service and professional teachers, and I was always conscious that I had responsibility and, indeed, accountability to them all.

You say that your managerial accountability was to the county council, but presumably there were a variety of ways in which the accountability was mediated?
The theory of corporate management would hold a chief education officer accountable to the full council and certainly not exclusively to the education committee of the authority, but his accountability would be corporate as well as personal because he would be a member of the chief officer management team. That's the theory. In practice I felt myself primarily accountable to the education committee and particularly its chairman, and because the education committee used the services of other chief officers, there was an accountability to the management team in that context.

Is the Chief Executive in a stronger position than the former clerk with a monitoring role rather than a co-ordinating role, perhaps even a managerial role in relation to other chief officers?
I was clear that the Chief Executive was my senior officer. But there

are different styles in the office of Chief Executive, and in Avon I think it would be fair to say that the Chief Executive saw himself as having a co-ordinating and monitoring relationship with chief officers, rather than the managerial direction of them. That's the genuine concept of a team, and in a large multi-purpose authority demanding a variety of specialist service management skills, it ought not to be necessary to manage the managers, though it is certainly important to ensure their co-ordination, and understanding of each other.

The idea of professional accountability is an interesting concept, in that it implies that accountability flows down the hierarchy or at least out into the professional field as well as flowing upwards.

Yes, I'd hesitate to think in terms of 'down' and 'out', but perhaps 'across' and 'into'. The CEO's role, as I have suggested earlier, seems to me to be that of leader, adviser and confidante to heads of schools and principals of colleges. I don't believe that a modern CEO can be an autocratic or, indeed, messianic educational director in these days of increasing professional expertise in the schools. It's the professional teachers in an authority who create the character of the service. It is the job of the CEO to express and articulate that character rather than to assert his own.

I wonder whether you found any conflict between managerial accountability and professional accountability?

I remember being advised by the Director of Education in one county in which I worked that his job was akin to that of a juggler engaged in keeping several balls in the air at one time. After watching the work of experienced senior colleagues in Bristol particularly, I realised that what was involved in the juggling of the senior local government officer's job was, in fact, the balancing of the professional interests of the service for which he was responsible with the political demands of councillors. I must confess it's rather like walking a tightrope.

It might be suggested that corporate management, in taking away some of the decision-making from the education department, means walking the tightrope without a balancing bar?

Yes, but you've recognised the possibility of a balancing bar. The balancing bar in this situation ought to be the chief officer management team of which the CEO is a member. The management team as a corporate body must ensure that all departmental staff dealing with the education service have a proper regard for the professional standing and managerial responsibilities of heads of schools and colleges.

So, were you in the Avon context able to reconcile these two account-abilities?

Not altogether. Not so much because I failed to persuade my fellow chief officers that heads of schools and colleges were their colleagues too, although that took time, but because the reality of corporate management never existed. There wasn't a single unified manage-ment of the education service, rather a series of management controls exercised by the various administrative departments of the authority without sufficient consultation between them or co-ordin-ation of them.

Would you say that accountability of heads was largely to you as CEO, or was it much more diffuse with the development of the corporate management system?

As you say, it was much more diffuse, but regretted both by me and I know by heads and principals. Clearly, their accountability to an individual in an authority would be simpler, more direct and more professional. Their situation and mine in Avon was made difficult because other departmental officers claimed the responsibility of heads to themselves for the management of resources.

Was one effect of that a feeling of ambiguity for the heads of institutions?

Because a head was obliged to serve so many masters, yes. It creates a monstrous hydra-headed structure which prevents the development of close personal relations with institutions and leads to attitudes of 'them' and 'us'.

Can professional decision-making and discretion survive these stronger claims for accountability?

The teaching profession has developed a considerable expertise over the last few years in terms of curriculum and school organisation. There is still room for improvement on the part of the heads in the management of their resources. If heads fail to earn confidence in their management of resources and fail to achieve their own managerial discretion, particularly in a time when resources are short, then the central control of those resources becomes inevit-able.

ROLE OF THE DIRECTOR OF EDUCATION

What is the CEO's distinct contribution to the education service?

It's essential for the future welfare of the service that he has the confidence of his teaching force, and that almost certainly means that he must have taught and know the workings of a school. He has to represent the interests – indeed, the responsibilities – of the service to elected members and local government officers who will have more generalised concerns, and he must carry conviction with them that he and his immediate staff are managerially competent to handle the disproportionately large share of local government resources the education service demands. No longer then is his distinctive contribution, as I see it, primarily as an educationist, though he must be that. He must also have the skills of modern leadership, of representation and negotiation as well as administration.

What future developments do you foresee for the role of CEO?
There is the danger that restricted expenditure and the need for efficient cost control will tempt authorities to appoint men with little or no educational experience. Aspiring CEOs will have to acquire modern management skills during their apprenticeship and may well have to rethink the traditional path of gaining experience and on-the-job training simply in an education department. At the same time, they will face the challenge of earning the loyalty and respect of the teaching staff – it's all too easy to lose touch when involved in the bureaucracy of local government's version of corporate management.

Index